Restoration

The Year of the Great Fire

ALEXANDER LARMAN

First published in 2016 by Head of Zeus Ltd

Copyright © Alexander Larman, 2016

The moral right of Alexander Larman to be identified as the author of this work
has been asserted in accordance with the Copyright, Designs
and Patents Act of 1988.

1 3 5 7 9 8 6 4 2

A catalogue record for this book is available from the British Library.

ISBN (HB) 9781781851333
ISBN (E) 9781781852668

Designed and typeset by Broadbase

Printed and bound in Germany by GGP Media GmbH, Pössneck

Endpapers: Coronation procession of Charles II by Dirck Stoop
(Print Collector / Getty Images / Museum of London);
Whitehall from St James's Park by Hendrick Danckerts
(© UK Government Art Collection)

For Nancy and Rose

Contents

Introduction

When the diarist and naval clerk Samuel Pepys wrote his first entry of the year on 1 January 1666, the day had offered little in the way of any particular interest. He was awoken at five in the morning by a colleague, worked solidly 'without eating or drinking' until three in the afternoon, and then, after a dinner mainly spent discussing business with another clerk in the Naval Office, went 'late to bed'. He was not at all vexed by the industry of the day. A summing-up of 1665 in his previous day's journal recorded him as having more than trebled his capital, from £1,300 to £4,100, and even the 'great melancholy' of the plague did not affect him; he boasted, 'I have never lived so merrily', thanks to the company of his friends and the presence in his life of Elizabeth Knepp, an attractive actress with whom he enjoyed a flirtation. He had hopes that the next year would bring more of the same merriment.

At the end of 1666, the tone of his diary struck a different note. Although he was worth a good deal more money – £6,200, according to his careful accounting – Pepys was irritated to find that he had spent considerably more than the previous year through his 'negligence and prodigality'. He knew that in this he was representative of what he castigated as the 'sad, vicious, negligent' court, which had been responsible for 'this year of public wonder and mischief... [one] generally wished by all people to have an end'. Public affairs were in 'a sad condition', with the country's enemies 'great, and grow[ing] more by our poverty'. Those 'sober men' like himself had become 'fearful of the ruin of the whole kingdom this next year'. It was a far cry from his optimism of twelve months earlier.

If the Restoration itself can be compared to the supposedly blissful early days of a marriage between king and country in their respective roles of husband and bride, then by the end of 1666 the honeymoon was over. The relationship had become one bedevilled by mistrust and suspicion. The euphoria that had greeted the return of the monarch had been based less on rational expectation of what his reign would bring, and more on a mixture of hope and a misguided belief that he would prove a more able ruler than his father, uniting Parliamentarians and Royalists in an England keen to put the schisms of the civil war behind it. The literate middle classes, represented by Pepys, who wrote about the year with both wit and an insider's view of court, observed those above and below them initially with optimism but also with a growing sense of disquiet. Death stalked the age, whether through ill-advised foreign adventures, poverty and plague – or simply brutal capital punishment.

The year itself began with the concluding months of the

Great Plague, which killed more than 200,000 people across England, and climaxed with the destruction and chaos of the Great Fire in September, which meant that London had to shake off centuries of history and rebuild itself as a modern and outward-facing world city. Yet this was also a year when many English people believed that the end of the world was nigh, because of the devil's number – 666 – that it contained. A solar eclipse in July struck panic into the hearts of many, who muttered darkly about this new, licentious age, in which those at court adopted foreign customs and the king was married to a Catholic. England's relations with her European neighbours continued to be troubled. The disastrous Second Anglo-Dutch War was fought in vain pursuit of mercantile advantage; it saw one of the longest naval skirmishes ever fought, the Four Days' Battle of early June 1666.

Still, if the end of the world really was coming, people were determined to enjoy themselves first. Pleasure, despite (or because of) the constant sense of mortality, dominated the age. Freed from the repressive shackles of the Commonwealth, those who could afford such luxuries wore gaudy, figure-enhancing and expensive new clothes and drank rich imported wine. New theatres were built for Londoners of all classes to go to see the suggestive new comedies whose authors often seemed to enjoy the same hard-living, hard-loving lives of their rake-hero protagonists. At home, people pursued illicit love affairs, safe in the knowledge that they would escape legal retribution; some even enjoyed carnal relations with members of their own sex, a risky move that nonetheless seemed tacitly sanctioned by the permissiveness of the time.

This was not, however, an age purely of indulgence and excess. Literature flourished, helped by the rise in mass printing and affordable books and pamphlets. People could buy witty and sometimes obscene poems written by a louche group of young aristocrats, many of whom had royal favour. They could also appreciate the emergence of politically and religiously engaged writers, from John Milton to John Bunyan, who eschewed the court (often by dint of being in prison) and wrote more weighty and ambitious works such as *Paradise Lost* and *The Pilgrim's Progress*. The foundation of the Royal Society a few years earlier meant that serious matters of science and philosophy were central to the national conversation. Charles himself was a keen student and had his own private laboratory at Whitehall. Scientific innovators such as Robert Hooke formulated laws that would shape humanity's view of the physical universe for centuries thereafter; an apple fell from a tree in front of a twenty-three-year-old Isaac Newton. Even medicine evolved, albeit in a more limited fashion.

The poet John Dryden called 1666 an *annus mirabilis*, with the agenda of promoting himself to royal favour. The more sanguine John Evelyn described it as 'a year of nothing but prodigies in this nation: plague, war, fire, rains, tempest: comets'. Beyond the clichés of orange-selling wenches and bewigged dandies lay a changing world that was as frightening and uncertain as it was seductive. The year 1666 stands at the dawn of a new age in which the Restoration reveals itself in all its tantalizing, contradictory aspects.

My first concerted experience of writing about the Restoration period came when I was researching *Blazing Star*, a biography of John Wilmot, 2nd earl of Rochester. Rochester's life – to understate, a tumultuous affair – was gripping material for any biographer, but the strange, beautiful and damaged time that he inhabited was every bit as compelling. Over and over again I was frustrated at having to jettison a fascinating story, or at not being able to follow an intriguing character in order to prevent the book becoming a slippery morass of sub-plots and background detail. When I finished writing *Blazing Star* it was with a sense of unfinished business. I had more stories left to tell, and wanted to carry on exploring them. I wanted to create a combination of social and narrative history, offering both an overview of an age and a more detailed glimpse into the lives of those who inhabited it.

Restoration is the result of my attempt to finish what I had begun. After a research and writing process that has been at once tortuous, fascinating and liberating, I feel like a time traveller from an antique land, ready to tell tales from the past that are, by turns, amusing, horrifying and utterly unexpected. There were many other years in the Restoration period that could have made – and no doubt will make – fascinating books, but it seems appropriate, on the 350th anniversary of one of the most turbulent years in English history, to have visited 1666 and to have tried, through the stories of the people involved in it, to make sense of what happened there.

We will meet a cross-section of individuals from royalty to labourers, prostitutes to poets (with scant difference between them in some cases) and will tarry awhile with the outwardly respectable and the flamboyantly wicked. We will visit the decadent court, and peep inside the humblest houses, to say nothing of the fearsomely filthy prisons in which some of our main protagonists dwelled, deservedly or otherwise. We will patronize the theatres and the fairs, but also spend time at home admiring the fashions of the day. We will sail with the English fleet to do battle with the Dutch, and we will take care to avoid the ravages of the plague. And, finally, we will stand and watch the awesome spectacle of the Great Fire, the moment at which it seemed London might be destroyed forever. I hope that 1666 will prove to be as exciting a world to explore as a reader as it has been to research and write about.

A Note on the Text

I have attempted as far as possible to keep intact the archaic grammar and syntax of the writing of the period when referring to quoted material – save where comprehension would be adversely affected. Spelling has been modernized for ease of reading.

All currency values should be multiplied by approximately eighty to get a sense of what the cost would be in present-day terms. Modern values have been estimated using the excellent website measuringworth.com.

Any errors of fact are my own.

The State of England

'Is this the seat our conqueror is given?'
– John Dryden, *The State of Innocence*

By 1666, London was unquestionably the greatest city in England. Its population at the time of the Great Fire was around 400,000, which made it fifteen times bigger than any other English city and second only to Paris in Europe. By comparison, Oxford had a population of around 10,000, including 3,000 students. Cambridge had slightly fewer. The city closest in size to the capital was Norwich, with 30,000 inhabitants, which had risen to prominence in the Restoration on account of its thriving cloth industry. Half of royal revenue came from London, and virtually everything that was manufactured was made in the capital. The population of England itself was around five million, meaning that almost one in ten inhabitants had either been born in or had headed to London in order to live and work there. It was glamorous, dangerous and home to the king and his court – and a magnet for the ambitious and the curious. One such figure was the French physician, philosopher and man of letters Samuel de Sorbière.

Sorbière might have expected, at the age of nearly fifty, to be enjoying the life of a respected academic, lauded by his Parisian peers for his work in the spheres of medicine and literature. Instead, his visit to England had ended with him being exiled to Brittany and censured by the crème de la crème of French society, including the king, Louis XIV. He had provoked a diplomatic storm that led to the Conseil d'État, the supreme court of justice, taking dramatic action against him. His considerable public career, which had included friendships with Thomas Hobbes and the French philosopher Pierre Gassendi and the achievement of being the first French translator of Thomas More's *Utopia*, seemed to have come to an ignominious end. Biding his time in penury and solitude, he had plenty of opportunities to think about what he had done that had led to this state of disgrace. The answer was both banal and tragic: he had visited Restoration England and told the truth about what he had seen there, in his book *A Voyage to England*, which caused a diplomatic storm upon its publication in Paris in 1664.

Sorbière had form in upsetting the inhabitants of the countries he visited. His translator, François Graverol, laconically noted in his memoir of Sorbière that an earlier visit to Italy 'had not the success he imagined' as his curiosity and limited grasp of the language often manifested itself in a bluntness that verged on rudeness. Nonetheless, when Sorbière arrived in England in 1663, his first impressions were positive. He was intrigued by what awaited him, saying of his destination 'there is no country in the world so well known'. After a seven-hour journey across the Channel, he arrived at Dover and was picked up by a stagecoach driven by a man 'clothed in black and appointed in all things like another Saint George'; impressed, Sorbière described the coachman as 'a merry fellow', who 'fancied he made a figure and seemed pleased with himself'.

When Sorbière arrived in London a few weeks later, he lodged in Covent Garden, an area frequented by French visitors. He pronounced it 'certainly the finest place in the city'. Wandering further afield, he was surprised at the 'vastness' of London. He noted that it had more houses but fewer people than Paris, 'and that in many other things it's not to be compared to it'. He spent a crown a week on his rooms, which he considered reasonable for accommodation near to Whitehall and Westminster, and felt himself fortunate that he was centrally situated; as he said, 'it takes a year's time to live in it before you can have a very exact idea of the place'. He praised the shops, which he described as the finest and the most varied in the world, but criticized the public buildings as unremarkable, belittling the two major churches, Westminster Abbey and St Paul's, by remarking 'we have not much to say of them neither'.

Sorbière encountered some of England's most notable figures during his visit. He said of the king's cousin Prince Rupert that he was 'kind, modest [and] very curious', although he also believed that Rupert should have been 'more haughty' and kept 'himself at a greater distance'. Sorbière became aware of Charles's interest in science and navigation, but hinted that the king's interests seldom lasted long and that when he became bored, he swiftly moved on to something more diverting. As with his mistresses, Charles was fickle in his attentions.

It is a mark of the ruler's accessibility that, when introduced to Sorbière by the diplomat Sir Robert Murray, Charles
addressed him in French and spent an hour with him in his
private rooms. Sorbière was later to say of Charles: 'this prince
made great improvement of his long adversity, from which he
has drawn all the conclusions which he seems to have taken
for settling the peace, tranquillity and embellishment of his
country upon a solid foundation'.

The Frenchman enjoyed a privileged experience at court,
visiting Westminster, the Courts of Justice and some of the
country's most impressive estates; he 'forgot nothing that was
feasible'. Even as he noted that 'the court of England is not so
great as ours', he praised the nobility and gentry, reserving his
disdain for the ordinary people who, in his eyes, 'are naturally
lazy, and spend half their time taking tobacco'. His account
seemed to suggest that the country would have been a better
and happier one if the aristocracy had disposed of the common
man altogether and created a prelapsarian state where wealth
and taste were the only credentials worth bearing. The reality
could not live up to his hopes.

For rich and poor alike, life in London in 1666 was noisy and
dirty; the sounds of animals, cart drivers, children, street
sellers and craftsmen melded together in an urban cacophony,
and waste from the furnaces used by tradesmen hung heavy
over the city. The diarist John Evelyn bemoaned the 'clouds of

smoke and sulphur' that polluted the centre. The black, foul-smelling expanse of the Thames – a filthy, polluted waterway where corpses of animals and even humans were deposited – bisected the city. Seventeenth-century winters were more severe than those of twenty-first-century Britain,* and the river was liable to freeze over, as it did in the winter of 1665–6. Despite its squalor, the Thames had an important symbolic place in London's heart. It provided a backdrop for some of the city's most notable civic events, including the annual Lord Mayor's parade, which took place every 29 October and was intended to display the autonomy and wealth of the City of London. During the pageant, a flotilla of boats,† each representing one of the City's guilds, made its way from the City to Westminster, watched by crowds of thousands along the way.

If the annual parade (which continues to this day) showed London at its most glittering, everyday reality was less glamorous. Both the streets and the river were full of human and animal excrement, and they were crowded and took time to traverse. If you wished to cross the Thames on foot or on horseback, your only option was London Bridge, the king having refused earlier petitions to allow the building of another bridge downriver between Lambeth and Westminster. Thronged with livestock, carts and workers, it could take anything up to an hour to cross on a busy day. Some people even lived on the bridge, in houses with shops on the ground floor. Many

* The so-called 'Little Ice Age' lasted across Europe from the sixteenth to the nineteenth century, and was characterized by heavy snowstorms and freezing temperatures.

† The boats used in this voyage were known as 'floats', in due course giving their name to land-borne transports.

preferred to take one of the hundreds of boats that sailed up and down the Thames, touting for business every day except Sunday. These looked either like Venetian gondolas, or 'skiffs', or larger barges. Travel on these was precarious and frightening, with the ever-present danger of capsizing into the fast currents of the murky depths.

Meanwhile, on dry land, London's teeming, filthy streets offered rich pickings for the opportunistic thief. Evelyn described them as 'narrow and incommodious in the very centre and [the] busiest places of intercourse'. Some preferred to travel on horseback; for society's wealthiest there was the ostentatious option of a private carriage, drawn by as many as six horses, which were generally hired rather than owned. Carriages were expensive; Pepys eventually indulged himself by paying £53 for one, which was roughly equivalent to a year's salary for a reasonably successful draper or haberdasher. Clearly he decided that this was a better investment of his money than the five shillings or so a carriage cost to hire for a day.

The ill or indolent preferred to be borne around the city by sedan chair. This method of transport had first appeared in England in the Elizabethan age, the arrival of a sedan chair at a grand house was an indicator of the wealth and status of the occupant.* By 1666 they were more commonplace, and those for public use could be hired from a stand in St James's Park; they were also supplied by upmarket restaurants and taverns for the comfort of their wealthy patrons. The extremely rich had their own, but a footman's cry of 'Chair!' in a smart

---

* They took their name from the town of Sedan, in northeastern France, where they originated.

part of town invariably brought forth four or five competing 'chairmen', anxious to secure a lucrative fare. Typically, the occupant sat on a leather or upholstered seat, and was borne on two metal poles by two strong chairmen. At night they were accompanied on their journeys by 'link boys', who carried torches to guide the chairs to their eventual destination. Apart from this illumination, the streets were generally dark, making progress difficult. It was tiring work, especially if a well-fed man was being carried, but well paid – a day's hire cost four shillings. A ride in a sedan chair was comfortable enough in good weather, if a little bumpy. If it rained, however, the journey could be wet and foul-smelling – more torment than pleasure for the passenger exposed to the elements.

Those of lower status preferred to take their chances with the hackney* carriage, the Restoration equivalent of a taxi. These coaches accomodated up to six people at a rate of eighteen pence for the first hour and twelve pence thereafter. They were dark inside, and could be stiflingly hot in summer, freezing in winter. Their coachmen, who were given a licence for life, were notoriously rude and unreliable, as well as inclined to fight one another. Traffic jams were as common for hackney carriages as for any other form of transport; Pepys noted in November 1666 that he had been obliged to give up after half an hour of sitting in motionless traffic and head out on foot instead. Wherever one's destination in town, the city's size made it difficult to negotiate, as Sorbière bemoaned: 'I am persuaded no less time [than two hours] will be necessary to

---

* The term 'hackney carriage' may be a derivation of the French 'haquenée', meaning a small horse, or a reference to Hackney, then a small village outside London.

go from one end of its suburbs to another.' If you were lucky and could find one, the little skiffs took fifteen minutes to cover the same journey from Whitehall to the City.

———— ❦ ————

There was an enormous difference between the socially wealthy and fashionable, who congregated in Westminster and around the court, and the self-made rich. The latter's natural habitat was the City where they zealously guarded their independence in the milieu in which they lived and worked. The middle classes tended to live in upmarket suburbs such as Aldersgate, where the average annual rent for an unpretentious home was between £6 and £10, with 'great houses' for the leading merchants costing as much as £30 a year.

These houses were owned by aristocrats and other wealthy landlords who saw the opportunity of making easy money from their tenants. Such men kept houses outside the city that they could escape to whenever they wished, or lived to the west or northwest of London. A select few, notably William Russell, duke of Bedford, chose to recreate magnificent country houses in London, simultaneously enjoying the city's amusements and a quasi-rural peace. Russell kept two homes, Bedford House on the Strand and Woburn in Bedfordshire. These mansions also boasted stables, thatched cottages and gardens and housed dozens of people, including servants, family members, courtiers and general hangers-on. If the king chose to visit – a conspicuous sign of royal favour – the household would have to absorb his substantial entourage, at considerable cost. Charles's lavish appearances at great palaces were becoming an anachronism, however, as he preferred to entertain at Whitehall rather than accept the hospitality of the nobility. This stood in stark contrast to Louis XIV of France, whose 2,000-strong entourage would turn up for visits lasting several days, even weeks, at a time, all but bankrupting his hosts.

While these substantial monuments to wealthy and worldly success mostly survived the Great Fire, thanks to their being located away from the path of the blaze, they were already out of place in an increasingly cramped city, inspiring envy rather than admiration among the have-nots. After the fire, their owners fled the filth and pollution of the city, and their former homes became embassies or enormous lodging houses, the forerunners of cheap hotels. The irony was that as the wealthy of the city sought the peace of the country, so rural dwellers flocked to London in search of employment and potential wealth. The vogue in Restoration comedy, as in William Wycherley's 1675 play *The Country Wife*, was to play on this juxtaposition and to depict the countryside sardonically, as a place where untested virtue was set against visiting urban sophistication.

Those who wanted to become great men at court – as well as those who already were – gathered at Whitehall. The place itself was a sprawling complex based around a Tudor palace that Henry VIII had appropriated from Cardinal Wolsey – after removing him from power in 1530 – and converted into royal accommodation. It stretched over half a mile between the Thames and what is today central London, and had some 2,000 rooms. One courtier, Edward Waterhouse, described it in 1665 as 'the centre of greatness and pomp, fashion and civility, honour and advancement', boasting a 'proper man', 'the delicate woman' and 'the eloquent divine' who will seek preferment 'by courtly tongue and apposite discourse'. Sorbière had mixed feelings about Whitehall; while comparing it favourably in terms of size to the Louvre, and speaking glowingly of its being by 'a fine park', St James's, and 'a noble river', he also described the palace as 'ill built... nothing but a heap of houses, erected at divers times, and of different models, which they made contiguous in the best manner they could for the residence of court'.

Outside the gilded world of the court, ordinary people led less adventurous lives, being obliged to work for a living rather than surviving on patronage or inherited wealth. However, those who had achieved success in their chosen profession – men like the naval administrator Samuel Pepys, working in what would today be called the civil service – were free, within reason, to choose their own hours of work. This meant in practice that many embraced lives of indolence, although they lived in fear of being reported to their aristocratic masters if they were seen to be enjoying the tavern or the theatre too much, or if they went hunting. Graver failings or ongoing incompetence could lead to dismissal, sometimes even to imprisonment, although this seldom occurred. A small bribe could normally ensure that no ill report was made of them, and they could resume their undemanding lifestyles untroubled by the threat of further sanction.

A senior civil servant in Pepys's position worked hours that his twenty-first-century counterpart might envy. It was not uncommon for such an individual to be at his desk between 5 and 7 a.m., depending on the time of year, work until around 9, and then head to a nearby tavern – perhaps Abraham Browne's establishment, the White Horse, on Lombard Street – for a reviving draught or two of beer. Refreshed, he might then return to his desk, before heading to an eating-house around noon for lunch. Depending on his level of industry, he would either take the afternoon off and go home, go to the theatre or some similar place of entertainment or return to the office. Pepys records staying at his desk until 9 p.m. on occasion, although his labours were normally interspersed with social visits, some more enjoyable than others.[*]

For individuals who did not work in these upper-middle-class jobs, usually made possible through family or social connections, it was a harder task to make a living through their own enterprise. Pepys's diary refers to a Philip Harman, who appears sporadically through 1666. Harman, who was born in 1636, represents the modestly successful self-made merchant class which began to establish itself during the Restoration. In his diary entry for 14 January 1666, Pepys describes Harman as 'a civil man' and 'careful in his way'. He was an independent

---

[*] See Chapter 6, 'Going Out'.

shopkeeper who kept an upholsterer's business in Cornhill. The area was closely associated with London's first coffee house, in St Michael's Alley, Cornhill, which had been established by a Greek émigrée named Pasqua Rosée in 1652. Harman and his fellow shopkeepers used her establishment as a social centre as much as a place to sip the newly imported, bitter drink.

Harman's and others' shops were denoted by brightly coloured signs, such as a bag of nails for an ironmonger, or Adam and Eve, indicating a greengrocer.* These signs were often more enticing than the reality of their grim, cramped interiors, showing that a primitive form of advertising was successful even back in the mid-seventeenth century. Their opening hours were essentially those of daylight, so they would probably have been open from around 8 a.m. to 5 p.m. in the winter and 6 a.m. to 9 p.m. in summer. Some houses also bore similar signs.†

The major source of goods for ordinary people was from the City-owned markets, which included Leadenhall, Smithfield and Honey Lane. The purpose of each was distinct; Smithfield for meat, Leadenhall for cloth and metal goods and Honey Lane for silk and cloth. They were open two days a week, Wednesdays and Saturdays, from 5 a.m. to 5 p.m. in summer and 8 a.m. to 3 p.m. in winter. Housewives were given the run of the markets for the first two hours, and thereafter the stalls were open to all comers. In the Great Fire of London,

* The implication being that his produce was as the fruits or vegetables found in the Garden of Eden.
† No system of street numbering was introduced in England until the 1770s.

Leadenhall Market would be only slightly damaged, and would need a comparatively small amount of rebuilding, and Smithfield would be unscathed. It would have been catastrophic for London's trade if either or both had been entirely destroyed.

Certain areas were associated with specific professions. Scribes and copyists lived in Paternoster Row, drapers and goldsmiths in Lombard Street and bakers inhabited Pudding Lane, which would become notorious as the starting point of the Great Fire. Lawyers were based in the Inns of Court near Holborn (as they still are to this today) and the clergy congregated around St Paul's and Westminster Abbey. Even the dishonorouble had their place: confidence tricksters and hawkers tried to avoid the attentions of the law by skulking in Tower Street.

New trades were growing up apparently overnight; before the Restoration, professions of 'coachmaker, harness-maker, orangeman, and coffeeman' were unknown, and such apparently niche occupations as ivory turner, silk dryer and periwig maker were now becoming accepted as part of mainstream society. Visiting such suppliers was a social day out as well. Shops doubled up as places where both men and women could gather and talk, without necessarily feeling the need to buy anything.

From the small hints that Pepys gives us we can build up a picture of Harman as a typical mid-level tradesman of the time. He was representative of the growing urban middle class, not quite an educated gentleman like Pepys or Evelyn, but he could read and write – he was made an executor of a neighbour in 1674, which suggests that he was literate. He might well have had some education at one of the City grammar schools, although almost certainly not at university, which was still very much the preserve of gentlemen. His wife Mary Bromfield's early death in July 1665 was by no means unusual for the period, although it is notable that she died in childbirth rather than from the plague which had devastated England.

Harman was not a wealthy man, and was subsequently rejected for being 'too poor' when he made another marriage proposal in 1668. But at least he had the wherewithal and means to rebuild his house after the Great Fire. Unlike an apprentice, who would have had to serve a master for seven years before being granted his freedom, Harman was able to earn a living without needing to rely on the patronage of others.

An upholsterer in the 1660s primarily catered for the tastes and whims of the wealthy. It was a profession that did not exist on a wide scale until the Restoration because there was not such a great demand for domestic upholstery in the same way until that time. It was expected that the luxuriously appointed private houses of the well-off would display furniture made from walnut, rather than oak, and showcase lavish decorations such as veneering or lacquering. Yet even those from the newly emergent upper middle class would have called on figures such as Harman for their domestic luxuries – for feather-stuffed cushions and for opulent beds and chairs. Harman was not from the top rank of upholsterers, but he was respectable enough for Pepys, himself an occasional patron, to refer to him as 'cousin', as much a term of social recognition as an allusion to any distant familial relationship that existed between the two men. It also carried the overtones of superiority that Pepys wished to preserve, given his greater wealth and social standing.

—⁂—

For the London poor, like their counterparts elsewhere in England, life was hard and they endured a difficult, miserable time, a desperate, hand-to-mouth existence. Forced to live in squalour, in narrow streets whose flimsy and inadequate houses offered little in the way of privacy, the poverty-stricken found themselves surrounded by stinking piles of waste. Refuse of all kinds, including human excreta, was thrown out of windows, and only the overhanging storeys of dwellings built up over too many floors could shield the unwary from the contents of a chamber pot. Vagrancy was punished with whipping, but not prison; it was felt to be too expensive to detain the poor, and there was a thriving market in keeping wealthy prisoners in their homes as a means of extorting money from them. The homeless had no such possibility of being able to pay for their keep.

There were many reasons why people fell into poverty, even before the Great Fire rendered tens of thousands homeless. Some were former sailors and soldiers, for example, who had not been paid because of lack of government funds, and were instead given 'tickets', promissory notes that they could draw against, but the high rate of fraud meant that all of these were treated as forgeries after June 1661. Such was the unrest this caused that an Act was passed in 1664 designed to prevent 'the disturbance of seamen', and to put an end to the 'divers fightings quarrellings and disturbances'. The Act invested the Navy Board with magistrates' powers; the penalty for protesting about being unpaid was seven days' imprisonment or a fine of twenty shillings. It is unlikely that any could have afforded such a fine, given their desperate circumstances.

Few, if any, were poor out of simple idleness. Many were unskilled labourers who were unable to find work in a city where there was no shortage of competition for labour. Pawnbrokers were aplenty, but once their clients' few valuables had been sold for derisory sums there was little remedy for their former owners. Theoretically, those in desperate straits could turn to their local parish for help, but such was the suspicion of those who had come to London to beg that an early Royal Proclamation forbade 'rogues, vagabonds, beggars and other idle persons from all parts of the nation [coming to] the cities of London and Westminster and the suburbs'. They were instead to be sent back to their home towns. This was a popular move, simultaneously relieving a financial burden on the capital and keeping many apparently undesirable men and women out of sight.

Authority was not always heartless, however. Direct appeals to the Lord Mayor often produced at least a small sum of money, and the London parishes sometimes offered deserving supplicants an annual pension that allowed for a few pounds a year. This was far from adequate, but it was better than nothing. Nonetheless, the Poor Law of 1662, describing the need to offer relief to the poor as 'very great and exceeding burdensome', was a harsh and authoritarian document; by 1666, there was even provision for 'disorderly persons and sturdy beggars' to be deported to the plantations of Jamaica for up to seven years, effectively as slaves. On these foundations of human misery was a glorious trading reputation created.

If it seems strange that an attitude of such obvious callousness was taken for granted, it should be remembered that those at the bottom of society had no education and would have almost certainly been illiterate, thus no letters or diary entries complaining at the injustices visited upon them exist. Their treatment in London was no better or worse than in any other European city; in contemporary Paris, the poor were known as 'the most vile' and regarded as the source of virtually every problem in the city, whether social, financial or moral. Without the ability to articulate their misery, they were considered little more than pests. In short, they were expendable. Hardly surprising, therefore, that they resorted to violence and theft in desperation, nor that the penalties that they faced for their crimes were often brutal and summary.

Sorbière, who cheerily believed that most of the English did not lack 'any necessaries of life', did not limit himself to London on his travels. He also found time to visit Canterbury ('the metropolis of the county of Kent') as well as Rochester and Gravesend. He was impressed by the latter, the port town of the Thames, and wrote of it, 'you daily meet with something new here to divert you'. A more enlightening experience, however, came when he went to Oxford, home to supposedly clever men. The journey from London took around two days by carriage, necessitating a stop at an inn en route. A harder but quicker journey could be made on horseback: this reduced the travelling time to eighteen, or even sixteen, hours, meaning it was just conceivable for a rider to make it to Oxford in a day, if urgent news needed to be carried.*

Sorbière was impressed by the Oxford colleges, of which he pronounced 'the meanest of them is not inferior to the Sorbonne', and compared the grandest of them, Christ Church, to the Palais-Royal in Paris. Even a 'small, ill-kept' physic garden was something akin to an orchard, he wrote. He was less taken by the city itself – '[it] would be nothing without the colleges', he sniffed – but praised the towns that he saw on the journey between Oxford and London, including Uxbridge, Beaconsfield ('Beconsfields'), High Wycombe (then known as 'High Wickham') and West Wycombe ('West Wickham'), saying that he was 'delighted with [their] sights'. Even the threat of highwaymen did not bother the doughty Sorbière, as he trusted the 'good regulations' that meant few bandits succeeded in their nefarious aims.

Outside London, towns tended to be self-sufficient when it came to their government, trading and customs. In fact, few people travelled beyond their locality unless they were heading for the capital or another large city in search of new opportunities. This was partly due to the dangers and uncertainties of the roads, where highwaymen and filthy conditions alike made long journeys difficult, and partly because of a sense of local identity that dominated each town and village. Strong regional accents were prevalent and each area had its

* Although in 1669 the so-called 'flying coaches' would reduce the London-to-Oxford journey to a single day.

own customs, superstitions and beliefs.

While we know much less – Sorbière's brief accounts excepted – about the state of other English towns and cities in 1666 than we do about London, it is still possible to gain some sense of what everyday life was like in such places as Bristol, York and Newcastle. These were important trading (and, in the case of York, ecclesiastical) centres, whose inhabitants lived, bred, quarrelled, ate, drank and worked as any other assembly of human beings in a sizeable town did. Bristol had a particular importance in that it was the major western seaport, consolidating its earlier reputation as a point of embarkation for voyages of exploration by becoming a major trading port. It was a place where appearances mattered enormously, even in death; both Evelyn and Pepys recorded the elaborate nature of christening and burial services there, and the biographer and lawyer Roger North said of a Bristolian that 'a man who dies worth three hundred pounds will order two hundred of it to be laid out in his funeral procession'. Similar wealth was to be found in the ports of Exeter and Plymouth.

Nearby Bath was fashionable and frequented by men of quality, albeit not on the same scale that would develop in the eighteenth century, as was its southeastern cousin Tunbridge Wells, a popular resort for the fashionable to escape the hubbub of London life. The poet and libertine John Wilmot, 2nd earl of Rochester, wrote a satire about it, lampooning the 'new scene of foppery' that saw the wealthy and gullible take the waters in the belief that they would cure the infertile and restore lost youth; as he acidly noted, 'ourselves with noise of reason we do please in vain: humanity's our worst disease'.

Other cities that would grow in size and importance during the Industrial Revolution were at this time little more than small towns. Liverpool, for instance, had a population of around 4,000, and was not seen as a port worthy of the name until the early eighteenth century, when the world's first enclosed commercial dock was built there. Manchester accommodated slightly more people – around 6,000 – and was known for the manufacture of such small luxury items as leather laces and shoe ties. Both paled in comparison as commercial centres next to their northeastern neighbour Kingston upon Hull,* which, although it did not yet have a dock, was a valuable port that imported iron, copper, corn and linen. All of these were much prized in London, bringing lucrative commercial rewards to the city.

Sorbière noted that he had talked 'with some of the genteelest and most polite people in the kingdom' and that 'my short stay in England, and ignorance of the language, perhaps have been a bar to making a right judgement of things', but his comments on the national character are revealing nonetheless. He saw the English as being 'of a very irregular and fantastic temper'. The common people, he wrote, exhibited 'a haughtiness and indifference towards strangers'. Warming to his theme, he criticized them as being 'very suspicious, and full of hollow-heartedness'. He noted also their 'capricious and melancholy temper, which is so peculiar to them', and he remarked that 'the English may be easily brought to anything,

---

* The poet and politician Andrew Marvell, who was born and brought up in the city, served as its member of Parliament for most of the period from 1659 until 1678.

provided you fill their bellies, let them have freedom of speech and do not bear too hard upon their lazy temper'.

In the course of his travels, Sorbière observed that the English might have been poor, but lacked little when it came to good cheer: 'you will meet with no faces there that move pity, nor no habit that denotes misery... they scarce want any necessaries of life [and] their pride keeps them back from pushing after superfluities, which others take so much pains to pursue'. He was struck by the 'excellent qualities' of Englishmen, their keen interest in blood sports such as 'bear-baiting and bull and dog-fighting', and praised their coolness and seriousness in comparison to the 'forwardness, which they call indiscretion' of the French.

Despite these laudatory words, Sorbière was scathing about English xenophobia. He recorded that when he tried to find accommodation for the night in a country inn on his journey to London, he was treated with contempt, and 'as little regarded as if [I] had been a bale of goods'. Such behaviour doubtless stemmed in part from ignorant suspicion of outsiders, but it may also have been characteristic of a people who had been cowed into obedience through fear during the years of the Protectorate. Taking a Frenchman as an interpreter, Sorbière discovered on his journey to Oxford that, only a few years after the Restoration, 'there are no people in the world so easily frightened into subjection as the English... as soon as ever you repress their insolence, you take away their courage'.

Strong words; strong enough, in fact, for one English divine, Thomas Sprat, to write a satirical response to Sorbière. In his *Observations Upon Monsieur de Sorbière's Voyage into England*, he praised the temper of the English as 'free, modest, sincere, kind [and] hard to be provoked'. Sprat, who had achieved preferment under Charles II as a prebendary of Lincoln Cathedral,* was naturally keen to defend the status quo as far as he could. He implicitly compared England with absolutist France under Louis XIV:

> The government which we enjoy is justly composed of a sufficient liberty and restraint. And though it may be suspected in a querulous and discontented age, a little to incline the people to disobedience, yet in a calm and a secure time (such as this at present) it serves admirably well to breed a generous, an honourable and invincible spirit.

Sprat was, despite his unprepossessing name, a significant figure in the new order in which he found himself, but when he said 'a universal zeal towards the advancement of such designs has not only overspread our court and universities, but the shops of our mechanics, the fields of our gentlemen, the cottages of our farmers, and the ships of our merchants', it is tempting to wonder whether his desire to act as a propagandist for the new regime had clouded his judgement. Many would desperately have wished that Sprat's 'calm and secure time' was an accurate reflection of the state of things, but in what would become the most turbulent year of Charles's entire reign, the 'honourable and invincible spirit' of England would be tested to its limits.

* He would eventually become bishop of Rochester.

For the country to maintain its facade, criticism of its aristocrats had to be limited. Referring to the tensions between Clarendon and the Earl of Bristol, which were clearly a matter of public record, Sorbière presciently noted, 'it looks as if the least spark of fire, when they meet with combustible matter, should make great conflagrations'. Sorbière was unimpressed by Clarendon, saying of him that he '[understood] the formalities of the legal system, but [had] little understanding of other things, and no knowledge of literature'. This insult caused diplomatic outrage, especially coupled with his other unflattering comments about the English. Sorbière was particularly unfortunate in his timing; tense diplomatic relations between England and France over the latter's support for the Dutch meant that it was inevitable that he should be made a scapegoat to demonstrate that the entente cordiale remained.

Sprat's attack on Sorbière seemed almost an official response from the court; the former defended Clarendon in the most generous of terms, saying, 'I will declare, that of all the men of great worth, who have possessed the office, since learning and the civil arms came amongst us, there was never any man that had so much resembled Sir Thomas More, and the Lord Bacon, in their several excellencies, as the Earl of Clarendon.' Sprat's fulsome praise concealed a more venal purpose – the Royal Society, which he belonged to, wished to have the all-powerful Clarendon as its patron – but the implication was clear; Sorbière was persona non grata and deserved all the scorn and ridicule that greater minds could cast upon him.

Ironically, Sorbière's eventual salvation, such as it was, came from two sources. The first was Charles, who had enjoyed his encounter with the Frenchman and felt that his treatment was unnecessarily harsh; he intervened on Sorbière's behalf with Louis and saw to it that he was recalled from his banishment after a few months. While Sorbière's reputation never fully recovered – he was not made a member of the Académie des sciences (the French equivalent of the Royal Society) – he continued to write and travel until his death in 1670. He never returned to England, but, had he paid another visit after 1666, he would have found an altogether different place from the one he had earlier described.

King and Court

'Who never said a foolish thing, nor ever did a wise one' –
John Wilmot, earl of Rochester, 'Epitaph on Charles II'

On 24 December 1666, James Barnes, a weaver who lived in Stepney, was prosecuted at the assize courts. His crime was to have said, 'Here is a health to George Monck, and the devil take the king'. The court arraignment described his words as 'malicious and devilish', stating that they were said 'in the presence and hearing of divers persons'. Whether or not Barnes's statement was intentionally libellous, or a remark made in a moment of drunken bravado, the details are telling. General Monck, 1st duke of Albemarle, Knight of the Garter and officer in charge of the navy, was one of the great figures of the Restoration, though a series of mistakes in the Second Anglo-Dutch War had seen him become a diminished figure by the end of the year. However, he still held some loyalty from those who believed he had acted as an important check on the sins of the court, a moral man in a sea of immorality. Barnes was eventually acquitted, perhaps because the evidence against him was weak. He was fortunate. Had he been found guilty, he probably would have been hanged.

It is also possible that the magistrates had some sympathy with his sentiments. Barnes's comments about his monarch, once a figure beyond reproach, chimed with an increasingly disillusioned public attitude towards Charles. In the space of a few years he had gone from being a popular, even loved, king to one regarded with hostility and contempt by his people, who saw him as blithely inconsiderate. As one disaster after another threatened to destroy the country, and with it the entire basis on which the Restoration was founded, it is astonishing to consider how swiftly the English monarchy once again nearly collapsed.

Things had been very different half a decade before. In a triumph for diplomacy and negotiation, rather than the divine right of kings, Charles Stuart was crowned Charles II on 23 April 1661. It was an event that many had thought impossible after his father's execution on 30 January 1649: a restored monarch once again resuming his place as head of church and state alike. The day itself, St George's Day, had been picked because of its patriotic associations. Those around Charles believed that the public wanted a grand spectacle, and this is what they were given, beginning with the king's eve-of-coronation journey from the Tower of London to Whitehall. This was not only 'a spectacle so grateful to the people', as the official description had it, but a self-conscious attempt to place Charles in the tradition of his forebears; medieval kings such as Edward III and Richard II had all trodden the same route before their coronations. Continuity with previous traditions was key, even if Charles became the last king to date to follow the time-honoured path. He rode through the streets to great acclaim; Pepys, who watched some of the journey from the upholsterer John Young's house at Cornhill, said, 'So glorious was the show with gold and silver, that we were not able to look at it, our eyes at last being so much overcome with it.'

The next day, the pageantry began early. After several days of rain, the morning was dry and bright, an auspicious omen. Royal advisers felt that the theatricality of having the streets run with wine had been successful on the day of Charles's Restoration, 29 May 1660, and so taverns and vintners were encouraged to pour wine through the conduits in the street, creating a suitably jovial, alcohol-soaked atmosphere. The regal procession headed to Westminster Abbey, where some spectators, including Pepys, had been waiting since just after four o'clock that morning, anxious to be present at the moment of history. They had to wait until 11 a.m., so that Charles could proceed in his newly accustomed pomp from Whitehall to Westminster to the acclamation of the crowd.

When he reached the Abbey, mounted on a horse with a saddle embroidered with pearls and gold, Charles was met with the lavishness that a king deserved, or expected. One nobleman's robes had cost more than £30,000, and the entire event was rumoured to have cost £200,000, voted for by a committee determined to retain 'the old names, and fashion' befitting a coronation. Scarlet and blue lent a regal flavour to the day. Charles was dressed in a hugely elaborate outfit that encompassed mantles of crimson velvet trimmed with ermine, satin undergarments and golden sandals with high heels designed to make him look suitably imposing. Sartorial splendour was a requirement for everyone attending. Pepys himself wore an expensive velvet costume made by the French tailor Claude Sourceau in collaboration with his English tailors, John Allen and William Watts, and costing the enormous sum of £2,271 19s 10d. The bill was not settled until the following year, and then only after repeated requests.

The ceremony itself was modelled closely on Charles I's investiture in 1626, although many of the jewels used, such as the Black Prince's ruby and St Edward's sapphire, had had to be repurchased by Royalist sympathizers after their disposal following the king's execution. Others had either been broken up, their precious metals melted down and the stones dispersed, or disappeared into European collections. Few had believed that a king would need such finery again. Yet a new crown was now placed on the royal head by the Archbishop of Canterbury, leading to 'a great shout', as Pepys put it, before the nobles and bishops present took an oath of loyalty. As they swore that they would be ever ready to support the crown, with all their power, foreign dignitaries looked on, interested to see how things would be in this new England. This accomplished, Sir Edward Walker, the king's loyal supporter and holder of the office of Garter King-at-Arms, asked three times whether anyone knew any reason why Charles should not be crowned. The Lord Chancellor then announced a general pardon for those who had fought against him in the civil war and Lord Cornwallis distributed silver medals to attendants; to his chagrin, Pepys did not manage to obtain one. The diarist left the event early because, as he wrote, 'I had so great a lust to piss'.

An event of this nature merited an extravagant feast, and a

banquet of a sort unseen in England for years was subsequently held in Westminster Hall. Pepys, as a naval administrator and Justice of the Peace, was sufficiently high profile to be invited to attend, and described it as 'a rare sight', full of ritual and spectacle. The Lord High Stewart, Lord High Constable and the Earl Marshal appeared on horseback, and the king's champion, Sir Edward Dymoke, issued a challenge to any 'false traitor', '[who] shall deny or gainsay our sovereign Lord King Charles the Second', and promised to fight him. The food was of secondary importance to the show, although Pepys managed to get his hands on 'four rabbits and a pullet', along with some bread. There was 'music of all sorts' played by twenty-four violinists, and much good-natured commotion, which lasted until 6 p.m., when Charles ceremonially washed his hands in water brought to him by attendants and left Westminster by barge. As he departed, the weather broke, and Pepys noted that 'it fell a-raining and thundering and lightning as I have not seen it do some years'.

Whether Charles believed that the suddenly inclement weather was a symbolic judgement on his resumption of the throne, or if he was simply too exhausted by the activity of the day to consider such superstitions, he could be forgiven for not taking the event as seriously as those around him. After all, it was not the first time that he had been crowned king. Following his father's execution, the Scots had pronounced Charles the rightful heir, and crowned him King at Scone – the traditional place of coronation for kings of Scotland – on 1 January 1651. It did Charles little good in terms of helping him to reclaim the English throne. Later that year, he found himself fleeing across the country after defeat at the Battle of Worcester, pursued by Cromwell's soldiers and with a bounty of a thousand pounds upon his head. So, for all the cheering and hand-kissing, a sense of déjà vu settled over the new king, relieved only by the attentions of his mistress Barbara Villiers, as he considered what had happened since he had returned to the country nearly a year earlier.

The restoration of Charles to the throne first became a possibility with the death of Cromwell in September 1658. His son Richard, later derisively nicknamed 'Tumbledown Dick', had none of his father's military strength or religious conviction, and lacked the will and the authority to continue the Protectorate. He resigned his post in May 1659, leaving England with an unpopular Rump Parliament composed mainly of army loyalists and Protectorate veterans. Without Cromwell acting as king in all but name, there was a vacuum where a ruler was needed, and vacuum created opportunity. The Commonwealth army, once the model of order and discipline, was in open disarray, its largest part commanded by Monck, a former supporter of Charles I-turned-arch-Parliamentarian. Monck's motives remained opaque up until 1 January 1660, when he and his army set off from Scotland and headed for London. Upon his arrival on 3 February, he asked for a dissolution of the Rump Parliament and the election of a new Convention Parliament, mainly Royalist in its construction, which was created in March. Although Monck was no turncoat, he believed that the return of Charles to the throne was the country's best chance of unifying itself, and so secretly began negotiations for his restoraton.

Charles had been miserably exiled for the past nine years, living off the scraps of his royal reputation in various European courts. His brother James, duke of York, even claimed that the beginning of 1660 represented 'the lowest ebb' of his hopes, as he slid into an understandable depression at his seemingly hopeless situation. To be offered the crown of England seemed a happy reversal, even with the conditions that came with it. The main ones were that he would issue a 'free and general pardon' to those who had opposed him in the civil war and interregnum; that all who had bought property confiscated from the Royalists would be allowed to retain it; that religious toleration, or 'a liberty to tender consciences', would be observed; and that the army would become the servants of the crown and paid monies owed in full.

Charles willingly agreed to these conditions as part of the Declaration of Breda on 4 April 1660. His mentor and counsellor Clarendon, then known as Edward Hyde, put together the document; he had been Charles's staunch ally throughout his wanderings and shared his excitement at the prospect of a restored monarchy. Charles wrote to Monck on 27 March: 'I know too well the power you have to do me good or harm not to desire you should be my friend.' His tact was both diplomatic and necessary. Had he refused any of the conditions that Monck suggested, his sole chance of a Parliament-approved and sponsored restoration would have disappeared. He lacked money, support, a home or status in his own country. Even his clothes were threadbare. To be offered them all, even conditionally, was an opportunity that he could not refuse. However, Charles would not fully accede to the 'free and general pardon' that Monck asked for. Instead, he specifically exempted 'such persons as shall hereafter be excepted by parliament', allowing him to take revenge upon those whom he saw as responsible for what he called the 'crying sin' of his father's murder, his long exile and the deaths of many of his friends and supporters.

Monck assented, knowing that those who Charles wanted removed from the scene were not his natural allies. The Declaration of Breda was made public on 1 May, with Parliament unanimously approving the king's restoration. This was helped by a tactful letter that Charles had written to the Speaker of the House of Commons, Sir Harbottle Grimston, in which he said that the powers of both monarchy and Parliament 'were best preserved by preserving the other'. Flattering the 'wise and dispassionate men and good patriots', he ended his letter by alluding to his exile, saying, 'we, and we hope our subjects, shall be the better for what we have seen and suffered'. There was joy in the streets; Pepys wrote that people fell to their knees to drink the king's health, in his words 'a little too much'. His own feelings were ambiguous and tinged by self-interest. He received preferment in the new regime, but he had earlier rejoiced in the execution of Charles I, saying, 'were I to preach upon him, my text would be "the memory of the wicked shall rot"'. This led him to confide fearfully in his diary, later in the year, that an old school friend, Mr Christmas, might have remembered his comments; others were dismissed from their positions for less.

Knowing that his restoration was assured, Charles began the journey back to London, landing in Dover on 25 May 1660. More than fifty thousand people had watched his departure from Holland on the renamed *Royal Charles* flagship; its former name, the *Naseby*, was considered a tactless reminder of the civil war. Charles understood the value of demonstrating friendliness and good grace to all; he noted the importance of not offending 'anybody who may be made to good service'. He was accompanied by Pepys, who assisted Edward Montagu, commander of the fleet supervising the king's return. Pepys recorded that the king's conversation during the voyage home dwelt on the sufferings and privations that he had undergone over the previous years, especially his flight across England after the Battle of Worcester; it moved the diarist so much that he wrote that he was 'ready to weep'. It was unsurprising that Charles chose never again to leave England.

When he arrived in the country that he had not seen for nearly a decade, Charles knelt and kissed the ground, thanking God for his safe return. After he was greeted with, as Pepys put it, 'all imaginable love and respect' by his sponsor Monck – who deserved as much credit as the Almighty for his return, and was addressed by Charles as 'Father' – the king set out for London, accompanied by near-hysteria along the way. Aware of the symbolism that his return carried in the tradition of penitential kings, he headed first to Canterbury, where he inducted Monck, Montagu and two others into the Order of the Garter, pointedly rewarding the former Parliamentarians and loyal Royalists alike. He entered London on 29 May, his thirtieth birthday, to a deafening clamour of guns, bells and 'such shouting as the oldest man alive never heard the like', as one observer put it. The slow pace of his journey gave his new subjects the chance to see their king. The sheer size of

Charles's entourage did not allow swift progress: he travelled with 20,000 men, and it took them seven hours to enter the City via Blackheath when they finally arrived.

Hundreds of thousands thronged the roads and streets, desperate to catch a glimpse of Charles. Amongst the crowds of people watching Charles's return would have been the children of some of those who had tried to capture or kill him a decade before; others were his would-be captors themselves. Yet, as John Evelyn wrote, 'all this without one drop of blood, and by that very army, which rebelled against him... such a Restoration was never seen in the mention of any history, ancient or modern... nor so joyful a day, and so bright, ever seen in this nation... I stood in the Strand and beheld it and blessed God.' In other parts of the country, joy at the Restoration was similarly felt; in Boston, Lincolnshire, the unpopular flag depicting the arms of the Commonwealth state was taken down, dragged through the streets, whipped by the beadles, urinated and defecated upon and finally thrown on a bonfire built 'for joy' by the locals at the news of Charles's return to his country.

When he arrived in London, one of the first places that Charles visited was the Banqueting Hall on Whitehall, the site of his father's execution. He seemed not to bear a grudge, stating in his speech that he was 'set to endeavour by all means for the restoring of this nation to freedom and happiness'. He even joked to one of his intimates that it was his own fault he had been away so long, and that he had not met anyone 'who did not protest that he had ever wished for his return'. The twenty-ninth of May was declared 'a perpetual anniversary thanksgiving', and the days of persecution and bloodshed appeared to be over.

They were not.

——— ⊶⊷⊶ ———

Charles liked to maintain a calm, jocular exterior to his subjects, but inside he was a serious, sometimes melancholy figure who vividly remembered the traumatic experiences he had undergone, and continued to desire revenge for the wrongs done to him. He had returned to a country where the celebrations concealed those, mainly Presbyterians and Puritans, who bore him little love, and where his own position was still precarious. The possibility that some disaffected Englishmen would combine their strength with those in Scotland and Ireland and rebel was entirely real. It was little wonder that Pepys said of him that 'the King seems to be a very sober man'.

Egged on by Hyde, now created Earl of Clarendon and Lord Chancellor,* it was time for a demonstration of royal power, and there seemed no better opportunity than the punishment of his father's – and by extension his own – enemies. The Act of Oblivion and Indemnity that Parliament passed in August 1660 offered a pardon to all who had served against the king, with the sting being that it also meant severe punishment for anyone who had been responsible for the regicide of

* Another, grubbier, reason for Charles's keenness to shower Hyde with honours was that his brother James had secretly impregnated and married his daughter Anne, and, regretting his actions, had attempted to have the marriage annulled by Parliament.

1649. The great figures of Cromwell's government often owed their fortunes and favour to their willingness to be complicit in Charles I's execution. Initially, thirty-three men were exempted from the general pardon, but more were added as became convenient for the new regime.

While Charles took pains to present himself as a merciful and unvindictive figure, his true wishes could be discerned in a speech given by Orlando Bridgeman, Chief Justice of the Common Peace, who declared that the blood of Charles I 'cries for vengeance, and it will never be appeased without a bloody sacrifice'. The trials of the surviving 'commissioners' who had signed the death warrant of Charles I resulted in the execution of more than a dozen regicides, including Colonel Adrian Scrope and Gregory Clement, both of whom were hanged, drawn and quartered at Charing Cross on 17 October 1660. Others were imprisoned or pardoned, while some fled abroad. Clarendon sent emissaries to Europe to hunt down the fugitives, as in the case of the Parliamentarian Miles Corbet, who was found hiding in the Netherlands, sent back to England under close guard and eventually executed in 1662.

The condemned regicides made speeches from the gallows defending their actions as matters of principle, and called upon God to be their witness. One man, Thomas Scot, boldly declared, 'I say again, to the praise of the free grace of God; I bless his name he hath engaged me in a cause, not to be repented of, I say, not to be repented of.' After their moment of defiance, they were hanged, drawn and quartered, the traditional punishment for traitors. Evelyn referred to the 'miraculous providence' of the same God as he saw their bloodied remains prominently displayed in public. Residents of Charing Cross, where many of the executions took place, complained that the smell of gore was making the air putrid. Charles occasionally attended the executions himself, Evelyn justifying his presence by claiming that he was merely observing the deaths of men who had wished to kill him as they had killed his father.

The most ghoulish moment of all came on the anniversary of Charles I's death, 30 January 1661. The corpses of Oliver Cromwell and others responsible for Charles's execution were exhumed, taken to the Old Bailey, posthumously given the death sentence, and then hanged and decapitated, their heads being stuck on poles. Effigies of Cromwell had already been hanged and burnt on bonfires the previous year, but the real thing would prove to be far more effective as a symbolic rejection of the Commonwealth. For all his charm and superficial affability, Charles was implacable when it came to dealing with his enemies or those who would emulate them. After the executions and imprisonments that followed his accession to the throne, it was made clear that mercy would be tempered with a dedication to the settling of old scores that would put a pagan god to shame. He let it be known that he would use 'all rigour and severity' against anyone who would 'manifest their sedition and dislike of the government, either in action or words'; a visit to Charing Cross showed that he was not exaggerating.

Others of lesser standing than the regicides also proved troublesome. There are several records of people being put on trial for speaking out against the new king, among them Edward and Alice Jones, a Westminster shoemaker and his wife, who, while accepting that 'it was the King's time now to reign', described this as taking place 'upon sufferance for a little time', and that 'it would be theirs again before it be long'. Margaret Dixon from Newcastle was indicted for claiming, perhaps more perceptively than she realized, that 'there is none that loves [Charles] but drunk whores and whoremongers... God's curse light on him'; and Cuthbert Studholme from Carlisle greeted the news of the Restoration by seizing his sword and announcing 'this is the sword shall run Charles Stuart through the heart blood'. Although such episodes, as well as a failed uprising in London by the Fifth Monarchists, a fundamentalist sect, in January 1661, posed no serious physical threat to Charles, their existence was a constant reminder that the propaganda war was not yet won, despite the expense and pomp of the king's return.

Charles knew that harmony was essential for his new kingdom, and so was keen to ensure that those who had supported him in the years of exile were well rewarded. Monck was the most notable recipient of royal favour: he received an annual pension of £9,000 and was created a Gentleman of the Bedchamber and Duke of Albemarle. Even those around Monck received preferment, his protégé William Morice being created secretary of state; Charles was aware that bridges had to be built, and so rewarded both those who had been his constant supporters in exile and those who were pivotal in the running of the country.

Many traditional landowners had been dispossessed, notably those Royalists who had remained loyal to the king during this period of internal turmoil, and tensions over landownership remained acute during the early years of the Restoration. Disputes between old and new proprietors were not uncommon. Landowners who had been passed over joked bleakly that 'the king had passed an act of oblivion for his friends and of indemnity for his enemies', but Charles was discerning in those to whom he offered preferment. As well as the likes of Monck and Clarendon, just as important were people like Thomas Killigrew, a former playwright who had been at the king's side during the years of exile and was created Groom of the Bedchamber, as well as being given the unofficial role of court jester. Pepys later observed that 'he may with privilege revile or jeer anybody, the greatest person, without offence, by the privilege of his place'.

Charles was able to show generosity because he was, temporarily at least, in the best financial situation he had enjoyed since his childhood, thanks to the annual grant of £1.2 million that Parliament voted him to run the government. (In practice, he never received anything like this amount, not least because Parliament had miscalculated several sources of income, meaning he had to introduce taxes to compensate.) His father's estates and property were also returned to him, most notably the royal residence of the Palace of Whitehall, and also – following a vote by the House of Lords committee – his goods and chattels, jewels and paintings. Any of the present owners who resisted had them removed by force.

Charles's attitude to handing out titles and favours at the

start of his reign mirrored the profligacy with which he had scattered them in exile, but, while they had then been baubles to buoy his followers' spirits, now they were concrete signs of royal favour. At times, his naivety showed. Charles happily doled out titles and land in Ireland around, ignoring the delicate political balance that had existed ever since Cromwell's violent incursions into that country. One ally, Henry Legge, was awarded the impressively impractical amount of '3000 acres of profitable land in Connaught' – an area that lacked even three acres of profitable land at the time. However, the reason for Charles's actions was clear: being seen to recognize those who had backed him for the past decade was a sure way of continuing to maintain loyalty at a time when the future of his throne was by no means secure.

His relationship with Parliament in this regard was, beneath the amicability of the Restoration settlement, one of uncertainty. Charles still retained the power to dissolve and convene Parliament as he wished, but, remembering the lessons of his father, he knew that such actions could not be taken arbitrarily. Apart from anything else, he needed money over and above the amount he had already received, but this could only be voted to him by the state, thus creating an uneasy relationship of co-dependence between the two. In the initial euphoria of his return, this was brushed aside, but the consequences soon became clear.

The House of Commons, for instance, had not received the king's writ and so was technically illegal, although the so-called Convention Parliament's presence in the months after the Restoration was a vital cog in the bureaucratic wheel, and a bill was produced in June 1660 making it legal. A Cavalier Parliament was elected the following year, and would remain in place until 1679. The process of managing a theoretically loyal parliament, against a shifting backdrop of the deaths of some members and the ennoblement of others (and their concomitant departure for the Lords), was a delicate one. Protocol dictated that Charles's first regnal year should be 1649, that of his father's death, but it was impossible to pretend that the intervening eleven years had never occurred.

There were other pressing problems to deal with. The New Model Army had to be decommissioned; mindful of how Monck had used the army to bring about reform and change, Parliament paid its soldiers off and disbanded the force, before handing over responsibility for the diminished corps to the king. A small standing army was created by royal warrant in early 1661, incorporating former Royalist regiments and Commonwealth creations whose loyalty seemed assured, such as the Coldstream Guards. The absence of a strong army and navy would cause problems for Charles before long, but he was grateful for the removal of at least one source of friction. The same could be said of the church; while there had been little appetite for the brand of Puritanism espoused by Cromwell, defining what the Anglican faith should – and should not – be was a headache for Charles in his assumed role as head of the church. Despite his talk of 'liberty to tender consciences' at Breda, religious tolerance could only go so far. Like much else, this would soon have unpleasant repercussions.

As a man, Charles had a handsome, if slightly grave, aspect. He was described by the courtier Sir Samuel Tuke as being 'somewhat taller than the middle stature of Englishmen' – he was around six foot three, unlike his father, who had been a good foot shorter – and had a complexion that was 'somewhat dark, but much enlightened by his eyes, which are quick and sparkling'. The stresses of his years abroad had marked his face with deep lines around his nose and mouth, giving him an air of wariness and suspicion underneath his bonhomie. Although Tuke claimed that his face was 'leaner' than it was when he was younger, and therefore less attractive, it was complemented by hair of 'a great plenty' and 'shining black'. He enjoyed riding, playing tennis, walking in the parks and dancing, and, as Tuke said, 'to the gracefulness of his deportment may be joined his easiness of access, his patience in attention and the gentleness both in the tune and style of his speech'. Such were the personal attributes of a man whose accession to the throne of England had made him one of Europe's most desirable marriage prospects. For Charles, finding a wife was less an act of romance than an act of political necessity.

As king, Charles inherited a series of turbulent alliances and enmities. While his personal relations with the Dutch were strong, the memory of the First Anglo-Dutch War (1652–4) was still fresh, and the vexed question of trade routes lingered, with both countries vying for mercantile supremacy; the issue would not be resolved until the Second Anglo-Dutch War of 1665–7. Obtaining a wife would bring him an ally, but also enemies. France seemed an obvious source of union – his sister Henrietta was married to his cousin Louis XIV's brother Philippe – but France and Spain were traditional foes, and whichever one he chose to support would turn the other against him immediately. However, his family connection with Louis tipped the balance, and so, emboldened by his decision, Charles decided to act decisively by entering into an alliance with Spain's other long-standing enemy, Portugal. He did this by contracting a marriage of political convenience.

The twenty-three-year-old Catholic princess Catherine of Braganza of Portugal was a highly sought-after royal bride for the monarchs of Europe, who knew that she offered a stupendous dowry (rumoured to be around £360,000), international influence and trading privileges, as well as acting as a useful military partner. After a union brokered by the diplomat Francisco de Mello, Charles married her in Portsmouth on 21 May 1662, in some haste, having met her for the first time only the day before. She spoke neither French nor English, so they communicated awkwardly in the little Spanish Charles had gleaned on his travels.

She seemed an unlikely wife for the worldly king, having led a cloistered life in which piety and regular confession played important roles. Contemporary portraits, such as that by Jacob Huysmans, show a shy-looking, rather plain young woman, attired in expensive clothes and jewellery as befitted a queen, but without regal bearing. Her hair was swept back on the sides of her head like a pair of wings, a style common in Portugal but unheard of in England at the time, and upon first seeing her, Charles was said to have remarked to his courtiers in astonishment: 'Gentlemen, you have brought me a bat.'

There was, initially at least, some fondness between them. Charles even commented to Clarendon that she was 'as good a woman as was ever born'. But their marriage produced no children. Catherine suffered three miscarriages, and thereby deprived Charles of a much-desired legitimate heir. Many regarded her with suspicion and distrust because of her religion – Charles's father's marriage to the Catholic, Queen Henrietta Maria, had done little to impress his people – and her lack of English. She and her attendants in turn disliked the men of the court and their habits, especially their penchant for urinating in public. She was miserable, bored and homesick, all the more so because Charles, if a neglectful husband to her, was certainly a great lover of other female company. His protégé Rochester would later sneeringly denigrate his patron as a 'merry monarch, scandalous and poor', who 'rolls about from whore to whore'.

Charles's compulsive fornication had its roots in his years of exile in Europe, when sex was probably one of the few distractions from boredom, depression and poverty. It became habitual, even addictive, and when he returned to England he saw no reason for anything to change. He needed congress like a drug addict needs a fix; as Pepys wrote in October 1665, 'this lechery will never leave him'. Unlike his father, who had no mistresses and was happily married, he embraced every carnal opportunity that came his way. While Charles's friend George Savile, Lord Halifax, claimed that his 'inclinations to love' were the result of 'good health and a good constitution', the truth was more mundane. As Rochester put it, 'love he loves, for he loves fucking much'.

In addition to the scores of casual liaisons he had with the anonymous women who were brought in secrecy to Whitehall every night, he fathered at least four acknowledged illegitimate children before he came to the throne. The first, James, was eventually created Duke of Monmouth, while the others, Charlotte Fitzroy, Charles FitzCharles and Charlotte FitzCharles, became, respectively, leading figures in society and a nun. He had his pick of ladies at court when he returned; few women in London would have failed to succumb to his advances. Some were optimistically put forward by their parents as potential marriage material while Charles was still a bachelor, while other, more pragmatic families attempted to use their beautiful daughters to further their own interests with the king. Some husbands even offered their own wives to advance their careers. The rewards were limitless: patronage, gifts and money flowed towards those fortunate enough to share the king's bed.

However, even the great seducer could meet his match, and that came in the beauteous, scheming form of Barbara Villiers, a sexual renegade whose physical and sexual attributes were equalled by a personal vileness that endeared her to few (Evelyn called her 'the curse of our nation'). She had first encountered Charles while he was still in Holland, when she and her husband, the lawyer Samuel Palmer, joined the throng of those attempting to receive royal favour. Palmer was armed with a gift of £1,000 and his undying support; his wife's charms were sufficient recompense in themselves. Charles was enraptured. Portraits of Lady Villiers, many of them the work of the admiring court painter Sir Peter Lely, show a remarkably attractive woman with a full, sensuous mouth, magnetically captivating eyes and luscious dark hair. It seemed unsurprising to many that she should become the king's acknowledged mistress. Pepys recognized as much himself when he wrote in July 1660 that Charles intended 'to make her husband a cuckold'. So it proved: she soon became pregnant, and her first child, Anne, was born in February 1661. Barbara's reputation at court was assured.

A smitten Charles lavished on her an annual pension of £5,000 and considerably more in gifts and jewellery. She spent equally enormous sums in an evening's unsuccessful gambling. Palmer was created Earl of Castlemaine in 1661, possibly as a reward for accepting the situation with good grace, and Barbara was referred to as 'Lady Castlemaine' thereafter. The relationship soon became public, leading to widespread disapproval of the licentious royal court. Pepys, who himself privately lusted after Barbara, wrote in his diary in September 1661 that 'at court things are in very ill condition', and claimed that this was caused by 'poverty and the vices of swearing, drinking and whoring'. Presciently, he claimed: 'I do not know what will be the end of it but confusion.'

Queen Catherine suffered almost serial humiliation, watching one bastard after another being born to Barbara in the early 1660s. The cruellest slight came in 1662, when, against her and Clarendon's wishes, Barbara was created Lady of the Bedchamber, thereby allowing Charles constant access to his 'maîtresse en titre', and allowing her to flaunt her position as the king's consort. Catherine attempted to veto this appointment, was overruled by Charles and had to suffer her rival's presence at court. The first time the two women were introduced by Charles led to near-hysteria on the part of Catherine (she threw a violent fit), but thereafter he compelled her to acknowledge Barbara both socially and privately. Barbara celebrated her victory by commissioning her portrait by Lely painted in several guises, including Minerva, the Roman goddess of wisdom and war, and, most notoriously, in the painting *Madonna and Child*, in which she flaunted her bastard son by the king, Charles FitzRoy.

Charles's treatment of his wife, while appalling on a personal level, should be viewed in the light of aristocratic mores of the time. Parading one's mistress in public was something done by gentlemen of quality, and Charles was nothing if not a man of quality. But the consequence of the relationship was to alienate the king from Clarendon, his most consistent counsellor and mentor, who was faced with the demeaning task of asking Catherine to accept the appointment of her rival. While Clarendon accepted that it would be absurd for Charles to be 'ignorant of the opposite sex', he saw that the unrestrained Barbara was an embarrassment to the court, and begged Charles to give her up. In doing so, he drew an uncharacteristically stinging response from the monarch: 'if you desire to have the continuance of my friendship, meddle no more with this business... whosoever I find to be my Lady Castlemaine's enemy in this matter, I do promise upon my word to be his enemy as long as I live.' Barbara went a step further, saying of Clarendon that she hoped one day to see his head on a spike. She openly agitated for his downfall, and ultimately would not be disappointed.

Clarendon, the cleverest and most able of Charles's counsellors, was nonetheless flawed. Bad-tempered and irritable as a result of chronic gout, he found it difficult to adjust to a world in which he wielded a vast amount of power. His greatest achievement was to bring Charles home from exile and onto the throne, and a more modest man might have retired afterwards, rather than seeking further public office. Clarendon, however, believed that he could continue to contribute to the greatness of England, most notably drawing up the four penal laws of 1661–5, the so-called Clarendon Code, that were intended to safeguard the Anglican church. He had the ill fortune to be a rigidly moral man in an age that rejected conventional ideas of morality, and made numerous enemies before long. The first attempt to impeach him – by George Digby, earl of Bristol, in 1663 – failed, but Clarendon presumed, vainly, that he continued to enjoy royal favour and took every opportunity to lecture Charles, as if he were a schoolboy, on the folly and profligacy of his behaviour.

One of his grand ideas was to introduce a Privy Council, in which he would take the role of a proto-prime minister. He described this position as 'the most sacred, and hath the greatest authority in the government next the person of the King'. His aim was to limit the power of Parliament, and to have the Privy Council take responsibility for the navy and treasury. This would have meant that, rather than the king being subject to the influence of potentially hostile Parliamentarians, he would instead be reliant on the advice of a small group of trusted councillors. However, Charles did not share Clarendon's vision, reasoning that it was as bad, if not worse, to be influenced by a few all-powerful politicians than by Parliament, to whom he declared in 1664: 'I need not tell you how much I love Parliaments... never King was so much beholden to Parliaments as I have been.' The Queen Mother, Henrietta Maria, echoed Charles's own beliefs when she commented that the council 'shadowed the King too much, and usurped too much of his authority, and too often super-seded his own commands'.

Clarendon's position of influence was to be superseded in turn by two men, one directly and the other indirectly. His direct rival was Henry Bennet, earl of Arlington, a confidant of Barbara Castlemaine's, who endeared himself to the king by faithfully fulfilling his requests. The clergyman Gilbert Burnet said of Bennet that he had 'the art of observing the King's temper, and managing it beyond all the men of that time'. Appointed secretary of state in 1662, he became a major figure at court; his closeness to the monarch was such that his Whitehall lodgings were connected to the royal apart-ments by a secret staircase. Much to Clarendon's chagrin, he was compelled to find Bennet a parliamentary seat, and so he became a less than committed MP for the constituency of Callington in East Cornwall in 1661.

Clarendon's other, greater, nemesis was George Villiers, duke of Buckingham, 'the father and mother of scandal'. The most notorious of the noblemen at court, Buckingham had such a reputation for dissipation that he was rumoured to have masturbated in the geometry lessons of his former tutor, the philosopher Thomas Hobbes, as a child. Brought up as a surro-gate brother to Charles at court after the violent death of his father in 1628, he was the epitome of the new order that now ruled in Whitehall. The lawyer and biographer Ralph North said of him that he 'commonly turned day into night and night into day, and knew no order of life of time but... the calls of his appetite, and those were either lewd or profane'. Buckingham was far from the only one at Whitehall who could be described in this way.

Clarendon and Buckingham hated each other. Clarendon believed, probably correctly, that Buckingham was venal and unworthy of holding high office; and Buckingham saw Clarendon as a poisonous voice in Charles's ear, accusing him of treachery and papist sympathies. Clarendon, meanwhile, hired spies to follow Buckingham and report on his behaviour. Buckingham was helped immensely by the contempt in which many at court held Clarendon, who now found himself an anachronism. Buckingham, by contrast, lived up to Burnet's censorious comments that: 'He had no principles, either of religion, virtue or friendship... pleasure, frolic and extravagant diversions was all that he laid to heart... he was true to nothing, for he was not true to himself.' He thrived in this new era because he was a pragmatist who was bound by no existing set of beliefs. He eventually became so influential that Pepys said of him, 'The King is now become... a slave to the Duke of Buckingham.' It was an unequal struggle, and one that could only result in Clarendon's defeat.

As his courtiers plotted and sought to tear each other apart, Charles surveyed the kingdom he had built with satisfaction. For all his accessibility and charm, there was a wilful side to him, too. Like his father, he believed that kingship allowed him to do as he pleased, and that the consequences and feelings of others did not matter; the difference was that he was better at hiding this belief. As 1666 began, Charles had his tame 'little queen', his sexually voracious mistress, a mixture of wise greybeards to counsel him and younger men to entertain him, and lavish banquets and entertainments by the score. Although some thought his unfettered dedication to pleasure in all its forms was distasteful and ostentatious, those at the epicentre of court considered the new, hedonistic age to be an exciting and rewarding one, and Charles its suave and all-welcoming figurehead. For a man such as Rochester, newly created Gentleman of the Bedchamber and one of the king's companions in licentiousness, England was his playground. A more suitable setting could hardly be imagined.

For others, the new age realized all of their worst fears.

Anglicans and Dissenters

'Better to reign in hell than serve in heaven'
– John Milton, *Paradise Lost*

For most of 1666 the writer and preacher John Bunyan languished in Bedford jail, in harsh conditions. Prisons in the seventeenth century were unpleasant places, especially for the impecunious, and Bunyan later described his incarceration as being spent in 'a jail like hell itself'. Overcrowded, squalid and beset by the threat of plague, such places tested both the physical and moral strength of those imprisoned within them. For Bunyan, who as a child had claimed to be possessed by the devil, inner fortitude was all he had to draw upon in his hour of need. As he said, 'I saw in this condition I was a man who was pulling down his house upon the head of his wife and children; yet thought I, I must do it, I must do it.' He was an unwilling but principled victim of the repressive religious policy of the time; a policy, in its own way, every bit as harsh as that of the Protectorate that it had replaced.

His tale of childhood possession might seem to be either horrifying or a tragic case of mental delusion, but Bunyan claimed in later life that he took pleasure in being 'taken captive by the devil at his will, being filled with all unrighteousness'. This demonic control manifested itself in spectacular fashion; he horrified his humble Bedfordshire family by his actions, and claimed he was unequalled when it came to 'cursing, swearing, lying and blaspheming the holy name of God'. However, his wicked behaviour was checked by other visions; he said that he was 'greatly afflicted and troubled with the thoughts of the fearful torments of hell-fire'. This tension between his base human instincts and a responsibility to a higher power lasted throughout his life. Nonetheless, he might have been surprised to find that it led not only to his imprisonment, but to a potential death sentence.

After an undistinguished period serving in the civil war on the Parliamentary side, Bunyan married and worked as a tinker for a number of years. While he was never a drunkard or an adulterer, he attempted to forget the nightmare visions of his infancy and to live as carefree a life as he could, enjoying everyday activities such as playing the game 'cat' on Sunday afternoons.* It was during one of these games that he claimed he heard 'a voice from heaven', saying, 'Wilt thou leave thy sins and go to heaven, or have thy sins and go to hell?' Thus began an engagement with religion and preaching that would last the rest of his life. In 1656, he published his first pamphlet, *Some Gospel Truths Opened*, which attacked many of the religious orthodoxies of the day. He began to preach around Bedford, delivering long extempore sermons to audiences of several dozen people. After his first wife died in 1658

---

* An early precursor of cricket and rounders, in which players would attempt to hit a small piece of wood (the 'cat') with a larger bat.

Bunyan remarried. His second wife was an eighteen-year-old named Elizabeth; he was thirty at the time. Their marriage was soon disrupted by what became the regular pattern of his incarceration.

Bunyan would eventually spend twelve years in Bedford jail. On several occasions he was offered the chance of swift release if he promised to abandon his preaching and obey the Conventicle Act of 1664, under whose terms religious gatherings of more than five people outside the Anglican church were banned. But Bunyan refused, proclaiming, 'If I was out of prison today, I would preach the gospel tomorrow by the help of God.' He was true to his word; briefly released in 1666, he continued to preach, and so was rearrested and imprisoned once more. Matters were not helped by his publisher Francis Smith's shop being raided, and Bunyan's books being seized, adding to his reputation as a dangerous man.

Although Bunyan's life in prison was difficult, his faith made him persist. He not only preached to his fellow inmates, many of whom went on to become Dissenters themselves upon their release, but also began work on his allegorical masterpiece *The Pilgrim's Progress*. The book is an extraordinary dream epic that follows the journey of the everyman figure of Christian, the pilgrim, through temptation and distraction in the forms of Vanity Fair and the Slough of Despond until he reaches the longed-for Celestial City, an arrival heralded by the words 'So he passed over, and the trumpets sounded for him on the other side'. Bunyan's incarceration permeates the book, which begins with Christian saying, 'As I walked through the wilderness of this world, I lighted on a certain place, where there was a den; And I laid me down in that place to sleep: And as I slept I dreamed a dream.' His readers would have known that 'den' was a reference to a cell, but Bunyan manages to make his confinement a release; his body might have been imprisoned, but his mind and spirit were free. First published in 1678 by the Nonconformist Nathaniel Ponder, the book became a cause célèbre and made Bunyan famous, if not wealthy, as well as inspiring countless writers, theologians and philosophers.

It was a mixture of bad fortune and unshakeable integrity that led to Bunyan's initial apprehending in 1660, when Nonconformists began to be arrested for sedition. Although the Act of Uniformity was not passed until 1661, Bunyan was initially sentenced to three months' imprisonment in 1660 for 'perniciously abstaining from coming to church to hear divine service, and for being a common upholder of several unlawful meetings and conventicles to the great disturbance and distraction of the good subjects of this kingdom'. Because there was no law with which to charge him with dissent, Bunyan was prosecuted under the Religion Act of 1592, a long-forgotten but unrepealed act that was used as a catch-all to punish people considered a threat to the state, in particular Puritans.

Although the Restoration had led to the end of Cromwell's militant Puritanism, which in its day had punished swearing with imprisonment and playing football with whipping, there was little sense that the tolerance initially promised upon

Charles II's return had really permeated the country at large by 1666. Those who had rejoiced six years earlier had included the Anglican clergy, deposed by the Commonwealth; those who had mourned included Quakers, Catholics and atheists – not because the interregnum had been a happy and tolerant time, but because the longed-for freedom of religious expression never came.

Charles II's own religious leanings, insofar as he had any, were towards Roman Catholicism, both as a result of his upbringing by his Catholic mother Queen Henrietta Maria, and of the time that he spent observing the practice of the faith while in exile in France and Spain during the Commonwealth. Charles's long-standing interest in the Roman form of Christianity also had its basis in his remembrance of the kindnesses shown to him by his Catholic subjects when he was on the run in 1651. Furthermore, in 1661, he had married a Catholic wife, Catherine of Braganza, the daughter of John IV of Portugal. But Charles knew that to openly embrace Catholicism – a hugely unpopular faith among the ordinary people – would lead to a schism in England that would threaten both his crown and the Restoration itself.* He found himself treading a delicate line between private expression of theological uncertainty and public upholding of the conservative tenets of the Church of England in the Restoration era. In the latter respect, his behaviour left much to be desired; he was notorious at court for falling asleep during sermons (on one occasion, a fellow sleeper was admonished by the preacher, 'My lord, you snore

---

* As the hysteria of the following decade's Popish Plot would confirm.

so loud you will wake the King') and, when not asleep, he was more likely to offer lucrative preferment to a cleric who was charismatic and witty than one who was learned and earnest.

Nonetheless, Charles acceded to the throne in the belief that his reign would be one of religious tolerance, with his subjects at liberty to make their own decisions as to how to worship. This was initially made manifest in the Declaration of Breda of May 1660, when he promised that his subjects would enjoy 'liberty of conscience', and was then repeated in October of that year in the Worcester House Declaration, during which Charles asked Parliament 'to exercise with a more universal satisfaction that power of dispensing which we conceive to be inherent in us'. If this was not quite a fully ecumenical offer of tolerance, it went considerably further than any English king had before.

Even the Presbyterians were offered an olive branch, with such prominent figures as Edmund Calamy and Thomas Manton being offered the bishoprics of Coventry and Rochester respectively, which they refused with good grace. Charles's religious intentions upon taking the throne were certainly honourable; realpolitik, however, would soon make life difficult for those who refused to accept the status quo.

In 1662, under pressure from Clarendon, Charles had accepted that he needed to impose a uniform religion on his people. The laws that were passed would become known as the Clarendon Code; they encompassed the 1661 Corporation Act, the 1662 Act of Uniformity, the 1664 Conventicle Act and the 1665 Five Mile Act. Although the acts bore Clarendon's name, he was far from an uncritical supporter of them, but he nonetheless took responsibility for enforcing them on an often unwilling populace.

The central text of this new style of religion was the revised edition of the Book of Common Prayer, which had been introduced in 1662 and quickly established itself as the standard liturgy of the Church of England. Its preface emphasized that this was the version ordained by Charles, and stated that his 'pious inclination' had led to 'the preservation of peace and unity in the church'. The Book of Common Prayer was designed for use on all occasions, from everyday worship to marriages and funerals, and even – fittingly in what would be a time of maritime warfare – prayers for the navy, including 'short prayers for single persons that cannot meet to join in prayer with others by reason of the fight or storm'. The implication was clear: the Book of Common Prayer was to be as much a social and political document as it was a religious one.

Revisions to the prayer book had been discussed at the Savoy Conference of 1661, convened by the Archbishop of Canterbury, Gilbert Sheldon. A dozen representatives of the Presbyterians and a dozen Anglican bishops attended the event, as well as nine assistants for both sides. These men wielded power and influence that most politicians, dealing with earthly rather than heavenly concerns, could only look at enviously, and parish priests ensured that every man, woman and child in their dioceses knew and respected their authority. Sheldon himself was arguably second in power and influence only to Clarendon, at least until the latter's downfall in 1667. Aged sixty-three in 1661, and still vigorously involved with all aspects of English religion and society, Sheldon took a rigid line on the rejection of Puritanism and Nonconformity and an equally firm stance on upholding the traditional Anglicanism that had been widespread in the country until two decades earlier. Sorbière was impressed by his reforms and called them 'the boldest thing that could have been attempted', especially insofar as they were anti-Presbyterian.

Many of the proposed revisions, including an amended liturgy and a list of 'exceptions', were presented by the minister Richard Baxter. He claimed that 'we are called by the name of Presbyterian (the odious name), though we never put one petition for Presbyterianism but pleaded for primitive episcopacy'. Sheldon and the other Anglicans, however, ignored most of his ideas and suggestions, with only a few minor amendments being made to the following year's Prayer Book. Perhaps inevitably, the 1662 Act of Uniformity was followed in turn by 'the Great Ejection' in which more than two thousand Puritan ministers refused to take the oath were expelled from the Church of England. The day of expulsion of these ministers from their parishes, 24 August 1662, was dubbed 'Black Bartholomew's Day'* by Dissenters. The episode marked the appearance of the concept of 'non-conformity' in English public life, to denote the stance of those dissenting Protestants who refused to 'conform' to the strictures of the Act of Uniformity.

There was some public dissatisfaction with the 1662 Book of Common Prayer, led by Presbyterians who desired a good deal more autonomy on the part of the priest in what to

---

* A reference to it taking place on St Bartholomew's Day (24 August), the anniversary of the infamous massacre of Protestants in France in 1572.

incorporate and omit in the service, and who also disapproved of the congregation taking a more active role in the proceedings than merely repeating the word 'Amen'. Churches and cathedrals that had been either desecrated or simply neglected during the interregnum had been reopened for worship; the implication was that in terms of religious observance it was business as it had been under Charles I. Following on from the 1661 Corporation Act, which made it obligatory for all clergymen to reject the Solemn League and Covenant of 1643 and to take Anglican communion, the 1662 Act of Uniformity asserted the authority of the new prayer book. This became the means of either weakening or strengthening the power of the individual clerics.

The new Anglican clergymen were theologically and socially conservative, and had been carefully vetted to ensure their loyalty to the new regime. So much for a cleric being, as Rochester put it, tongue firmly in cheek, 'a meek, humble man, of honest sense'. Those who dissented were removed from their positions. The Chippenham clergyman Isaac Archer, a former Presbyterian, became an Anglican priest in 1663 for reasons of self-preservation, and his diary details his shame and reluctance at having to conform to the Book of Common Prayer, which he did out of a mixture of financial necessity and self-confessed weakness. Archer wrote glumly in February 1666 that Chippenham '[has] grown worse now of late than when I came here first' and saw his own lack of spiritual commitment mirroring his parishioners' love of alehouses and drinking.

Nonetheless, if one was prepared to toe the line of

conformity, it was possible to make a decent living out of being a clergyman in 1666. Clerical life was safer than the army and less taxing than farming, and was a popular option for many literate men. The satirical poet John Oldham later complained that it was easier to find a parson than a porter in the streets. While some local clergy moaned about the expense of having to entertain their parishioners twice a year (the Buckinghamshire vicar Henry Oxinden called this a 'foolish custom' and griped about the cost of providing local people with bread, cheese, beer and tobacco), others found that they could provide for themselves more than adequately.

One typical Essex vicar, Ralph Josselin, earned around £225 a year; this was made up of his ecclesiastical income of around £80, his salary as the local schoolmaster of £65 a year and another £80 or so a year from the rental of his land. This figure rose dramatically for some London clergy, who, if they received aristocratic or even royal preferment, could earn three or four times this amount, and a few made even more. Gilbert Sheldon amassed so much money during his lifetime that he was estimated to have spent around £65,000 of it on various charitable and architectural projects, including the construction of the Sheldonian Theatre in Oxford, where he was appointed chancellor of the university in 1667. Built between 1664 and 1668, the impressive construction, designed by Christopher Wren as his second commission, cost an estimated £15,000, in addition to a one-off endowment of £2,000 towards it.

It is not overstating the case to say that in 1666 everyone in England was defined by religion, whether or not they adhered to the tenets of the Anglican church. Most believed that the events contained in the Bible were literally true and historical and were as tangible as, say, the reign of Elizabeth I. Churchgoing at least once on Sunday was compulsory: if no 'reasonable excuse' was offered, a fine of one shilling was levied for non-attendance. But the Sunday service was enjoyed as much as a social event and an opportunity to catch up on local gossip and news as it was observed as a religious duty. There was pleasure to be had from hearing a good sermon, especially if it happened to be delivered by the local bishop. The diary of the Lancashire shopkeeper and tradesman Roger Lowe makes repeated reference to his visits to Wigan to hear the prelate (presumably George Hall, bishop of Chester) rail against 'atheisticalnes'. A Nonconformist, Lowe also stated that he refused to stand at Gospel, a tradition introduced by the conformists of the 1660s, describing the practice as 'a mere Romish foolery'. Lowe was happier with such texts as Lewis Bayly's *The Practice of Piety*, a popular work about Christian piety and practical living, which on 21 December 1661 he recollected reading to a friend's sick wife; he noted that 'as I was reading, she gave up the ghost'. The language he used to describe her death was a conscious allusion to the King James Bible, with which he was undoubtedly familiar. Virtually every literate household possessed a copy of the Bible, and even those that did not were intimately familiar with it thanks to readings in church and elsewhere.

Under the Commonwealth, some of those who would

previously have regarded themselves as Protestant Christians had felt oppressed by the Puritan strictures of the time. As a result, many small communities, especially in the north of England, had embraced a simpler, almost pagan style of worship. In the early 1660s, the Church of England believed such practices to be in desperate need of reform. However, Charles's attempts to bind his people with the common thread of the Anglican communion were to be frustrated, at least in part, by the libertine atmosphere of the royal court. Many who lived outside the metropolitan bubble were appalled by what they saw as the unchristian behaviour of its denizens.

One such was the Nonconformist pastor Joseph Alleine. Alleine spent the period of the Commonwealth studying and then worked as assistant pastor at St Mary Magdalene in Taunton, turning down offers of preferment on the grounds that he was a man of God above all else. However, the 1662 Uniformity Act was not to Alleine's taste. He was ejected from his ministry and became an itinerant preacher. By 1666, like many Nonconformists, he had grown accustomed to persecution and imprisonment, having been in jail sporadically from 1663 onwards.

Like Bunyan, Alleine used his prison cell as a pulpit as he preached to his few remaining followers through the bars, but while he was incarcerated he was repeatedly beaten and mocked for his adherence to his outmoded style of faith. His friend Richard Baxter described Alleine's time in jail as 'full of troubles and persecutions nobly borne'. Alleine's plight was not helped by the 1665 Five Mile Act, which dictated that clergymen were forbidden to live within five miles of a parish from which they had been expelled unless they swore an oath of loyalty to Charles and to preach only from the Book of Common Prayer. Many reluctantly acquiesced to this, reasoning that it was better to live an apostate than die penniless and ostracized, but Alleine's deeply held beliefs could not be crushed by mere social convention. His *Letters from Prison*, which first appeared in 1664, proved a rallying cry for many oppressed Nonconformists.

Alleine emerged from his last spell in prison in 1668. Exhausted by the hardships that he had faced, he died in November of that year at the age of just thirty-four, a martyr to the Nonconformist cause. He was far from the only one who suffered. Anyone suspected of following an unorthodox religious path was liable to be imprisoned, beaten and convicted of an offence they may have been scarcely aware they had committed, making a mockery of Charles's earlier ideas of tolerance and justice. Life for such Nonconformists could be extremely harsh. Charles Nichols, a friend of Henry Oxinden, wrote to the Buckinghamshire cleric throughout 1666 after having escaped from jail, and his letters (necessarily undated and without address) speak of his 'patient[ly] rejoicing in tribulation and submissive contentment... [I] swallow up all complaints in thanksgiving... except against myself that I am and have done my Master no better service'.

Nonconformists like Alleine, Nichols and Bunyan were not the only men to fall foul of the spiritual strictures of the new regime. Thomas Hobbes had built his reputation on making pronouncements that few others would dare articulate, thanks to his close relationship with the king, whose tutor he had been in the 1640s. Hobbes's 'atheist'* views and open espousal of absolute rule were popular among the free-thinkers at court, but utterly at odds with the prescriptions of the Act of Uniformity. The final straw came on 17 October 1666, when the House of Commons introduced a bill against atheism and profanity in which Hobbes and his book *Leviathan* were singled out, along with the works of the Catholic priest Thomas White. The order demanded that the Commons be empowered 'to receive information touching such books as tend to atheism, blasphemy or profaneness, or against the essence or attributes of God'.

Hobbes was sufficiently alarmed by this that he burnt some of his private papers, even as he argued, with some success, that he could not be called a heretic on intellectual grounds. He claimed: 'So fierce are men, for the most part, in dispute, where either their learning or power is debated, that they never think of the laws, but as soon as they are offended, they cry out, *crucify*.' He also drew up a history of the English law on heresy, which he thought would help prove his innocence should he become the target of the commission on atheism. Nonetheless, he was terrified at the idea of being arrested, committed to an ecclesiastical commission and declared a heretic in public. Charles's intervention lifted the threat of imprisonment that was hanging over Hobbes, but he was unable to publish any significant work of philosophy

---

* In 1666, an atheist was one who believed in God but had doubt in the concept of divine providence; Hobbes argued that there was no such thing as an incorporeal spirit and that revelation stemmed from human experience, rather than being something ordained by a deity.

in England again. Instead, he published his works in Latin in Amsterdam, beyond the threat of censorship.

Hobbes continued to enjoy an exalted international reputation until his death in 1679. Sorbière had visited him in 1663, on his ill-fated visit to England. The two renewed an acquaintance that had stretched back as far as 1647, when Sorbière had arranged for Hobbes's book *De cive* to be published in Amsterdam, as well as translating it into French in 1649. Sorbière had even gone so far as to describe Hobbes as his hero, and gushed, 'while I was contemplating the stupidity of most mortals, after thinking that men differed by next to nothing from brute animals, you appeared'. Sorbière had not seen Hobbes for fourteen years, but pronounced him as having 'very little alteration in the face, and none at all in the vigour of his mind, strength of memory and cheerfulness of spirit'. It was to Hobbes that Sorbière turned when his book about England caused uproar, as he begged him to appeal to his former friend Clarendon; what Sorbière did not know, however, was that Clarendon, a figure of the new order, and Hobbes, a stubborn representative of the old, were at loggerheads, and no compromise could be reached.

Religious turmoil was not limited to England. In 1650, during his exile in the Netherlands, Charles had signed the Treaty of Breda with a group of Scottish Presbyterians known as the

Covenanters,* who were implacably opposed to Cromwell. In this treaty, Charles undertook to establish Presbyterianism as the national religion and to recognize the authority of the Kirk's General Assembly in civil law in England and in Scotland, in exchange for much-needed support. Charles's rejection – some would say betrayal – of the Scottish Covenanters after the Restoration went down badly, as many felt that he had reneged on his promises. In the southwest of Scotland, an area associated with Covenant sympathies, as many as 270 church ministers refused to accept the new regime. Tension mounted through the early years of the Restoration until violence finally erupted in the shape of the November 1666 Pentland Rising. The revolt itself was comparatively small-scale, but nonetheless illustrated how Charles was out of touch with the various dominions of his kingdom, as well as showing the ferocity with which the Scots clung on to their religion.

The rising began on 15 November, led by Colonel James Wallace. It started because of a scuffle in St John's Town of Dalry, in what is now Dumfries and Galloway, after troops attacked an elderly man who had failed to pay a fine for not attending church services. Local Covenanters and the population at large confronted and disarmed the soldiers, whereupon a crowd set out on a journey to Edinburgh to present a petition to the Parliament there, demanding equality of expression and religious freedom. At its largest, the crowd consisted of around 3,000 people. A smaller number of no more than 1,000 were intercepted in the Pentland Hills by Tam Dalyell, commander-in-chief in Scotland, and a one-sided battle was

---

* On account of having sworn a 'covenant' to uphold their faith in Edinburgh in 1638.

fought in which fifty or more of Wallace's small army were killed, and the rest were executed or imprisoned. It earned Dalyell a reputation for brutality and the nickname 'Bluidy Tam'; his allegedly cruel treatment of those in prison became another rallying point for the anti-Episcopalian, Presbyterian Scots, many of whom may have wondered how a man whom they had been the first to pronounce king could have turned against them in so brutal a manner.

The Covenanters were not the only religious group to be disappointed by Charles. Others who were discriminated against included the Quakers,* a sect founded in 1647 as the Religious Society of Friends by the Dissenter George Fox in 1647/ The Quakers preached pacifism, a rejection of the rites and regulations of the Anglican church and an emphasis on individual communion with God that could be found anywhere and at all times. By 1666, Fox's creed was sufficiently popular for it to have acquired around 35,000 followers. Members of the sect scorned discretion, wearing wide, broad-brimmed hats in all places and using the anachronistic term 'thou' rather than 'you'. The Quakers had been watched closely since before the Restoration, as Fox and his kind were felt, in their own way, to be as great a threat to the new stability as any Catholic or Presbyterian Dissenter. Anti-Quaker pamphlets were widely disseminated. A typical example from 1655 was subtitled 'The Devil's Pilgrimage in England' and contained an account of

---

* The name 'Quaker' derives from a mocking reference by the magistrate Gervase Bennet when he imprisoned Fox in 1650; Fox had quoted Isaiah 66:2, saying 'I bade them tremble at the word of the Lord'. The Quakers referred to themselves simply as 'friends'.

their meetings, mentioning 'shriekings, shakings, quakings, roarings, yellings, howlings, tremblings in the bodies and writhings in the bellies', to say nothing of the 'strange and wonderful Satanical apparitions, and the appearing of the Devil unto them in the likeness of a black boar, a dog with flaming eye, and a black man without a head'. Charles himself began his reign with a certain amused tolerance for Quakers, releasing 700 individuals previously imprisoned by Cromwell in 1660, but the 1661 rebellion by the Fifth Monarchy Men,* an extreme Puritan group who believed that the world would end in 1666, soon put paid to this.

The 1662 Quaker Act made it illegal for Quakers not to swear allegiance to the king; as swearing fealty to a monarch was against their creed, conflict was inevitable. Parliament often called for military intervention to break up their gatherings if they were felt to be a threat. A later act, the 1664 Conventicle Act (itself derived from the 1592 act under which John Bunyan had been imprisoned) was specifically designed to punish Nonconformists by forbidding non-Anglican religious gatherings of more than five people. Quakers were actively persecuted and subjected to penalties that included heavy fines, imprisonment and even transportation to America as a final punishment. The Nonconformist Act of the following year, which accused them of 'the great endangering of the public peace' and 'the terror of the people', seemed the last and strictest edict against them. Nonetheless, the Quakers were not to be cowed.

* A reference to a prophecy in the Book of Daniel that the kingdom of Christ would come after four ancient monarchies, the Babylonian, Persian, Macedonian and Roman.

The intellectual and spiritual quest at the heart of their mission was epitomized by the Quaker writer Margaret Fell, who in 1666 published her pioneering defence of the role of women in church, 'Women's Speaking Justified', while imprisoned in Lancaster jail for allowing Quaker meetings to be held in her home. Her work not only argued for the spiritual equality of the sexes, but reinterpreted passages of the Bible to show that it did not vindicate the subordination of women by men. She went on to claim that women had as much of a right to be Quaker ministers as men, describing their ministry as a spiritual or 'called' one rather than one ordained by royal favour. The implicit contrast with bishops such as Sheldon, grown fat and wealthy on patronage, could not have been more obvious.

Even as she excluded the foolish and carnally orientated of her sex from preaching, and advocated living 'peaceably with all men', Fell struck a blow for equality and women's rights hundreds of years before the suffragette movement. Hers was an extraordinarily bold and provocative statement, and she was praised by her fellow Quakers. She became, after Fox, the most prominent of all the Quakers, and remained a vital force of Nonconformism until her death in 1702 at the age of eighty-eight.

Echoes of Charles's original intentions of tolerance still resonated. One religious group whose members were, if not welcomed, tolerated more than they might have expected, was the Jews. Cromwell had seen the Jews as a secretive cabal, but he was wise enough to realize their potential as intelligence gatherers, with the result that they were allowed back into the country for the first time since the end of the thirteenth century in 1657.* However, their presence in Britain was still threatened by anti-Semitism, which was as institutionalized as it had ever been and stemmed from a mixture of commercial jealousy and simple lack of tolerance. There was no official recognition of them as a race.

Charles had had some useful dealings with Jews during his years in exile, especially with a character known as 'the little Jew'. The Portugese-born Augustine Coronel-Chacon, who would live in Britain after 1660, assisted Charles both with his financial transactions and in arranging his advantageous marriage to Catherine of Braganza. Coronel-Chacon,† like some other Jews based in the Spanish Netherlands, had offered Charles loans and financial assistance during his exile. Perhaps rashly, Charles had promised that, in exchange for these much-needed funds, he would observe tolerance for Jews on his eventual Restoration: 'We shall extend that protection to them which they can reasonably expect and abate that rigour of the laws which is against them in our several dominions.'

While the initial attitude towards the Jews on their return was one of confusion mixed with hostility, by 1666 they occupied a more settled place in British society, this despite the efforts of men like Thomas Howard, earl of Berkshire, who had tried to have the Jews expelled from England once more. In 1664 the Privy Council had passed an Order in Council which effectively offered them a permanent place in Britain,

* When they had been expelled for a mixture of offences including denying Christ, usury and allegedly eating babies.

† Coronel-Chacon died in 1666, having been made bankrupt in 1665; perhaps his financial savvy was limited to dealings with the king and did not extend to his own affairs.

'so long as they demean themselves peaceably and quietly with due obedience to His Majesty's laws and without scandal to his government'. The Order was carefully worded; 'due obedience' and 'scandal' were matters of discretion, rather than law, and it was generally believed that if the Jews ever stepped out of line they would again be expelled. Nonetheless, the public's attitude to Jews had shifted from contempt to a lack of interest; the most notable thing about them was their conspicuous synagogue on Creechurch Lane in Aldgate, which Pepys and others visited to experience both the strangeness of the building and of the worship that took place within it. However, Jews remained resident aliens rather than full citizens, a state of affairs that would continue to the next century and beyond.

As for other faiths and creeds, they remained largely unknown in Restoration England. There had been some academic engagement with Islam since the 1630s, when a chair for Arabic studies had been established at Cambridge, but there was no acknowledgement of Muslims in the wider social or religious context of the time. Instead, the emphasis was on attempting to encourage 'the Turk', as they were popularly known, to convert. This had been spearheaded by Fox and the Quakers as far back as the early 1650s, when a mission had gone to Istanbul and Palestine to preach the gospel. Although their efforts were unsuccessful, one of their number, Mary Fisher, managed to obtain an audience with the Ottoman Sultan Mehmed IV in 1658. Although she did not change the course of religious history, she was listened to with courtesy and kindness.

The Quaker attitude towards Islam remained one of engagement throughout the Restoration. John Perrot, a follower of Fox, wrote the pamphlet *A Visitation of Love and Gentle Greeting of the Turk* in 1660, which advocated a peaceable conversion to Quakerism. Perrot visited Istanbul the following year and said of his hosts, 'I am very favourably persuaded of you, that you will rationally and in an open and easy understanding be given to credit and believe this declaration unto you.' Despite his attempts to stress the similarities between Islam and the Quaker faith Perrot's proselytizing mission was unsuccessful. But he had at least tried to find ecumenical common ground between Christianity and Islam, whereas the Anglican faith did not recognize 'Mohammedanism' and made no attempt to engage with its adherents. Such contact as was made was occasioned by the necessities of trade, rather than any particular desire on the part of the court or Parliament to discover more about Islam. Charles was, for better or worse, no Richard the Lionheart.*

It was this conservatism – the harsh might call it cowardice – that summarized the Restoration attitude towards religion. Those individuals, such as Fox and Bunyan, who dared to challenge the status quo ended up being marginalized or punished for their pains. Again and again, Charles ended up reneging on promises he had made while in exile, with the result that a country that had already suffered a deep schism when it came to religious practice was not brought together in any

---

* Charles received the Moorish ambassador Kaid Mohammed ben Hadu to court in 1682, suggesting that, had he lived longer, there might have been a greater engagement with Islam.

meaningful way. The extent to which Clarendon, rather than Charles, was responsible for the religious reforms is debatable, but as the head of the Anglican church it was ultimately the king who bore the burden of responsibility for the timidity and ineffectuality with which much-needed religious change was introduced.

Charles had no special interest in religion himself, and so lacked the zeal with which a godlier figure (such as his father) might have driven his convictions through. Instead, he turned his attentions to matters of science, even as these found themselves jarring with centuries of received superstition. This tension between innovation and conservatism was a microcosm of his reign.

Science and Superstition

'So charming ointments make an old witch fly'
– John Wilmot, earl of Rochester,
'A Satire Against Reason and Mankind'

While Charles, Buckingham and Rochester epitomized the licentious and bawdy aspects of the Restoration period, others pursued quieter lives, none more so than the natural philosopher Isaac Newton. Newton never married, and probably remained celibate all his life. Voltaire would say of him that he 'was never sensible to any passion, was not subject to the common frailties of mankind, nor had any commerce with women – a circumstance which was assured me by the physician and surgeon who attended him in his last moment'.* Instead, his attention was entirely given over to science, and he remained devoted to his first love.

Such fidelity produced significant results. Writing several decades after the Restoration, in the 1720s, a Whig politician named John Conduitt provided the following reverential vignette of the early life of the man whom he had succeeded as

---

* Newton wrote to John Locke in 1693 alluding to a conviction in illness that 'you endeavoured to embroil me with women', and apologized for his subsequent conclusion that ''twere better if you were dead'.

Master of the Mint, and whose niece he had married:

> In the year 1666 he retired again from Cambridge to his
> mother's house in Lincolnshire. Whilst he was pensively
> meandering in a garden it came into his thought that the
> power of gravity (which brought an apple from a tree to the
> ground) was not limited to a certain distance from earth,
> but that this power must extend much further than was
> usually thought. Why not as high as the Moon said he to
> himself & if so, that must influence her motion & perhaps
> retain her in her orbit, whereupon he fell a calculating what
> would be the effect of that supposition.

In 1666, the twenty-three-year-old Newton was fast building
a reputation through his work on mathematical theory and
optics. Admitted to Trinity College, Cambridge, in June 1661,
he had obtained his degree in August 1665, shortly after which
the university closed down as a precaution against the Great
Plague. Over the course of the following two years, studying
privately at his mother's house at Woolsthorpe in Lincolnshire,
Newton developed the theories that he would eventually
formulate fully in his *Principia Mathematica*, which was not
published until 1687. In 1667 he returned to Cambridge as a
fellow of Trinity. On 29 October 1670 he was elected Lucasian
Professor of Mathematics, a position he would hold until 1702.

Whether or not Conduitt's anecdote of the circumstances
attending Newton's formulation of his most famous theory, the
law of universal gravitation, is reliable in date and substance,
it captures the sense that existed in the 1660s of science

being a source of unparalleled potential. Under the influence of Francis Bacon in England and René Descartes in France, empirical methods of scientific inquiry had begun to emerge during the first half of the seventeenth century. Bacon's name would be invoked as an inspiration behind the founding, in November 1660, of the Royal Society as a 'College for the Promoting of Physico-Mathematical Experimental Learning'. It initially consisted of scientists, philosophers and others, including Christopher Wren, the natural scientist Roger Boyle and the astronomer William Ball. Granted a Royal Charter in 1662, it was subsequently renamed the 'Royal Society of London for the Improvement of Natural Knowledge' in 1663. Its initial premises were at Gresham College near Holborn, but in 1666 it moved to Arundel House near the Strand, the former home of the bishops of Bath and Wells.

The foundation of the Royal Society was greeted with approval by many in Europe, who envied its existence. Sorbière, dissatisfied with the Académie des sciences, wrote to a friend in England in 1663, observing, 'if chance and zeal of a few private persons has advanced our arts and sciences to the point we have attained, what will not be achieved by the skilful guidance of so many able men, the outlay of numerous peers, public authority and the magnificence of a powerful and wise monarch?' He was sufficiently impressed to plan a visit to England to meet members of the new society. It proved to be a memorable journey (see pages 2–4 and 7–14).

The men who made up the nascent Royal Society were an assortment of the brilliant and the worldly, attracting deep interest and fierce opposition on both an intellectual and a personal level. The 1666 issue of the Society's journal, *Philosophical Transactions*, exemplifies the eclectic nature of their interests and accomplishments: it records the scientist and ornithologist Christopher Merret's 'experiment of making cherry trees, that have withered fruit; to bear full and good fruit, and recovering the almost withered fruit', and the physician Richard Lower's early forays into the field of blood transfusion, as practised upon Arthur Coga, a 'mildly melancholy insane man', in London in May that year. The latter operation was controversial, as no transfusion had ever taken place between human beings before, previous experiments having been restricted to dogs and sheep. While the operation was successful, the unfortunate Coga was unwilling to repeat the procedure.

Not all of the experiments were so dramatic. One of the Royal Society's number was Robert Hooke, the natural philosopher and architect who was named Curator of Experiments at the Society in 1664; in this role, he offered impressive public demonstrations of the power of natural science, revealing everything from the nature of air and its pressure to the workings of the law of elasticity, which was subsequently known as Hooke's Law. He was also a leading innovator in the field of microscopic research, examining subjects as diverse as plant cells and the anatomy of fleas through the powerful microscopes that had recently arrived in Britain. *Micrographia*, the 1665 work in which he described his research, was both influential and popular. Pepys bought an early copy (writing on 2 January 1665 that it was 'so pretty that I bespoke bought it'), and described it as 'a most excellent piece, of which I am very proud'. On 21 January, having stayed up until 2 a.m. to devour its contents, he called it 'the most ingenious book that ever I read in my life'.

Hooke and Newton were both experimental scientists and innovators of genius. The relationship between them, however, was not one of mutual respect but of mutual loathing. Newton's famous statement that 'if I have seen further it is by standing on the shoulders of giants' originated from a letter to Hooke in which he mocked the latter's small stature.

Other members of the Royal Society had controversial public reputations. Pepys was caustic about many people in his diary, but few attracted his scorn quite so much as the actress Abigail Williams, mistress of the Irish mathematician and peer William Brouncker. He wrote of her on 16 March 1666 that '[she] without question must be my Lord's wife, and else she could not follow him wherever he goes and kiss and use him as publicly as she do'. Pepys referred to her as 'the woman I hate' and described her as 'a whore herself'; he also speculated that Brouncker had at least two mistresses, possibly more.

Brouncker epitomized academic and intellectual life in 1666. On the one hand, he was familiar with the pleasures of London living. Yet he was considerably more than a mere womanizer. He was the first President of the Society, and one of the commissioners of the navy. His lucrative sinecure as naval commissioner had been bestowed upon him by the king as a reward for designing him a yacht, rather than for conspicuous bravery at sea. His mathematical achievements, however, including his work on exploring the meaning and development of pi – and solving the complex mathematical formula known, erroneously,* as Pell's equation, which was widely held to be impossible – were considerable. Pepys even said of him in 1668, '[he] is the best man of them all'.

When Brouncker, as president, made his inaugural address to Charles upon the king presenting his Charter and thereby creating the Royal Society, he declared that this was 'the first foundation of the greatest improvement of learning and arts that they are capable of, and which hath never heretofore been attempted by any'.

The Society's members were not all based in the capital. Robert Boyle, perhaps its leading figure, left London for the more sympathetic surroundings of Oxford. It was here that he made some of his most important discoveries, such as those in the field of hydrostatics, the movements of fluids. His book *Hydrostatical Paradoxes* was described by Pepys on 10 June 1667 as 'a most excellent book as ever I read, and I will take much pains to understand him'. Boyle's departure from London was in part due to his lack of interest in court advancement and political intrigue, but also reflected his desire to concentrate purely on his scientific career; his many publications included *Origin of Forms and Qualities according to the Corpuscular Philosophy* (1666), in which he expressed his credo on the first page, talking of 'this curious and inquisitive age, where men have become thoroughly tired of the wrangling and idle-theory

---

* The incorrect attribution of the equation to the mathematician Thomas Pell rather than to Brouncker arose as a mistake on the part of the eighteenth-century Swiss mathematician Leonhard Euler.

spinning of the schools'.

Boyle sought to offer something altogether more substantial, extolling what he described as a 'more solid, rational and useful philosophy', and he went on to play a crucial role in pioneering the use of the scientific method in chemical experiment. This was especially evident in his invention of the vacuum pump that led to his discovery of the eponymous Boyle's Law, which describes the inverted relationship between the volume and pressure of a gas. Alongside his scientific interests Boyle maintained a devout religious belief, promoting the translation of the Bible into Arabic.

Some of Boyle's intellectual pursuits were more esoteric in nature. Along with Newton and Elias Ashmole, the antiquary and astrologer (and subsequent founder of Oxford University's Ashmolean Museum), he was keenly interested in alchemy and its quest to find the so-called 'philosopher's stone' – thought to be anything from a means of turning base metal into gold to the very elixir of life itself, which could grant immortality. In this, Boyle and his contemporaries were following such writers as the polymath Thomas Browne. Boyle's alchemical research had begun as early as the 1650s, as he sought the philosopher's stone to further both his scientific and religious understanding; he hoped that its discovery would allow him to commune with angels, as well as receiving insights into the secrets of existence.

To this end, Boyle remained highly guarded about his work, concealing his discoveries through a complex system of ciphers and codes. Although he did not succeed in his aim of turning lead into gold, it is now believed that alchemy played a significant role in the development of early modern chemistry, not least in the way in which Boyle explored the use of a liquid form of mercury, the so-called 'Philosophical Mercury' that could dissolve gold slowly.

Newton was also a student of alchemy.[*] Like Boyle, he believed that the quest for the philosopher's stone was his solemn duty. His research was extensive, even verging on the monomaniacal. Knowing that the cynical pursuit of so-called 'alchemy' was the preserve of the criminals and confidence tricksters who thronged London's notorious Tower Street,[†] and punishable by severe penalties including hanging, he kept his conclusions secret. He bestowed on them mysterious code-names such as 'Neptune's Trident' and 'the Spectre of Jove'. A subsequent fire in his laboratory destroyed much of his material. It is possible that the extensive exposure to mercury that Newton suffered in the course of his alchemical experimentation led to a nervous breakdown in 1692, a year after Boyle's death, when he would write unprompted letters of abuse to his friends.

Not all the intellectuals of the day approved of the Royal Society. Hobbes, a bitter enemy of Boyle, remained apart from it. Sorbière recalled a discussion with Charles in which it was said, ''tis agreed on all hands, that if Mr Hobbes were not so dogmatical, he would be very useful and necessary to the Royal Society; for there are few people that can see farther into things

[*] So much so that the economist John Maynard Keynes said of him, 'Newton was not the first of the age of reason, he was the last of the magicians.'

[†] They included Rochester, hiding out from the law in 1675 under the pseudonym 'Alexander Bendo' and posing as an Italian mountebank.

than he, or have applied themselves so long to the study of natural philosophy'. Hobbes also made an enemy of the Oxford mathematician John Wallis. Sorbière, who took his friend and mentor's side, had this to say: '[Wallis] has not used him well; seeing after he had, pursuant to the way of learned man, who make themselves ridiculous to courtiers, by their controversies and malignity, endeavoured to refute Mr Hobbes's mathematics, he fell upon his scheme of politics, and pushed the matter so far, as to make him a bad subject'.

Charles felt respect for and loyalty to his former mathematics tutor and even granted him a pension of £100. Certain members of the Royal Society, however, felt that his theological and philosophical views were dangerously free-thinking, even libertine, in their content. Sorbière, as an outsider, felt able to criticize those individuals whom Hobbes found wanting – especially Wallis – of whom he wrote: 'the doctor has less in him of the gallant man than Mr Hobbes, and if you should see him with his university cap on his head... you would much inclined to laugh at this diverting sight'.

In praising 'the excellency and civility of my friend', whom he extolled as 'a perfect gentleman as well as a great philosopher', Sorbière unwittingly exposed an embarrassing truth about the Royal Society, namely its need for cash that underpinned its lofty scientific ideas. Its members were brilliant and distinguished in their fields, but they were not, in the strictest sense, 'gentlemen'; thus Sorbière's attack on Wallis as being less than a 'gallant man' was more pointed than he might have realized. With his limited understanding of English etiquette, Sorbière did not appreciate that the Society was less in the gift of the monarch than he supposed, remaining a private rather than public organization. In 1666, it was dependent for its continued existence on aristocratic patronage, most obviously from the (then) all-powerful Clarendon, and its members were all too aware of their comparatively lowly status. Clarendon had been wooed for his support by Brouncker, who had promised that he would be regarded as 'the greatest and most accomplished minister that this nation had ever celebrated'. The embarrassed members of the Royal Society retaliated in kind, with the aforementioned Thomas Sprat criticizing Sorbière for misunderstanding and misrepresenting the newly formed learned body. Wallis and the others would have their revenge in due course, however, when Sorbière's publication of his account of his visit to England led to international controversy and his punishment.

The Restoration was rich in scientific innovation and thought, but it was also a period in which credulity and superstition dominated everyday life, fanned by religion and by historic observance of customs and traditions that not even a forward-looking monarch such as Charles could overcome. Superstition still attached to the person of the king himself, who was widely believed to have the power to heal. The royal touch was held to offer a cure for the disfiguring condition known as scrofula, an infection of the lymph nodes often caused by tuberculosis, and Charles participated in a ceremony for the curing of the so-called 'king's evil' in which he would touch people suffering from scrofula and give them a gold coin. It was by no means a new tradition, having existed in England since Edward the Confessor six centuries earlier, although the only monarch to have practised it with anything like the fervour Charles did was Mary I. The twice-weekly ceremony took place on Wednesdays and Fridays at the Banqueting Hall in Whitehall. If Charles was away, a temporary court was set up and Charles would touch the afflicted from there. It is believed that he touched some 4,000 people a year.

The annual cost of giving away gold coins was estimated at around £5,000, a huge sum of money for an impoverished monarch, but Charles continued to perform what must have been an exhausting and unpleasant task throughout his reign, and was celebrated for his prowess. (Even Rochester, so sceptical about most things royal, took his eldest son, Charles, to the king to be touched in 1672.) Robert Herrick, never shy about finding an opportunity to praise his sovereign, wrote a notably hyperbolic poem, 'To the King, to cure the evil', which contains the following treasured lines:

> Adored Caesar! And my Faith is such,
> I shall be healed, if that my KING but touch.
> The Evil is not Yours: my sorrow sings
> Mine is the Evil, but the Cure, the KING'S.

It may have been the case that, especially in the early days of the Restoration, there was a desire to portray the king as near-divine in his healing powers. In reality, however, there is scant evidence of Charles having the healing touch. There is the odd recorded case of a patient recovering after having been touched by Charles, but such individuals probably suffered from less serious ailments such as severe acne or simply bad skin, which would have cleared up naturally with or without the king's touch.

There were others who touched, but most did so without acclaim or publicity. An exception was the Irishman named Valentine Greatrakes, or 'Greatorex' (the name possibly puns on 'rex' meaning king), who was said to have stroked and cured hundreds, including the Astronomer Royal John Flamsteed. Greatrakes set himself up against both royalty and the fellows of the Royal Society: his 'healing' probably owed rather more to his use of a clean linen cloth on his patients than to any supernatural powers. Never shy when it came to self-publicity, Greatrakes, who became known as 'the Stroker', wrote an open letter to Boyle in 1666 in which he announced himself in London society, and declared that he was possessed of a miraculous gift. This was hubris in the extreme. Charles, who had been made aware of the presence of a usurper of a royal privilege, and had previously turned a blind eye to it, realized that something had to be done. However, he was not interested in having the braggart imprisoned, but instead dealt with him in a more restrained fashion. Greatrakes was invited to court and ordered to stroke an ailing spaniel. The dog showed no signs of recovery, and Greatrakes returned home in disgrace.

While most people had a core belief in Christian values, they still clung to older tenets and superstitions. In particular, astrology played a considerable part in many people's lives, as it had done for hundreds of years. People in very different walks of life – from farmers and doctors to aristocrats and statesmen – made use of astrology as a basis for decision-making. Crucially, it was not seen as incompatible with Christian belief – most contemporary astrologers were careful to describe themselves as churchgoers – but there was a clear, if necessarily unspoken, pagan aspect in the fretful study of the heavens.

It was fervently believed that one's health was dictated by the star that one was born under, and, much influenced by the 'astrologer and physician' Nicholas Culpeper, who had been active from 1640 until his death in 1654, many sought to pair ailments with herbs and treatments that were governed by one's star; for instance, water-based remedies were recommended for those born under a 'water sign' such as Pisces or Cancer. There is little evidence that any of these treatments worked, although Culpeper's medicinal use of herbs continues to influence practitioners of alternative or holistic therapies to this day.

Astrology was also central to the all-important almanac, which, after the Bible, was the most important book in many households. Almanacs were publications that listed the events due to take place in the coming year, including such occurrences as high tides, farmers' planting dates and major fairs. Their predictions of astrological events, including everything from solar eclipses to poor harvests, were taken extremely seriously. Almanacs sold in vast quantities – around 400,000 in 1666, a staggering number given that the total population of the country was around four million. It was estimated that one family in three bought an almanac every year. Published by the Stationer's Company,* they were big business, and much pirated. In 1664, the York bookseller Francis Mawburne was fined £95 for distributing 4,000 illegal copies of almanacs from his shop, which had the effect of flooding the market and damaged the sales of the 'true' almanacs. They were such an integral part of popular culture that, earlier in the century, plays by the likes of Shakespeare and Ben Jonson contained punning allusions to famous almanac makers of the day, individuals such as Richard Allestree, which would have been immediately obvious to their audiences.

In 1666, the leading astrologer was the one-eyed William Lilly, although his reputation had declined from its heyday of 1647, when his three-volume astrological compendium, *Christian Astrology*, managed to sell an astounding 30,000 copies in a matter of months, something unthinkable a century – or even a half-century – before. However, Lilly failed to make his enthusiasm for the Restoration and Charles sufficiently public, and he was accused of being involved in a plot to cause the Great Fire, or at least having had foreknowledge of it and failing to alert the authorities.

There were in fact grounds for this accusation; in 1651 Lilly had written an anti-royalist book, *Monarchy or No Monarchy*, that contained hieroglyphics drawn by him that predicted both the fire and the plague of 1665. He wrote a note in which he claimed that these hieroglyphics were written in an imitation of the Egyptian priests, and which 'in enigmatical types,

---

* A Livery Company in London that held a monopoly over all printed matter distributed and sold in the country.

forms, figures, shapes, doth perfectly represent the future condition of the English nation and common wealth for many hundreds of years yet to come'. John Evelyn later noted that enough people were convinced that Lilly knew something supernatural that 'many were so terrified... that they durst not go out of their houses'. The evidence was sufficiently strong for him to be summoned in front of a Commons Committee investigating the causes of the blaze, but Lilly's argument that he could not have known the precise dates of the fire fifteen years in advance, saying, 'it was the only finger of God; but what instruments he used thereunto, I am ignorant' – as well as his claim that his judgement 'might be concealed from the vulgar and made manifest only unto the wise' – was accepted and he was not charged.

As a diminished figure, Lilly was open to mockery, and the conservative bent of many almanacs meant that he was out of sympathy with the prevailing pro-royalist interests of the time. Many astrologers realized that, with Charles's popularity still high, it was sensible to ascribe such meteorological events as solar eclipses to the divinity of the monarch, and they profited accordingly. Not, of course, that all their predictions were accurate. The astrologer Thomas Trigge predicted that the English were 'a people from the beginning ordained for victory' in the Anglo-Dutch wars, and that the 'ravenous' Dutch would have to 'stoop, and (with reverence) lick our English dust'. However, when victory was not forthcoming, the astrologers did not eat their words; instead, Trigge accused the unfortunate Lilly (who had also predicted an English victory) of having jinxed the battles, and described him as having caused 'miserable and unheard of ruin and desolation'.

However, ruin and desolation were far from the usual predictions, which were generally upbeat and positive, sometimes even naively so. While the year 1666 contained the number of the beast, astrologers concluded that this did not refer to Charles II, but, rather, to the perfidious Dutch, and that they could expect their defeat at the hands of the English to follow soon enough. One almanac writer, John Booker, went a step further, announcing that the year's numerical designation was a clear sign that the Beast himself – the pope – was doomed and that his downfall was imminent. As Lilly half-heartedly suggested that 1666 would lead to an ecumenical understanding between Protestants and Catholics, his fellow astrologers were all too happy to openly wish for the downfall of the hated papists.

It was perhaps inevitable that, in the licentious spirit of the age, a satirical almanac would soon emerge; 1663 had seen the appearance of *Poor Robin's Almanack*, a scurrilous publication that mocked astrology and its practitioners, all the while maintaining an essentially conservative perspective on society and attacking the unusual and the eccentric. It caught on, becoming very popular in a short space of time and selling 20,000 copies a year by the 1670s. Part of its appeal was its combination of 'straight' information, such as saints' days and agricultural advice, with jokes and lampoons; thus there was a 'villains' days' section that included the real or imagined birthdays of everyone from Richard III and Caligula to Tom Thumb and Dr Faustus. The practical information that *Poor Robin's Almanack* contained was sometimes tongue-in-cheek (a recipe for making coffee begins 'take two quarts of the water of Styx'). However, it was a usefully light-hearted companion to some of the more po-faced pronouncements of the 'serious' almanacs.

The 1666 editions of *Poor Robin's Almanack* demonstrate that satire had permeated popular as well as literary culture. The publication of such an almanac would have been unthinkable under Cromwell. A typical example is the 'Observations on March', when it is stated that:

> Now the Physicians' Harvest approaches, to give men's purses a purge; but those who are only drunken sick, a good sleep will set them on their legs again, without the help of other physick. The Fishmongers now are in full trading by reason of Lent, but the Butchers have little to do, unless to study how to be revenged on the Weavers. There will be no brawling amongst the Lawyers at Westminster Hall all this month; therefore those who love scolding had best go to Billingsgate to hear it. Quarter day is nigh at hand, which causes a great rejoicing amongst Landlords, and much discontentment and vexation in them that have Rent to pay.

The amiably irreverent tone, mocking everyone from lawyers to physicians, continues throughout the almanac. The royalist tone of its sympathies may be discerned in another section, 'A discourse of the heaven', in which it is stated, 'you must understand that the Heavens are fashioned round, yea round as is a Porridge pot, or a Kettle, and therefore our Secretaries would at the first be called Roundheads, because they would be taken to be Heavenly people'. The passage may have been intended to amuse and to entertain, but its implication was clear: if you sympathized with the new regime, then laughter was not just permitted, but encouraged. If you did not, you were better off being discreet and avoiding drawing attention to yourself.

⸺ ❧ ⸺

Superstition and old wives' tales also extended into the medical treatments of the day. Doctors believed in the 'humours' of blood, phlegm, black bile and yellow bile that had to be kept in balance with one another, and if a patient was believed to be suffering from a humoral imbalance, a range of treatments – including purging, bleeding with leeches, enemas and 'cupping' (placing hot cups on a patient's back and quickly piercing the resulting blisters) – were prescribed. These invariably led to further weakening in the patient, and sometimes even hastened death. The drugs offered were of little more use: the approved *pharmacopoeia*, or list of prescribed medicines, included powders and potions made from such ingredients as human skulls (normally obtained from recently executed criminals) and animal claws.

While the relatively wealthy could visit one of the city's apothecaries, licensed shopkeepers who both prescribed remedies and sold them over the counter, the poor and ignorant could not afford expensive medicines, and preferred to take refuge in superstition, turning to so-called 'wise women'.

Some, like the writer and occasional physician Hannah Woolley, had an idea of what they were talking about, but many others were opportunists who treated their patients with a mixture of dubious herbal remedies and mumbo-jumbo. Their presence was often welcome at times of childbirth, given that the official midwives, who were usually licensed by bishops, could be expensive, and therefore beyond the financial reach of many. However, the unlicensed wise women were vulnerable to accusations of witchcraft if anything went wrong during the birth – a fraught, bloody process which as many as two-thirds of all babies did not survive.

If children did survive, they found themselves in a world where medical pamphlets offered a variety of weird and less than wonderful cures. The distinguished physician Thomas Willis's 1666 publication, *A Plain and Easy Method*, advocated placing live frogs 'renewed as they die' on plague sores, and extolled the medical virtues of a drink made up of wormwood and syrup of citron. However, some pamphlets were ahead of their time. Some advocated the diagnosis of illness by examination of a patient's urine, a practice known as uroscopy; this had been denounced by the College of Physicians as nothing more than 'piss-pot science', a judgement which dismissed a practice dating back to the Byzantine Greeks, and had indeed been adopted by the physicians themselves two decades before.

Whether such medical publications were accurate or simply fraudulent, they were big business; in the first half of 1666, there was a total of fifty-two new medical-related publications, including one offering 'a new method of chemical philosophy and physic, being a brief introduction to those two noble studies'. These manuals were hugely profitable for the booksellers of the day, selling to an audience only too eager to discover such doubtful products as Daffy's Elixir (a herbal remedy said to cure illnesses including kidney stones and rheumatism) and the popular Buckworth's Lozenges, which advertised themselves as combating 'coughs, consumptions, catarrhs, asthmas and all other diseases incident to the lungs'. All of these substances were also guaranteed to combat plague.

Although the great men and women of court regarded superstition with scorn, the England of 1666 remained a nation preoccupied with everyday incursions of fate, whether divine, devilish or otherwise. These could take a harmless enough form – according to folk belief, dropping a fork meant that your beloved was thinking about you – or have a more serious nature. Comets and eclipses, as predicted in almanacs, were regarded as invaluable guides to the future.

The Essex vicar Ralph Josselin – clearly no lover of Quakers – wrote of how he observed the workings of providence: 'A man I was hiring declined me to go to a Quaker, I know not his motives, there he fell ill of the smallpox and died... the Lord watched over me and mine for good.' Sudden death, whether divinely ordained or otherwise, could be interpreted as the wages of sin; an account appears in the collection of broadside ballads* and tales, the *Pack of Autolycus*, of a maid being struck dead after stealing from her mistress and claiming that she had been owed the money and more besides; a particularly vivid detail is that her body was said to have been 'black as pitch'

---

* A broadside was a single sheet of cheap paper printed with a song, ballad or news.

from where the devil's claws had seized her lying hide.

Then again, the country at large regarded the existence of the diabolic as an everyday part of life. Claiming demonic possession was an accepted (if normally useless) means of defending oneself against a particularly heinous charge in court. There was a widespread belief in the existence of witchcraft; in 1664, the judge Sir Matthew Hale had found two women guilty of the offence, and in his verdict he announced not only that the scriptures affirmed the existence of witches and devils, but also that the world at large continued to believe in them. The intellectuals of the day agreed with him; Joseph Glanvill, a fellow of the Royal Society, argued in 1668 that:

> If any thing were to be much admired in an age of wonders, not only of nature (which is a constant prodigy) but of men and manners, it would be to me a matter of astonishment, that men, otherwise witty and ingenious, are fallen into the conceit that there's no such thing as a witch or apparition, but that these are the creatures of melancholy and superstition, fostered by ignorance and design.

This belief meant that, while the outright mass persecutions of the East Anglian lawyer and witch-finder Matthew Hopkins* two decades before were no longer practised, the existence of evil was not only believed, but considered a real threat to everyday life. Charles himself shared the general

---

* Hopkins was a witch-hunter who presided over the executions of around 300 women between 1644 and 1647; this was more than half of the executions for witchcraft that occurred between the fifteenth and eighteenth centuries.

belief in witches, unsurprising, perhaps, for the grandson of James I, who in 1597 had written a book called *Demonology*, which drew on his personal involvement with witch trials in north Berwick, and which claimed that 'assaults of Satan are most certainly practised, and the instrument thereof merits most severely to be punished'. The Act of Indemnity and Oblivion that began the Restoration specifically exempted from the new king's pardon 'invocations, conjurations [sic], witchcrafts, sorceries, enchantments and charms', meaning that it continued to be open season on lonely old women who kept cats and were believed to be in league with Satan. This was hardly new; the Witchcraft Act of 1604, introduced by James, had made execution the norm for anyone who invoked evil spirits.

Not everyone joined the rush to condemnation. Hobbes commented, 'I think not that… witchcraft is any real power', although he protected himself from accusations of dabbling in the supernatural by claiming 'they are justly punished for the false belief that they have that they can do such mischief, joined with their purpose to do it if they can'. Likewise, Newton, initially a committed believer in the existence of witchcraft, eventually rejected the existence of demons and evil spirits, saying, 'to believe that men and women can really divine, charm, enchant, bewitch or converse with spirits is a superstition of the same nature with believing that the idols of the gentiles were not vanities but had spirits really seated in them'.

However, public opinion stood against them. In March 1662 a notorious witch trial took place in Bury St Edmunds,

Suffolk, presided over by Matthew Hale, Chief Baron of the Exchequer. Hale, commonly regarded by posterity as a fair and even-handed lawman, watched the conviction and subsequent hanging of two elderly widows on little more than hearsay and gossip, and the judgement ensured that persecutions and punishment would continue for many years to come. Bury St Edmunds had been a centre of the mass executions carried out by Matthew Hopkins in 1645, and witnessed witch trials intermittently until the 1690s; the last trial for witchcraft in England would take place two centuries later, in 1863. For all the Restoration court's determination that this would be a new age, fear, intolerance and violence proved to be a powerful means of keeping their subjects in their place, just as strict adherence to the new forms of religion managed to keep Dissenters muzzled. In this, perhaps, the brave new world of the Restoration had more in common with the Commonwealth regime than most cared to admit.

Yet even as witch-finders roamed the land and neighbours betrayed neighbours out of spite, a greater catastrophe yet would engulf the nation, one that neither scientific innovation nor superstitious invocation could combat.

The Great Plague

'Another Plague year would reconcile all these differences'
– Daniel Defoe, *A Journal of the Plague Year*

The first issue of London's first newspaper, the *London Gazette*, was published on 5 February 1666 by Henry Muddiman, a journalist and publisher who had been awarded a lucrative royal monopoly at the Restoration on all official journals of court or parliamentary business. The newspaper is still published today, as a journal of record for clerical, army, political and royal news and proclamation, and is consequently the oldest surviving newspaper in the country. However, its first issue was greeted with more than just the usual sense of anticipation at the arrival of a new title. It represented the end of a grotesque and violent episode in English history during which some 200,000 people had died, and the welcome resumption, after the best part of a year, of some form of normality. If, that is, things could ever be normal again.

Since the Black Death of 1348 and 1349, in which millions perished, mass death through plague had been an ever-present fear for those in England. Outbreaks of disease had continued to recur throughout the fifteenth and sixteenth centuries, peaking in 1479–80, during which a combined epidemic of bubonic and pneumonic plague wiped out up to one in five of the population, or around 500,000 people. Anyone who was thirty-five or older in 1665 remembered the last signifi-cant epidemics, between 1636 and 1638, which killed around 50,000 in London alone. And most had some recollection of a recent recurrence in 1647, which saw nearly 20,000 die across the country; those of a patriotic or pessimistic bent might have ascribed that to the defeat of the Royalists in the civil war.

Just before Christmas in 1664, a comet was sighted over London. The king remarked in a letter that it was 'no ordi-nary star' and Pepys commented on 15 December how its appearance had led to 'mighty talk of this comet that is seen at nights'. His superior Lord Sandwich in the Naval Office told Pepys that this apparition 'was the most extraordinary thing that ever he saw', and it was still visible over a week later, albeit 'whether worn away or not I know not'. Like many others, Pepys enjoyed the spectacle, rising early to try to catch the best view of it. Another observer was the Sussex vicar-turned-amateur physician John Allin, who wrote to a friend living in the country: 'The chief discourse is of a blazing star – the city was last night sitting up to see it.' It proved an unfortunate portent.

The superstitious believed that the comet's arrival was an ill omen, and were not afraid to say so. The astronomer John Gadbury from the Royal Society noted darkly in his pamphlet *De Cometis: or a Discourse of the Natures and Effects of Comets* that 'this comet portends pestiferous and horrible winds and tempests', and Dissenters saw it as a portent of impending doom; Theophilus Hastings, earl of Huntingdon, was told by a friend that it represented 'astral portents of great calamities', as well as a judgement upon the 'gallants' of court. A second comet that appeared in March did nothing to quell these excited mutterings.

In December 1664, the inhabitants of one of the poorest parts of the city, St Giles-in-the-Fields, were faced with a troubling development. The parish 'searchers' – elderly women paid a pittance to alert the authorities to the causes of sudden deaths – determined that their neighbour, 'Goodwife Phillips', had died of plague. As was common in rumours of this kind, her husband and the family were shut up inside the house, and 'Lord Have Mercy On Us' was written on the door. This minimized their chances of survival, especially with the meagre five shillings they were allowed to live on, but it was believed to reduce the danger of the infection spreading further. But it was already too late.

At Christmas 1664, Nathaniel Hodges, a physician working in Walbrook in the City, attended a young man who was displaying some disturbing symptoms. Hodges had moved from a successful academic career at both Cambridge and Oxford universities to work in London. Appointed to the College of Physicians in September 1659, he was representative of the new breed of doctors for whom science and superstition were separate, and who treated illnesses with medicine and surgery rather than trusting in old wives' tales. Nonetheless, even Hodges was alarmed by what he encountered. He saw that his patient bore the symptoms of severe and rare illness.

He observed 'two risings about the bigness of a nutmeg' on the man's thighs, 'upon examination of which I soon discovered the maliganty [sic], both from their black hue and the circle around them, and pronounced it to be plague'. Although his patient was cured by his prescription of 'Alexiterial medicines',* Hodges feared that it was far from an isolated incident. He would soon be proved right.

The infection's arrival in London was probably caused by contaminated rats coming to the city from the Netherlands, where bubonic plague had also sporadically occurred since the beginning of the seventeenth century. There had been a particularly bad explosion of illness at the end of 1663 in Amsterdam, which had continued through to 1664 and caused around 50,000 deaths. With the arrival of trading ships bearing bales of cotton, it was inevitable that the disease would spread round the cramped, unhygienic streets and lanes of London with all the unwelcome alacrity of an urban pestilence. By May 1664, Dutch ships had been quarantined and were no longer allowed to travel to England; however, the rules were often unofficially bent, not least when finery and horses were sent over for the royal court. The ship *King David of Rotterdam* was even officially exempted from the quarantine as it was carrying goods 'useful for the king's fleet'. By the end of 1664, apart from an isolated incident in East Anglia, a navy informant commented that the quarantine had been effective, and that the progress of the plague had been contained. At the start of 1665, there seemed little to be concerned about. There was

---

* A contemporary term for an antidote.

another case in early February, and then nothing again until the middle of April, when another two cases were detected in St Giles. However, by the end of the month, rumours were spreading that the plague was beginning to take hold, albeit in the poorest areas; Pepys noted in his diary of 30 April 1665: 'two or three houses are already shut up. God preserve us all.'

Initially, the well-to-do remained remote from the situation. The 'pestered places' in which the poor congregated were notoriously crowded and unhealthy, and full of fever and disease at any time. Those in charge of the city had no dedicated hospitals for those suffering from infectious diseases; instead, the poor were ordered to keep the exteriors of their houses and shops clean, on pain of fines. Yet the steady spread of the illness led to action. Infected houses were closed for forty days from the date of confirmed plague with a 'watcher' outside to ensure that nobody entered or left, and a nurse to care for the inhabitants. What little sustenance the occupants could afford would be passed through the window. Many died of starvation, as well as of illness and maltreatment by the nurses; Hodges wrote, 'what greatly contributed to the loss of people thus shut up was the wicked practices of the nurses, for they are not to be mentioned but in the most bitter terms...these wretches, out of greediness to plunder the dead, would strangle their patients, and charge it to the distemper in their throats'.

If they were not murdered by their supposed carers, other problems awaited those shut up indoors. The disadvantage with this plague order – which had existed since the time of James I – was that it all but guaranteed the inhabitants of the house would die, and failed to protect their neighbours; the plague was carried by fleas and passed through the air, and no quarantine could combat its movement. A widespread belief that the poor were the targets of a harsh system – Hodges even noted that 'it came by some to be referred to as "the poor's plague"' – led to rioting, with one closed tavern, the Ship, having its front door forcibly removed and the inhabitants allowed to 'go abroad into the streets promiscuously with others'. Even as Charles promised 'the severest punishment' for 'offenders in the said riot', it was beginning to dawn on those in charge that they faced a perfect storm of civil disobedience and a steadily increasing infection that they were powerless to combat.

The plague soon spread across town, reaching Bearbinder Lane in the City in early May. Even as doctors argued over the causes of the illness, and how best to treat it, a general order was given out on 4 May that all infected houses should be shut up. Yet the mild and pleasant spring weather, which encouraged people to spend time outdoors, was a far greater enemy than any individual victim, since it caused the plague to spread with terrifying speed. By the middle of June, it had made further inroads into the City, claiming another four lives in Cripplegate. One, ironically, was the servant of a physician, Alexander Burnet, who had sent his man away to the City 'pesthouse' in St Giles Cripplegate before voluntarily quarantining himself and his household. By the middle of June, there had been nearly 200 deaths from plague, of which more than half were in St Giles parish. The death toll was rising inexorably: thirty-one people had died in the week of 30 May to 6 June in St Giles, and sixty-eight perished the week after.

One apothecary, William Boghurst, undertook a study of the tell-tale symptoms of the epidemic. Like Hodges, he noted the round, raised marks on the body, either purple or scarlet in colour, and eventual swellings (or 'buboes', leading to the name 'bubonic plague') that normally arose in the armpits or groin, as well as shivering, vomiting and headaches. Boghurst recorded an eclectic range of symptoms including hysterical laughter, cold sweats, 'griping' or cramping of the guts and diarrhoea. A combination of these symptoms meant 'infallible signs of death now at hand, and they seldom came single', as Boghurst noted. It was easy to tell who was fatally affected: 'I most commonly gave judgement whether people would live or die at the first visit.' It soon became common knowledge that buboes meant the presence of infection; Pepys wrote in his diary of 22 July that Burnet's servant had died 'of a bubo on his right groin, and two spots on his right thigh, which is the plague'. Some even referred to them as 'God's marks', perhaps ironically, as their effects were anything but godly.

Death from the plague was a hideous, drawn-out process. Those afflicted took about five days to die, vomiting blood and suffering agonizing pain and seizures. Occasionally, the buboes burst and the patient did not die of plague, but in their weakened state, in the squalor and filth around them, they seldom had long to live. There was a stigma attached to anyone of 'the better sort' who died this way, and there were instances of well-meaning individuals concealing the true causes of a person's death. Simon Patrick, the rector of St Paul's Covent Garden, claimed that the daughter of his parishioner Dr Ponteus had died of natural causes, rather than of plague. This allowed her to be buried in Christian fashion: a kindness, certainly, but a misguided one. The contagion was a more than effective leveller, claiming victims from every stratum of society from beggars to the wealthiest.

While money itself could not save anyone's skin, it could buy the means to escape from London. Pepys had noted on 21 June, 'I find all the town almost going, the coaches and wagons being all full of people going into the country', and he dispatched his wife Elizabeth and her mother to Woolwich on 5 July. The next day, Charles himself left the city for Hampton Court, although not before issuing a command for the mayor and aldermen to remain. His court would later relocate to Salisbury before arriving at Oxford on 27 September, around the peak of the contagion.

In the king's absence, Sir John Lawrence, the Lord Mayor, was in charge, aided by Albemarle, who remained in London throughout 1665. They were faced with an increasingly desperate situation; the week of 27 June to 4 July saw 438 victims buried. As citizens perished in their hundreds, and with the monarch absent from the scene, all hope seemed lost. The only people who profited from the situation were coach drivers and boatmen, who charged exorbitant prices to transport Londoners away from their stricken city. It cost at least five shillings to leave town, a sum beyond the reach of any artisan or skilled labourer.

It is impossible to know how many people fled the capital at the height of the plague, but the doctor William Sydenham estimated that 'at least two-thirds of the inhabitants had retired to the country to avoid infection'. Even allowing for exaggeration, that still represents an exodus of tens of thousands of people from the city, leaving behind only the poor and the sick. Patrick noted that the centre of town was 'very empty', and that, while 'the ordinary sort of people continued there', a ghostly atmosphere hung over the plague-ravaged streets, 'all the gentry and better sort of tradesmen being gone'. And the countryside to which so many Londoners fled was itself far from safe. Many were attacked en route, either by opportunistic robbers who knew that the travellers were likely to be carrying their portable property with them, or by frightened locals who associated the urban influx with disease and death.

Not everyone left London, however. Pepys remained in the City, unable or unwilling to abandon his position in the Naval Office, and many high-end tradesmen, including goldsmiths and scriveners, knew that abandoning their businesses would spell economic ruin. As they lurked fearfully around the City, hoping that pestilence would not visit their homes, the usual quacks and mountebanks crawled out from under their rocks, offering ever more fanciful remedies. As panic rose, so did the scale and outlandishness of the deceptions that they practised on the terrified and gullible. Bills were distributed advertising themselves as selling 'the royal antidote' and 'never-failing preservatives against the infection'. The remedies proposed included such unlikely things as powdered unicorn horn and liquid gold. Even those who were not out for profit were still credulous; John Allin, the Sussex vicar, claimed to have discovered a plant called 'nostock',* which was said to be permeated

---

* The word 'Nostoc' was first coined by the Renaissance physician and botanist Paracelsus, a derivation from the Greek word *νόσος*, or 'sickness'.

'by a magic substance derived from fallen stars'.

While many so-called 'medical authorities' knew little more about healing the afflicted than their patients, others were of more assistance. When the pestilence was at its height in the summer and autumn of 1665, Hodges remained in London to aid his patients, assisted by the surgeon Thomas Harman. Many he correctly diagnosed as suffering from terror, rather than illness, but there was still the ever-present danger of infection from the genuinely sick. Fortifying himself with 'the quantity of a nutmeg of the anti-pestilential electuary',* he spent several hours each day examining the sick, before taking breakfast. His precautions were basic; he drank a glass of Spanish white wine, or sack, 'to warm the stomach, refresh the spirits and dissipate any beginning lodgement of the infection', and ensured that his mind was 'as composed as possible' in the presence of the unwell; he threw quicklime on to the coals in his home in an attempt to 'destroy the efficacy of the pestilential miasmata'. Hodges himself fell temporarily sick on two occasions, but claimed to cure himself by the methodical application of sack; he commented, 'I have never yet met anything so agreeable to the nerves and spirits in all my experience.' He later wrote of his experiences in an invaluable work that appeared in 1666, *An Account Of The First Rise, Progress, Symptoms And Cure Of The Plague, being the substance of a letter from Dr Hodges to a person of quality.*†

---

* An 'electuary' was a chemical paste disguised with a sweetener to hide the usually vile taste.

† Hodges also published a treatise in Latin in 1672 called *Loimologia, or, an historical Account of the Plague in London in 1665, With precautionary Directions against the like Contagion.*

Of the 1,500 doctors, physicians and apothecaries in London before the plague, only around 300 remained at its height. Hodges was one of the only two doctors who were chosen by the College of Physicians to continue to practise, and he was offered £100 in September 'for the prevention and cure of the plague'. If, of course, he could survive that long. He took notes from the College of Physicians, who counselled against bleeding weakened plague victims, and instead recommended a drug called theriac, a combination of viper's flesh, onion, garlic and opium, which was said to have healing properties. The use of the snake was believed to neutralize the effects of the poison in the plague. Those who were not sick, such as Pepys, still took 'plague waters', a drink containing various herbs and spices. It was also believed that smoking tobacco could ward off the illness; Eton schoolboys were caned if they missed their daily smoke before prayers. *O tempora! O mores!*

By mid-July, the humid and oppressively warm summer weather (described by Pepys as 'most extraordinary hot that I ever knew') was exacerbating an already chaotic situation. Thousands of people were dying each week, even as food shortages threatened to lead to mass starvation. There was no longer such a thing as a 'safe place' in London, as contagion had spread to virtually every part of the city. Those who had to remain there, whether from financial necessity or choice, spent little time outside. The streets were almost silent, the only sounds to be heard were coughing, choking and weeping, interspersed with the occasional cry of 'Bring out your dead!' In the early days of the plague, a bell had tolled at St Giles for every death, but now they were so frequent and so numerous that it remained silent. In neighbouring parishes, however, church bells continued to sound their grim tocsin. Nearly all public places, including schools, theatres and law courts, were closed, the only gatherings being the occasional church services that were designed to pray for victims of the infection. Prisoners were doubly unfortunate: not only were the inhabitants of Newgate and Ludgate denied habeas corpus and confined indefinitely, in some cases without trial, but the filthy and cramped conditions within the jails were a breeding ground for plague, leading to many a de facto death sentence – for hardened criminal and petty thief alike.

The continued lockdown on London meant that traders were unable to sell their wares, either in the City, or elsewhere. The alderman Sir William Turner, who specialized in the sale of fine cloth, lamented, in a letter to his Paris trading partners, 'I have little to say at present, there being nothing to do by reason of the sickness... everyone hastes out of town which causes that there is no sale for goods and merchants pay ill.' As the chaos stretched on into the autumn of 1665, he would complain that 'it makes a miserable trade'. Nonetheless, Turner and his peers at least had the means to leave London if they needed to, unlike the city's poor, who were forced to turn to the parish for basic subsistence. Even as the death toll continued to rise (reaching 7,000 a week by the end of August), the impoverished still needed the basic necessities of existence, and parishes were obliged to appeal to the wealthy and generous for financial assistance. Some of the more compassionate gave gifts; St Margaret's in the west of the City recorded an income of £1,117 in aid. Others were either absent or uninterested in helping their fellow man, even in these times of extraordinary need.

Pepys remained in his post at the Navy Board for the duration of the plague. He saw it as his duty to face his potential fate, writing to the naval commissioner Sir William Coventry to say, 'You, sir, take your turn at the sword… I must not therefore grudge to take mine at the pestilence.' England was engaged in a naval war with the Dutch, and Pepys continued to benefit from the lucrative contracts, gratuities and bribes that came with his job. Even a serious epidemic could not halt the business of warmongering. It was with some satisfaction that Pepys wrote in his diary on 31 July: 'thus I end this month with the greatest joy that ever I did in all my life, because I have spent the greater part of it with abundance of joy and honour, and pleasant journeys and brave entertainment, and without cost of money.' The 'brave entertainment' included a visit to his occasional mistress Elizabeth Bagwell, whose husband was away at sea; the risk of infection that Pepys ran in travelling to Deptford where she lived was worth it for the carnal dalliance, even as he returned home 'in a most violent sweat'.

As the endless round of deaths continued, a curfew was introduced. Householders were warned to remain indoors after 9 p.m. Burials took place in mass pits both day and night. Those who loaded the dead onto carts to be taken away were paid fifteen shillings a week by the parish, a large sum of money, but a necessary expense, given how few would take the risk otherwise. The burial pits were located outside the City walls, in Finsbury Fields and Stepney among other places, and the cart drivers dumped the bodies in them as quickly as they could with neither ceremony nor respect, in the hope that they themselves would avoid contagion. These pits held enormous numbers of corpses; the Finsbury Fields pit alone contained 2,200 bodies. The constant threat of sudden, hideous death led to a general feeling of depression and fear in the city. Pepys wrote on 14 September that he had 'great apprehensions of melancholy', despite trying to 'put off the thoughts of sadness as much as I can'. The arrival of cooler weather in the autumn of 1665 made no difference to the toll exacted by the plague; in the week of 12–19 September, it was believed that up to 15,000 people died. Even recording the names of all those who perished had become a major task for the parish clerks, straining their abilities and facilities to the limit. In some cases, as at St Botolph-without-Bishopsgate, the clerks themselves expired, leading to further administrative chaos. The only group who kept entirely accurate records of their members were the Quakers, who continued to visit the sick, despite the risks to their own health.

Those who remained in the city through choice, rather than necessity, began to consider themselves beleaguered soldiers in a seemingly never-ending siege. Since it was believed the plague was transmitted by 'bad air', street fires were lit in an attempt to purify the atmosphere. But the smoke and smog they produced polluted the city yet further, and lent the streets of London an apocalyptic appearance. Hodges later claimed that 4,000 people died as a result of these fires and their harmful emissions. In the midst of death, the grimmest form of gallows humour developed. One possibly apocryphal story, which Daniel Defoe later recycled in *A Journal of the Plague*

Year,* concerned a Scottish piper who drunkenly collapsed one night, was assumed dead and was loaded on to a cart with other corpses. Regaining consciousness, he attempted to attract the driver's attention by frantically playing his bagpipes. The noise that ensued made the driver believe that the Scotsman was in fact the devil, and he fled in mortal terror. Whether the piper continued to evade death is unknown.

Even some of those who were infected managed to summon up a final spirit of reckless – even malicious – defiance. Hodges recorded some of those in the city throwing infected bandages through the windows of their neighbours, and literally laughing in the faces of passers-by. He also saw some victims breaking out of their houses and running madly down the street, summoning up their remaining energy in a doomed attempt at some kind of escape. All this he ascribed to a form of madness: 'the plague seemed to have complicated in its production everything of a poisonous and destroying nature'.

While London was the part of England worst affected by the plague, the rest of the country did not escape infection. Although the 'Great Plague of London', as it was called in the early summer, began as an urban pestilence, it soon carried into the Midlands and East Anglia, and reached as far north as Newcastle and as far southwest as Dorset and Devon. Up to 100,000 people died of plague outside of London in 1665 and 1666, giving the lie to the idea that it was restricted to the capital. Colchester was especially badly affected, with 161

---

* This fictional account of the plague year was first published in March 1722; Defoe had been five at the time of its outbreak, and so the book was based upon the journals of an 'HF', probably his uncle Henry Foe.

people dying of plague in the week from 29 September to 6 October; this was more than seven times the number who died of other causes. The East Anglian naval commissioner William Doyly saw chaos break out as a result of captured Dutch prisoners, themselves already infected, spreading further sickness in cramped and unhygienic prison conditions. He wrote to his fellow commissioner John Evelyn to say 'the sickness is broken out most fiercely. The present mayor hath no authority to rule this numerous people.' Panic and lawlessness broke out, and the army had to be called in. It had little effect, as the dispirited and frightened population were summarily reduced by lingering plague, which remained in the town until early December 1666. The town, which had been a medium-sized one of around 5,000 inhabitants at the beginning of 1665, was reduced to barely half of that the following year.

Further north, an even more curious incident occurred. At the village of Eyam in Derbyshire, 160 miles north of London, there was an outbreak of plague towards the end of 1665, thought to have been carried on infected cloth delivered from London to a man named Edward Cooper. Cooper's servant, George Vicars, fell ill almost immediately and was dead within four days. To deal with the infection, the village acted quickly and took measures to stop the spread of disease. The village rector, William Mompesson, fearing the villagers were on the verge of fleeing and infecting the surrounding areas, ordered that a quarantine be enforced. Food and supplies were delivered regularly, but nobody was to leave or enter the village. On 11 October 1666, three months after the last reported death, it was assumed that the plague had left Eyam, and the village was reopened. The remote village lost 259 of its 350 inhabitants, but by keeping its fear and illness to itself it may well have prevented the plague from spreading across a wider area.

One of the few people to survive a bout of the plague was Alice Thornton* of East Newton in Yorkshire, a moderately well-to-do woman in her late thirties. She recounted in her diary that she had fallen into 'a very sad and desperate condition' around 16 August 1666 and was expected to die within three days, but 'it pleased God, upon the use of [the doctor's] medicines, that extremity a little abated'. Nonetheless, she was in 'continual faintings' and believed that 'my loss of spirits and strength was so great that it was expected that I should have fallen into a deep consumption'. Her strength was restored partly by 'a medicine made of muscadine', but also because of her religious beliefs and knowledge of her status as a wife and mother; bravely, she wrote that although she was in a bad state, 'death in itself being desirable', she was determined to 'perform to my utmost capacity with a good conscience towards all'.

One of the few places outside London untouched by plague was Oxford, where Charles, like his father before him, had his satellite court. Those around the king guarded access to him zealously: for Charles to have sickened and died would have prompted a monarchical crisis that might have seen England, already weakened by expensive foreign wars, reduced to little more than a backwater. Nonetheless, 'the merry monarch' continued to live as full a life as he could in the circumstances,

---

* For another incident from Thornton's unhappy life, see page 194–5.

enjoying the company of actresses (including the woman who would eventually become his most famous mistress, Nell Gwyn, who had followed the court to Oxford) and such entertainments as could be offered. The French diplomat Denis de Repas later wrote to the politician Sir Robert Harley about his experiences in the city at this time, saying, 'there's no other plague here but the infection of love; no other discourse but of ballets, dance and fine clothes; no other emulation but who shall look the handsomest... none other fight than for "I am yours"'. The antiquary Anthony à Wood commented on the 'nasty and beastly ways' of the courtiers living in Oxford.

Everyday life and government continued in Oxford as far as possible. Parliament met at Convocation House, the western section of the famous Bodleian Library, in October 1665, while the Lords met in the Geometry School, now part of the Bodleian's Lower Reading Room. Charles fixed upon Christ Church, the grandest of the colleges, as his own seat. The newsworthy items of the day were published in a newly created pamphlet, the *Oxford Gazette*; it was this publication that Muddiman eventually turned into the *London Gazette* when the court returned to the capital early the following year (see page 98). Yet national morale was lowered by the refusal of the king and his courtiers to return to the capital until there was no further risk of plague, and, after the first few months, a sense of hopelessness overcame many of those remaining in London. Without the totemic figure of Charles, the city seemed diminished and empty.

Finally, and mercifully, the death toll began to fall slightly. In the first week of December, as hard frosts set in, the number of confirmed fatalities fell from 333 cases to 210. As sub-zero temperatures continued over Christmas, it seemed as if many of the plague's carriers were being killed off by the freezing weather. The first week of January 1666 saw just seventy deaths as a result of the contagion. But fear of the plague still stalked the city. One of the pensioners of Charterhouse Hospital, Edward Swan, writing to the Buckinghamshire vicar Henry Oxinden in early 1666, remarked: 'I have not but once been out of our gates now almost complete seven months.' Swan expressed relief, nonetheless, at the reduced levels of mortality: 'it hath pleased the great good God to decrease the sickness very much this last week.' He also had observations to make on the economic impact of the plague: 'I believe money is as scarce with most men in East Kent as [it is] with us here.' Later in the year, Swan wrote to Oxinden again, inviting him to visit and recommending the inn at the Sign of the Red Lion in Aldersgate Street. He described it as 'very good accommodation... which has been free from any contagion all these times'. Suspicion and unease, however, would linger on in the capital throughout 1666.

Even as the death toll shrank and those who had fled their homes returned to London, other problems emerged, not least the disposal of the dead, for whom space in the graveyards had long since run out. Mass bonfires and plague pits were built, but so great were the numbers of the dead that these proved to be less useful than envisaged. Pepys, whose doctor Alexander Burnet had been one of the few initial survivors of the plague before eventually succumbing, noted in his diary of 30 January that 'it frighted me more than I thought it could have done, to see so many graves lie so high upon the churchyard'. This was a relic of the practice of burying bodies in vaults underneath the churches, which, by then, were running well over capacity. Pepys's own local church, St Olave's, had 146 corpses buried in its churchyard. These were often interred during the day, flouting the order that they should only be buried at night. A further command was given out by magistrates that the bodies should be covered in lime, but this was only half-heartedly carried out, with the result that the pervasive stench of contagion and rotting was still prominent at the beginning of 1666.

Eventually, with the plague reduced in scale, it was considered safe for the king and his court to return to London. On 1 February 1666, Charles was once again at Whitehall. On his way back to London, the bells had rung in celebration of the king's journey home; it made a welcome change from their mournful tolling to announce yet another death in the parish. When Charles resumed his place, the legislative business of court resumed. The law courts were convened and the shops reopened. Most of those who had left town in fear came back, reasoning that if it was safe enough for royalty then it must be safe enough for them as well. Barely two weeks after the king's return, life in London seemed to be going on as before; an anonymous crony of the aristocrat the Earl of Ogle wrote to him to say, 'the town is very full of people after this great mortality, there being no miss of any, and very few shops shut up'. 'No miss of any' was true, up to a point; no aristocrat, major courtier or politician died of plague. Those who had perished had been mainly the impoverished and the desperate, who had hoped that the Restoration would represent a change in their pathetic circumstances, but instead found themselves as oppressed by bureaucratic indifference as they had ever been by war or illness. The plague would linger on until the end of 1666, mainly in isolated pockets outside London – as at Eyam – but it soon became an unpleasant memory rather than a major concern.

The Great Plague was a traumatic chapter in the history of London, killing as many as a quarter of its inhabitants. But the city would soon recover. Hodges's account of the plague, *Loimologia: or, an Historical Account of the Plague in London in 1665*, declared that people 'had the courage to marry again, and betake to the means of repairing the past mortality; and even women before deemed barren were said to prove prolific'. Those who had either escaped its grasp, or even the fortunate few that had recovered from it, gave thanks and set about their daily business. Good health was never a given state, and being alive, and able to do anything of any consequence, was enough for many. And this spirit of *carpe diem* was one that those fortunate enough to have the means and opportunity to enjoy themselves were determined to take full advantage of.

Going Out

'Must we not pay a debt to pleasure too?'
– John Wilmot, earl of Rochester,
'The Imperfect Enjoyment'

In January 1666, Samuel Pepys became one of the first people in England to experience what would become a feature of modern life: he became infatuated with an actress. The object of the diarist's desire was Elizabeth Knepp, a member of the King's Company who became one of the integral figures in the troupe. Elizabeth probably joined the company in 1664: it is recorded that she was cast in the role of Lusetta in Thomas Killigrew's *Thomaso* that year – although, thanks to its inordinate length and complexity, it was never staged – and played the title role of Epicœne in Ben Jonson's play.

Between 1642 and 1660, English theatres had been closed by the Puritans. Their re-opening at the Restoration had been accompanied by a socially significant innovation: women took to the stage to play characters of their own sex for the first time. Until now, women's roles had been taken by boy actors and young men in female attire. The contemporary writer and satirist Tom Brown later described the playhouse as a 'land of enchantment... here, in the twinkling of an eye, you shall see men transformed into demi-gods, and goddesses made as true flesh and blood as our common women'. It was little wonder that these 'demi-gods' and 'goddesses' enjoyed huge acclaim, or that ordinary people were so infatuated by them.

The star actor of the day, Charles Hart, excelled in both tragedy and comedy, playing many of the great Shakespearean roles. He would go on to create such parts as Mark Antony in John Dryden's rewriting of *Antony and Cleopatra*, *All For Love* (1677), and the archetypal Restoration rake, Horner, in William Wycherley's *The Country Wife* (1675). Hart had begun his career as a boy actor before the civil war, and during the conflict had served gallantly on the Royalist side, earning himself a good deal of royal favour when he returned to the stage.

It was harder for actresses, who found themselves regarded as not much better than prostitutes, an occupation that many found themselves driven to between roles. Even a successful actress such as Elizabeth Knepp, who played both male and female roles, was caught between a curious mixture of artistic fulfilment and social conservatism. Actresses faced a tough struggle to establish their credibility. Even being married did not always ameliorate their situation. Pepys noted that Elizabeth's 'surly' husband Christopher, a horse dealer, treated her badly, perhaps because he felt threatened by his wife's independence as an actress.

Elizabeth was responsible for the entertainment between acts, singing and dancing and speaking prologues and epilogues as appropriate. She certainly knew Nell Gwyn, who was also acting in the King's Company from 1665 onwards, initially in Dryden's *The Indian Queen*, after having been an orange-seller-cum-pimp, and possibly an occasional prostitute herself. Nell became firstly the mistress of Hart, with whom she often played a pair of witty lovers on (and off) stage, and then eventually the king's consort in 1668. Elizabeth may or may not have had affairs in 1666, but if she was promiscuous she was more discreet about it than Nell; her only known extra-marital liaison came much later, with the actor Joseph Haines, and resulted in her death in childbirth in 1681. But Elizabeth lacked the opportunities for advancement that came Nell's way, being on the margins of the royal court rather than at its centre.

Pepys was captivated by her, although less out of compassionate concern than lechery. He became godfather to her son, and enjoyed her singing and flirtatiousness. He makes reference to her virtually every day in his diary in the first week of January 1666 and frequently thereafter, normally with lascivious overtones – 'she the pleasantest company in the world', and 'I very pleasant to her'. It is possible that Pepys and Knepp were lovers – his diary suggests that he kissed and fondled her – but it is more likely that Pepys exaggerated their encounters for his own enjoyment and satisfaction, and that she tolerated his advances out of a mixture of amusement and a wish for distraction while not consummating the affair. Pepys's wife was unimpressed; one diary entry included the unsurprising observation that: '[I] perceive my wife hath no great pleasure in her being here', and another (9 May) records that she was 'mightily vexed at my being abroad with these women... when they were gone, [she] called them whores and I know not what; which vexed me, having been so innocent with them'. Pepys's claimed innocence needs to be set against the fact that he would later write, in his diary entry for 21 April 1668, that he 'had the opportunity, the first time in my life, to be bold with Knepp'.

Whether or not he was aware of it, Pepys was participating in a new social phenomenon, that of libertinism. While the word later became associated with debauchery and rakishness,* its original sense extended beyond sexual freedom and the opportunity to fulfil one's selfish desires. The term 'libertine' was coined by the French theologian John Calvin, who used it to describe his political opponents in sixteenth-century Geneva. Philosophical libertinism, in the sense of the espousal of freedom of thought, may be said to have originated with Michel de Montaigne later in the same century. This was further developed in the seventeenth century when a group of philosophers including Gabriel Naudé and Louis XIV's tutor François de La Mothe Le Vayer were collectively known as the *libertins érudits*. They suggested that man was essentially a flawed and animalistic being who, rather than attempting to follow a moral code ordained by society, should surrender to his own desires and interests.

The selfish pursuit of fun was certainly one of the primary concerns of those who lived under the Restoration. In this new age the restrictive shackles of the Puritan regime were cast off in spectacular fashion. While the idea of England having been a restrained and godly place until the year 1660 is a misleading one – bear-baiting and gambling had been thriving since the

---

* As depicted, for example, in the sexual behaviour of the Vicomte de Valmont in Pierre Choderlos de Laclos' novel *Les Liaisons dangereuses*, first published in 1782.

sixteenth century, if not before, and young men had been losing their virginities to prostitutes since time immemorial – the abrupt lifting of restrictions on entertainment, and their venues, meant that a cornucopia of options presented themselves, ranging from the virtuous to the vice-laden. Whether you were after a spectacular public occasion, surrounded by hundreds if not thousands of your peers, or a more intimate encounter with a temporary companion, every moment could be taken up with some pursuit or distraction.

The greatest socially unifying factor in London was the theatre, a place described by one guide, *The Country Gentleman's Vade Mecum*, as attracting 'judges, wits, censurers… squires, sharpers, bullies and whores'. The newly reopened playhouses offered a new repertoire of bawdy comedies that were coming into vogue and which reflected the new permissiveness of the Restoration. Even the closure of the playhouses for much of 1665 and 1666 because of the plague failed to quell the appetite for riotous amusement, which began once again with their reopening. All society went to the theatre, from King Charles to 'ordinary apprentices and mean people', as Pepys described them. Theatre was thus the most egalitarian entertainment of the day, even if royalty and the groundlings were hardly rubbing shoulders. The revived theatre was not to everyone's taste: the Puritans continued to carp and John Evelyn wrote in October 1666 that he was 'very seldom going to the public theatres for many reasons now'; obligingly, he went on to give some of these reasons, which included the fact that 'they were abused to an atheistical liberty' and host to 'foul and indecent women now'. Few others shared Evelyn's distaste for the antics on stage. Venues such as the Theatre Royal in Drury Lane and the Lincoln's Inn Fields theatre could hold anything up to 700 spectators. These were, respectively, home to the two licensed companies of the day, Thomas Killigrew's King's Company at the Theatre Royal (the actors in which had to take an oath of loyalty to Charles, and were considered part of the royal household) and William Davenant's Duke's Company at Lincoln's Inn. It was a considerable coup to be granted a royal licence; recipients were given free rein over the plays performed, and the prices charged for tickets. The two licensees could hardly have been more different. Killigrew was an absurd and often drunken figure who provided a great deal of entertainment to the royal court; Pepys noted in February 1668 that he 'hath a fee out of the wardrobe for caps and bells, under the title of the king's fool and jester'.* But he was far from stupid; he had written plays himself before the civil war and, after the Restoration, he encouraged the work of such writers as Dryden, Aphra Behn and Wycherley. Additionally, he was an ardent supporter of Charles, and had even followed the royal court into exile.

Davenant, meanwhile, was a fascinating man. Under special dispensation from Cromwell, he had privately staged part one of what might be described as the first English opera, *The Siege of Rhodes*, in 1656, with the composers Matthew Locke and Henry Lawes. He had circumvented Puritan objections to dramatic presentation by describing the piece as 'recitative music', which was still permitted, thereby establishing

---

* This was reinforced by his 1673 appointment as Master of the Revels.

himself as England's first opera impresario. Aged sixty in 1666, he was a loyal Royalist whose previous literary endeavours had consisted mainly of tragedies and comedies; a series of panegyrics written to General Monck and Charles between 1660 and 1663 was the reason for his rise in royal favour.

The London playhouses were considered the finest in the country, although there was little competition. Restoration theatres represented a distinct shift away from the earlier traditions of open-air venues such as the Globe. Their interiors were lavishly painted and offered a level of comfort that mirrored the growing European trend for a more luxurious and enjoyable social experience. Pepys described the surroundings of the Lincoln's Inn theatre as 'very fine and magnificent'. Both the Royal and Lincoln's Inn were illuminated by hundreds of candles, and scenery was portable to allow for rapid set changes, which took place in front of the audience. The playhouses were designed around proscenium arches and thrust stages, which ran out into a common pit, and then there was a system of tiered boxes for the more discerning theatregoers. The royal box sat in the most prestigious location, on the first floor and directly opposite the stage, offering the king the best view of proceedings.

Tickets cost anything from one shilling for the ordinary visitors perched in the gallery or sitting on benches in the pit to four shillings for the men and ladies of fashion in their boxes, who were as interested in holding assignations and mocking their enemies as they were in watching the entertainment on stage. It was considered de rigueur for women to wear masks, initially for propriety's sake but soon because this added a frisson to their appearances in public. For more selective performances (as became necessary during the plague), there was a temporary playhouse constructed at Whitehall, under the supervision of the architect John Webb, which was variously known as 'the theatre in the Great Hall' or 'the Hall theatre'. Pepys noted the first production took place there on 20 April 1665, and this catered for royal command performances. If Charles, for whatever reason, decided against visiting the playhouse, then the playhouse must come to him.

Plays were advertised by a flag being hoisted up to the top of the roof of the theatre, a tradition that stretched back to Elizabethan days and was cheerfully revived. Once the audience had arrived – a process that could take hours, given that theatregoers began to pile into the theatre at noon, without any sense of order or decorum – the performance was expected to begin at between half past three and four o'clock, and lasted beyond sunset outside the summer months. It was as much a social as a cultural occasion, with people coming to gossip, eye up likely conquests and enjoy themselves on a day out; it took a very good entertainment to distract the audience. If the play was especially poor, the audience would signal their displeasure by pelting the unfortunate actors with rotten apples and oranges – as well as equally fruity invective. Little wonder that iron railings were soon erected at the front of the stage for their partial protection.

What the audiences came to see was an eclectic selection of entertainments. When Charles reopened the playhouses in 1660, there were no new plays for Killigrew and Davenant to present. Little of any significance had been written since the reign of Charles I; of that period's three greatest playwrights, Philip Massinger, John Ford and James Shirley, Massinger and Ford were long since dead and Shirley had retired when Parliament had suppressed stage plays in 1642. This necessitated a new repertoire and a new breed of writers to write them. Their works were then staged for a matter of days, rather than weeks or months, although the most popular ones were likely to be revived in subsequent years. The least popular, meanwhile, such as George Etherege's 1668 comedy *She Would If She Could*, were hastily taken off after a couple of performances, and the actors redeployed on other, more successful, works.

While the Restoration era is now synonymous with comedies its early years, however, were associated with heroic drama, most notably Sir Robert Howard's and John Dryden's *The Indian Queen* (1664) and its 1665 sequel, *The Indian Emperor*. This overblown genre, which was much mocked by the court wits and gallants, reached its apogee in Dryden's 1670 play *The Conquest of Granada*. Its ten acts of bombast were greeted with groans and hilarity in equal measure.* These plays were typically set in exotic, far-flung locations, requiring considerable creativity in both costumes and scenery, and featured noble heroes, warrior kings, virginal princesses and lengthy scenes of self-denial and self-sacrifice. As well as the good and the virtuous, however, these dramas also depicted villainous characters and whores, in whose gleeful pleasure-seeking certain members of the audience may have seen a reflection of their own unrepentant

---

* It led to the Duke of Buckingham's 1671 parody, *The Rehearsal*, which in turn inspired Sheridan's burlesque, *The Critic*.

libertinism. The most enduring comedies of the Restoration period, such as Wycherley's *The Country Wife* (1675) and Etherege's *The Man of Mode* (1676), were not produced until the middle of the following decade, and their rake-libertine protagonists, such as Horner and Dorimant, were played by star actors; similarities between these celebrity performers and the characters they portrayed were teasingly implied.

Other than drama, the most common form of entertainment in 1666 was prostitution. The theatre itself was an especially notorious hunting ground for whores, where brothel madams often took their newest girls to be inspected by theatregoers, and where the so-called 'Orange Moll', who was responsible for the sale of oranges and sweetmeats, also acted as a procuress for her girls, in case a punter was hungry for something else. Dryden wrote a sardonic poem, 'Poor Pensive Punk',* that talked of the girls' 'loose undress', as they received 'some cullie's soft address' while 'demurely [sitting]/Angling for bubbles in the noisy pit'. He was no great fan – unlike 'the merry gang' of court wits – of the 'place of traffic' where the whores sold 'their rotten-ware', and ended the poem with the telling couplet:

> For while he nibbles at her amorous trap,
> She gets the money but he gets the clap.

* 'Punk' was a term for a prostitute or harlot, first appearing in the 1590s.

By 1660, there were as many as 300 brothels throughout the city, ranging from high-end establishments in the centre of town (including one situated close to the House of Lords) to less salubrious places in the wilds of Smithfield, where the presence of whores was so commonplace that streets were christened Gropecunt Lane and Cock Lane. The 'prentices' and other menials were reduced to hurried couplings in the notorious stews of Covent Garden or, if they fancied their chances with the dockside prostitutes, Ratcliffe Highway by Wapping. The standard euphemism for these places of ill repute, wherever they were, was a 'house of resort'.

The Restoration had led to a surge in erotic appetites, as could be seen by the rise in pornography imported from France and Italy; the latter was heavy on depictions of sodomy, which remained illegal even while it was practised by many gentlemen of 'quality'.* It also reflected the continued desire for men to take their pleasure with whichever poor, broken-down wretch could be cajoled by a madam to spread her legs for a few shillings in order to give her grunting client a few seconds of satisfaction. Prostitutes were generally female; although there were a few streets where a likely lad could be found and hired for the evening, there were no male brothels of note.† If an aristocratic woman wished to be pleasured by a handsome young coachman or link boy, their attentions could be easily bought.

---

* Sodomy was so widespread that a later poem of Rochester's began 'Love a woman? You're an ass!' and went on to boast, 'There's a sweet, soft page of mine/Does the trick worth forty wenches.'

† Homosexual meeting places, the so-called 'molly houses', did not come into existence until the early eighteenth century.

Charles himself led by example when it came to sexual promiscuity. While he did not visit the various brothels in London himself, reserving his excursions to the 'stews' for his visits to the notoriously debauched Newmarket races, he was a connoisseur of women of easy virtue, whether it was Nell Gwyn, the beautiful but foul-tempered Barbara Castlemaine, or her sweet-natured and innocent protégé Frances Stewart. By 1666, Charles was sufficiently enraptured with Frances to commission the goldsmith Jan Roettiers to immortalize her on the coins of the nation as the face of Britannia. Pepys lusted after both of them, describing Barbara with both love ('without whom all is nothing') and loathing ('I know well enough she is a whore'). Of Frances, as early as 1664 Pepys sighed that she was 'the most beautifullest creature that ever I saw in my life, more than ever I thought her, as often as I have seen her'. He even believed that '[she] doth exceed Lady Castlemaine'.

Charles managed to keep his sexual dalliances largely hidden from the outside world, but his predilections were known by a growing number of Whitehall attendants and civil servants, including Pepys, who wrote an account of one mistress, Winifred Wells, whom he saw dressed in male attire in June 1666. The shocked diarist recorded how she and a companion were attired 'with coats and doublets with deep skirts, just for all the world like men, and buttoned their doublets up the breast, with periwigs and with hats, so that, only for a long petticoat dragging under their men's coats, nobody could take them for women in any point whatever'. Pepys was careful to describe this as 'an odd sight, and a sight that did not please me', but the glimpse of an attractive woman dressed in breeches, as if on the stage, almost certainly stirred him rather more than he was prepared to admit.

The most famous prostitute of the age – as opposed to a royal courtesan like Barbara Castlemaine – was Damaris Page, the so-called 'Crafty Bawd' who was made notorious by a semi-fictional series of pamphlets by the Grub Street writer John Garfield. *The Wandering Whore* made it clear that Page was Top Bawd, among the 138 bawds, 269 ordinary prostitutes and assorted pimps, untrustworthy clients and kidnappers depicted. By 1666, the crafty bawd was in her mid-fifties and no longer a working girl but a madam and canny businesswoman whose trade was vastly helped by the country's rapid naval expansion during the Restoration. Sailors were her natural clients; many of them were innocents who were lured into drunkenness and then press-ganged – a practice sanctioned in 1597 and formally introduced in 1664. Page was an adept recruiter of young men for the navy. By these means, she enjoyed connections to some of the highest in the land, such as the naval commander Sir Edward Spragge, who remarked to Pepys, 'As long as Damaris Page lives, I shall not lack men.'

In 1668, Page and some of the other leading madams, such as Elizabeth Cresswell, were targeted in a series of attacks known as the 'Bawdy House Riots' which began on 24 March. The significance of the day was that it was the traditional date for apprentices to visit brothels before a period of celibacy began during Lent. The riots were started by Dissenters angered that their conventicles were illegal but that brothels were tolerated; however, they soon came to involve thousands of young men, all of whom made for the brothel districts of Smithfield, Shoreditch and Moorfields. Armed with 'iron bars, poleaxes, long staves and other weapons', they set about demolishing any bawdy houses that they could find. The violence was in part a result of general mischief-making, but it was also a reflection of public anger at the status quo. Pepys overheard some 'idle fellows' commenting that 'they did ill in contenting themselves in pulling down the little bawdy-houses, and did not go and pull down the great bawdy-house at Whitehall'.

The riots lasted for several days, led by the Dissenter Robert Sharpless. They had the sympathy of the general public, especially in their demands for religious freedom and 'liberty of conscience'. Pepys wrote that 'none of the bystanders [found] fault with [the assailants], but rather of the soldiers for hindering them'. Attacks on brothels by apprentices had been a recurrent feature of seventeeth-century London before the Civil War, and were tolerated by the authorities as an element of 'the ancient administration of justice at Shrovetide', as the political theorist James Harrington described it. But the riot of 1668 was more serious than its predecessors, in both size and duration, and clearly presented more of a threat to public order. Damaris Page herself was targeted because of her involvement with press-ganging, and her premises attacked. Her enemies had to be dealt with severely, and so, after this contretemps, Sharpless and three others were arrested, arraigned and executed. Their conviction was brought about by Page's evidence being given undue weight in court, adding to the sense of an establishment stitch-up.

Those opposed to her were not done with their revenge. Page's name was attached to a so-called 'poor whore's petition', a satirical document purporting to be from her and Cresswell that asked 'the most splendid, illustrious, serene and eminent Lady of Pleasure', Barbara Castlemaine, to come to the financial assistance of 'the undone company of poor distressed whores', who were explicitly described as her 'sisters' in the petition. Pepys noted that Castlemaine was 'horribly vexed' by the letter. Damaris Page died in 1669, having made a great deal of money out of trading in pleasure.

Those who frequented prostitutes did so at their own risk. Garfield gave an account of how a typical transaction would go, including the detail that whores kissed vigorously and open-mouthed, and would typically offer the punter the opportunity to 'thrust his hand into the best cunt in Christendom', followed by the rest. Primitive condoms made of sheep's guts, leather or (most useless of all) linen, were available, but these offered little protection against infection, and were even less effective as contraceptives. It was equally risky for the women involved. Abortion was regarded as a form of contraception after the fact, but the risks involved in it were high, even if the services of a midwife or 'wise woman' were sought.

Both sexes, however, were at risk of what was called 'the great pox', as syphilis* was then named, to distinguish it from

---

* The word 'syphilis' was coined by an Italian, Girolamo Fracastoro, in an epic poem (written in the first half of the sixteenth century) in which he described the ravages of the disease in Italy. (The first well-attested outbreak of syphilis in Europe had occurred in 1495 and affected French troops besieging Naples.)

smallpox. The consequences of the disease ranged from the disfiguring to the fatal. Davenant, who contracted the illness as a young man from 'a black handsome wench', later suffered the collapse of the bridge of his nose. He was lucky compared to some, such as Rochester, who reached the tertiary stage of the illness, enduring madness and paralysis before dying in 1680. Syphilis was also hereditary – Rochester's son Charles, for one, suffered for the sins of his father – and a bitter legacy indeed. The cruel saying 'one night with Venus, a lifetime with Mercury'* was all too apposite. The prospect of such torments, however, apparently did nothing to stem the tide of clients eager to procure the sexual favours of the nocturnal wanderers.

Pepys, like many other men of the time, was both fascinated and frightened by whores, of whom there were rumoured to be around 1,500 at work in London in 1666. He wrote in his diary on 14 March 1666 that he took 'two or three wanton turns around the idle places and lanes of Drury Lane', but found no 'satisfaction', being scared off by 'a great fear of the plague among them'. Instead, Pepys frequently sought the company of the aptly named and more adventurous 'Captain Cock', a disreputable former Baltic merchant and naval contractor called George Cocke who was given to drinking and lewd behaviour and 'frolicking', as Pepys described the low-level adventures he enjoyed. Pepys's many extra-marital excursions involved not prostitutes but parlour maids and haberdashers, whom he encountered everywhere from churches to shops,

* Mercury was formerly used to treat syphilis, its toxic effects frequently proving as damaging to the patient as those of the disease itself.

and seduced in taverns before doing 'what I would with her', a state of affairs that the diarist admitted gave him 'great pleasure'. The attitude of simultaneous licentiousness and disdain for it that characterized the age was best reported by Pepys after the Bawdy House Riots, when Charles, on being told that whorehouses and brothels were both a blight on the country and a grievous temptation to the poor, replied airily, 'Why do they go to them, then?' Well might he ask.

⸎

If poverty or disinclination meant that you had no interest in the theatre or brothels, there were other amusements. There were puppet shows at Charing Cross, including Punch and Judy, newly imported from the Italian *Pulcinella* shows (anglicized to 'Punchinello'), and the royal zoo at the Tower of London, complete with exotic animals such as tigers, and lions, one of which, Crowly, Pepys described as 'now a very great lion and very tame'. Wandering players and showmen entertained those attending seasonal markets and fairs. These included festivities associated with May Day, which was reinstated when Charles was restored to the throne, and the rowdy Bartholomew Fair, which took place over two weeks from 24 August to 7 September in West Smithfield, and had existed since the twelfth century. It was a lively event, featuring entertainers of every kind from jugglers and fire-eaters to freaks and ballad-singers. Although it did not take place in 1665 and 1666 owing to the plague, it returned in 1667, and Pepys pronounced himself 'glad to see again' the spectacle there.

The Dutch visitor William Schellinks, who may have been moonlighting as a spy at a time of tense relations between the two countries, visited England in 1661, later publishing an account of his journey. He wrote about attending a concert at a music hall near Moorfields in London, where he listened to an organ, dulcimers and bass violins, and was enraptured by 'a remarkable performance by a buffoon or jester, who played a drunk and danced with a tame monkey and two or three burning candles, and made his exit by turning somersaults'. Exotic animals seemed to be an everyday part of life at this time; Schellinks also noted seeing a young lion and a camel at that year's Bartholomew Fair.

Public places to walk and talk were also popular. Ladies and gentlemen of quality would head to the New Spring Gardens at Vauxhall, which had been opened in 1660 and continued to attract a diverse range of visitors. The gardens were open daily, except Sundays, from May to September, and were popular with those who wished either to partake of the food on sale, which included such items as lobster and syllabub, or simply to enjoy an assignation there. Schellinks praised them as 'very large and most beautiful and interesting', and Pepys gave the New Spring Garden the nickname 'Fox-Hall', a play on 'Vauxhall'. He described it in a diary entry of 28 May 1667:

> I by water to Fox-hall, and there walked in Spring-garden. A great deal of company, and the weather and garden pleasant: and it is very pleasant and cheap going thither, for a man may go to spend what he will, or nothing, all as one. But to

hear the nightingale and other birds, and hear fiddles and
there a harp, and here a Jew's trump, and here laughing, and
there fine people walking, is mighty diverting.

The gardens occupied twelve acres, with pavilions, temples
and grottoes, and included everything from concert halls
to supper boxes, which were ideal for assignations. They
had supplanted the Old Spring Garden nearby, which Pepys
dismissed as expensive and lacking in atmosphere.

A more central place to take a relaxing stroll was St James's
Park, which, under the auspices of Charles was redesigned in
the style of French pleasure gardens by the Frenchman André
Mollet, featuring an enormous canal at its centre, and with
parrots and flamingos roaming free. The park was closed in late
1665 when the plague was ravaging London, and only reopened
in early 1666. Edmund Waller wrote a sycophantic poem about
it, 'On St James's Park, as Lately Improved by His Majesty',
which described it as a new paradise, praising Charles's 'manly
posture, and his graceful mien', and employed overblown
neoclassical metaphors in an attempt to curry royal favour.
(Waller wrote similar paeans in praise of the new buildings
at Somerset House in 1665 and a new statue of Charles I in
1676; had there been the opening of a royal envelope, no doubt
that would have occasioned a poem as well.) St James's Park,
like all the other grander spaces in London, was a royal park;
Charles's showed his broader commitment to creating green
spaces in the city saw him acquire another tract of land to
the northwest of St James's in 1668, which became Upper St
James's Park (now Green Park). The city's most famous green

space, Hyde Park, was restocked with deer, and great men and women took pleasure in circumnavigating the park in their carriages.

The gardens also — inevitably — became places of debauchery and lewd assignation, not least for Charles himself, who often took his latest mistresses there. Rochester would eroticize St James's Park in his notorious poem 'A Ramble in St. James's Park', in which he characterized it as a place where 'buggeries, rapes, and incests [are] made' and which is home to all manner of society, from 'carmen, divines, great lords, and tailors' to 'prentices, poets, pimps, and jailers'. The only thing that united them all was that it was a place where they 'promiscuously did swive'. It was at night that the park came fully alive, with its central location ideal for drunken gallants intent on sport — or for adulterous husbands seeking a clandestine location for a rendezvous with a mistress or paid companion before returning home.

Other outdoor activities also proved to be popular. After being outlawed during the Commonwealth, such games as football and tennis enjoyed a renaissance, with new rules being drawn up for them. A *Book of Games* by the ornithologist Francis Willughby attempted to introduce a sense of decorum to football. Willughby specified the presence of goals, 'a close that has a gate at either side', and rules, such as the ball (normally a pig's bladder filled with air) being kicked through the goal. It was a hazardous sport: Willughby noted, 'They often break one another's shins when two meet and strike both together against the ball, and therefore there is a law that they must not strike higher than the ball', and 'tripping-up of heels' was a constant irritant. It remains unclear how much notice was taken of Willughby's well-intentioned designs, with football, which was often played on town and village greens on Sunday after church, continuing to be a pell-mell exercise in (sometimes) good-natured violence. For those who moved in grander circles, Charles popularized yachting – a sport previously unknown in England – which he had first noticed, and participated in, during his exile in the Netherlands. The Dutch word for a fast, light sailing boat of this type, *jaght*, was later anglicized to 'yacht'. He was presented with one of these yachts, named *Mary*, upon his departure from Holland in 1660, among a number of gifts that the States-General of the Netherlands made to Charles to mark his restoration to the English throne.

The Restoration public also took pleasure in spectacles of a rather more unsavoury nature. Robbery and street violence at fairs and festivals were rife, and prizefights and wrestling bouts at such places as the Bear Garden in Southwark and Moorfields were bloody and vicious events. (Schellinks noted that fighters were 'allowed to kick the legs from under their opponent' to hasten their defeat.)

The torture and goading of animals for entertainment was widespread. Bears and bulls were baited with dogs and then tore each other to pieces for the riotous pleasure of the mob, something that Pepys described in August 1666 as 'a very rude and nasty pleasure'. Cockfights were an everyday occurrence, especially at the cockpit of Shoe Lane, or outside some of the seamier taverns of Southwark. Pepys had this to say of a visit to a cockfight in December 1663:

> To Shoe Lane to see a cock-fighting at a new pit there, a spot
> I was never at in my life: but Lord! to see the strange variety
> of people, from Parliament-man… to the poorest 'prentices,
> bakers, brewers, butchers, draymen, and what not; and all
> these fellows one with, another cursing and betting. I soon
> had enough of it… It is strange to see how people of this
> poor rank, that look as if they had not bread to put in their
> mouths, shall bet three or four pounds at a time, and lose it,
> and yet bet as much the next battle.

He went on to note that it was not uncommon for an individual
to lose ten or twenty pounds at one of these cockfights; not
only was this a considerable sum of money, but it was hugely
profitable for those who organized the games, and who ended
up pocketing most of it. Gambling, a sport that Pepys considered 'poor and unmanly', was a popular pursuit with both men
and women, whether wealthy or poor, and gaming houses took
thousands of guineas in an evening. Obscene amounts would
be wagered on the most trivial matters; Barbara Castlemaine
once lost £25,000 in one sitting.* The important thing to do
was to lose gracefully and with charm. Those who claimed
that they had been robbed made themselves look ridiculous.
Some even fought duels in a misguided attempt to restore
their lost honour. Duels, which were sometimes fought over
trifles (such as a disagreement over the price of coffee), eventually became so prevalent at court that they were outlawed in

---

* Around £2 million in today's money.

1666, although they continued to be conducted clandestinely.

———— ✺ ————

Outside London, there were more wholesome activities to enjoy. The tradesman Roger Lowe, who lived in Ashton-in-Makerfield in Lancashire, described a trip made in June 1666 with two of his friends to Whitleigh Green, where he played bowls; he enjoyed the sport, and frequently referred to it afterwards in his diary. Lowe was also a keen observer of festivals and holy days. On St Bartholomew's Day, he headed to Chorley with the aim of collecting a debt, but, having been unsuccessful in this endeavour, was easily persuaded to attend the fair in the town. Here, the highlight of his day was watching a pageant 'concerning the lives of man from infancy to old age'. Beyond such gentle pleasures as these, violent sports were as popular in the country as they were in the towns; in July, Lowe recounted going with a couple of friends to see a local cockfight, a clear indication that such entertainment was not confined to the capital. However, like Pepys, Lowe took little pleasure in the activity, claiming, 'I was ill troubled in my mind that I went.'

Lowe preferred the alehouse, which continued to occupy a central place in English life as a venue for drinking, talking and arguing. The tavern was the focus of many communities, both in London and in the country, and the landlord was often a significant local figure. In the case of Abraham Browne of the White Horse in Lombard Street in London, he was something of a celebrity. It is possible that he is the subject of the folk song 'Old Abram Brown', which offers the detail that he wore 'a long brown coat/that buttoned down before'. Browne had been landlord of the White Horse since 1641, although, like owners of other taverns, he had found business difficult during the Commonwealth. The Puritans did not close the public houses, as they had the theatres, but to have been found drunk in one of them was an offence punishable by whipping or a spell in the stocks. To allow drunkenness on his premises would have reflected poorly on the tavern's proprietor, who might himself have expected censure, and possibly even the closure of his establishment. When Charles came to power in 1660 and the strictures of the previous regime were lifted, Browne probably raised a celebratory glass.

Browne himself was an unusual character. Pepys described him as 'the simplest-looking fellow and old that ever I saw' and he would have been at least in his fifties by 1666, possibly even older. His first wife, Penelope, had died in 1651, having borne him children, and his second wife, Frances, whom it seems he probably married in the early 1660s, was said by Pepys to be 'a very pretty woman'. The marriage does not appear to have been a happy one. Pepys refers to Frances' 'long melancholy', and she eventually drowned herself in early 1667, after repeated suicide attempts.

The White Horse tavern was destroyed in the Great Fire of September 1666, whereupon Browne took over the running of the Bear. This was a famous establishment, in existence since 1319, and within easy reach of the theatres, brothels and bear pits of the day; fittingly, the sign of the tavern was a chained and muzzled bear. Browne saw the quality of his customers decline when he acquired the Bear, as its location at the foot of London Bridge meant that much of its clientele was made up of sailors and wayfarers, rather than more upright men (although Pepys still came to drink there). Browne eventually retired to Cheriton in Kent, and died in 1672.

It is likely that men of quality, such as Pepys and the court wits, drank imported Portuguese or French wine in taverns like the White Horse, which was sent over from the Continent in enormous vats and hogsheads and was served in flagons – glassware was too expensive and liable to break at the time. Wine was considerably more expensive than any other alcohol: 'sack', or dry white Spanish wine, was around twelve pence a quart, as was German red wine. Port was extremely popular as it had brandy added to it after fermentation, ostensibly to preserve it after its importation, but in fact with the intention of making as strong a drink as possible. Pepys recorded on 22 November 1666 that he had taken 'some bottles of new French wine of the year' and pronounced them 'mighty good', although, prudently, he wrote, 'I drank but little'. Three years earlier, he had praised 'a sort of French wine, called Ho Bryan'; in his acknowledgement of the excellence of Haut-Brion, he continued an English appreciation of Bordeaux wine that had lasted for hundreds of years, since Henry II married Eleanor of Aquitaine in the twelfth century. The owner of the chateau, Arnaud de Pontac, opened an upmarket tavern in 1665 near the Old Bailey, which he called the Pontac's Head, and which sold Haut-Brion at the extravagant price of seven shillings a bottle. Some taverns even had specially engraved glass bottles behind the bar to serve to their most honoured guests. English wine was occasionally produced, but only in limited quantities, and it was not sold commercially.

Beer was generally available in taverns, but was considered a poor man's drink. Where it was sold, it was available either by the barrel or the jug (the former mainly for home consumption), and was priced according to strength, with stronger beer costing threepence a gallon and weaker beer a penny-halfpenny. A popular alternative was a spiced brew known as 'mum', made from oat malt and wheat, which was sold in specialist 'mum-houses', often sweetened with sugar; Pepys recounted visiting one such establishment in 1664 in Leadenhall, and drinking so much mum that he 'broke up'. Likewise, spirits such as gin and rum, distilled clandestinely, were absent from the tavern, as their high strength and often adulterated contents could lead to blindness (hence the phrase 'blind drunk') and insanity, sometimes even death.

Instead, the traditional English drink was ale, which differed from beer in that it was not brewed with hops. Drunk by everyone from the infirm to schoolboys, it was either consumed at home, normally by the barrel or jug, or in one of the alehouses or taverns that thronged the city. It was regarded as such a vitally important beverage for the nation's health that even the poor of St Bartholomew's Hospital were entitled to three pints a day. In 1666, there were around 2,000 taverns in London, one for every 200 people.* These were not just places to drink, but places to eat, transact business, talk with one's neighbours and friends, smoke, and generally pass

* Today, there are somewhere between 4,000 and 7,000, making the number potentially one for every 2,000: hence the long queues at the bar.

the time of day. Ale was inexpensive, costing around twopence for a gallon of a weak brew, and a penny more for a gallon of a stronger substance. Water was not served, despite the streets being thronged with water sellers, as it was thought to be polluted and unfit to drink; the only people who bought it were the poor, with predictably grim results. The only places where it was served to be consumed were from freshwater wells in the gardens of grand houses, which were regarded as impressive marks of wealth and status.

In rural villages and small towns, the alehouse became a symbol of community rather than simply a place for a drink. Roger Lowe's diary paints a picture of an establishment that was effectively a club for poor and working-class men and women, where it was entirely possible to be both of Presbyterian sympathies (as Lowe, and most of the inhabitants of Ashton-in-Makerfield, were) and a confirmed ale-drinker.

Lowe's diary refers to many 'merry times' he spent in alehouses around Manchester and Liverpool. He clearly thought little of travelling as much as twenty miles to find refreshment. He refers in one diary entry to a typical local pub, Earlom's, where, for twopence apiece, his companions and he could purchase enough drink to be 'very merry', which sometimes led to a sense of being 'very feeble' afterwards. The alehouse was a place where views could be freely shared; Lowe tells of how, somewhat refreshed, his friends and he engaged in 'little unhappy discourses about religion, as we have been overtaken with too much passion; for each of us were of different judgements and each would vindicate his one way, and many times fall into exceeding passion'. The amount Lowe drank was prodigious; he described how he put away a two-quart (or five-litre) 'potle' of butt-end ale with another merchant to celebrate a deal, after which he continued drinking with the local vicar.

Drunkenness eventually became so prevalent that Charles II – himself no mean toper – issued a proclamation against it in 1664 in which he railed against the men 'who spend their time in taverns and tippling houses and debauches, giving no other evidence of affection for us but in drinking our health'. Then, as now, drinking was especially popular with students; Anthony à Wood recounts the story of how the new Vice-Chancellor of the University of Oxford, Dr John Fell,* who possessed something of a reforming spirit, tried to crack down on the problem by literally hauling students out of the taverns and alehouses of the city. Wood describes an encounter between Fell and an unfortunately named undergraduate:

> One... Drinkwater, an undergraduate of Exeter College with a red face was taken at the tavern by Dr. John Fell, vice-chancellor. He asked him his name. '*Drinkwater*,' answered he. 'Is this a place for *you*?' sayeth the vice-chancellor, 'who is your tutor?' 'Mr. Goodall'† replied he. 'Excellent and very ridiculous; get you home for this time'.

There seemed a clear correlation between what the cleric

---

* It was of Fell that the well-known lines 'I do not like thee, Doctor Fell/The reason why I cannot tell' were composed, apparently as an impromptu reply by the satirist Tom Brown, who was called up to translate a Martial epigram on pain of expulsion for a misdemeanour.

† As in 'good-ale'.

Gilbert Burnet described as 'the general joy that overran the whole nation upon his Majesty's Restoration' and the drunkenness of young men. Wood drily recounted how, as a result of the Second Anglo-Dutch War, 'Brandy [has been] much drank since this war began with the Dutch, and in Cornwall where before it was drank only in sea towns it is now in the middle of the country: and that because they have it cheap by the many prizes of brandy brought in'. Previously associated with medical treatment, the intoxicating qualities of brandy ensured that it quickly became popular at all levels of society.

Oxford was an especially notorious place for alcoholic excess, as colleges competed with one another to raise their debauchery to another level. Wood lamented the 'multitudes of alehouses', which led to the playing of dice and cards as well as heavy drinking. Students at St John's College saw it as their mission to attend chapel drunk, while Balliol men were rendered 'perfect sots' by their 'perpetual bubbling'. Three students of All Souls, then regarded as an especially bibulous college, became so inebriated at the Mitre tavern that they were said to have frightened the hostess to death. It was regrettably common for students to die of alcohol poisoning; one bishop's son was found dead with a brandy bottle grasped tightly in one hand.

Nor were their elders any better. The proctors, who were supposed to be responsible for discipline, took delight in showcasing their alcoholic and sexual prowess in the taverns, and at least one university ceremony had to be postponed because the vice-chancellor was too hungover to officiate. In Oxford, as elsewhere, the demon drink was one of the great levellers.

Not all were incorrigible bottle-fanciers. It was in Oxford in 1650 that England's first coffee house was opened, by a man called Jacob, at the so-called 'Sign of the Angel'. Jacob imported his coffee from Venetian merchants, who in turn had obtained it from Arab ports. Further coffee shops opened in Oxford during the 1650s, their atmosphere of civilized discourse and debate becoming a distinctive feature of the city. Coffee houses were known as 'penny universities', owing to the learned discussions that took place inside their walls, and the traditional price of a penny for a cup of coffee. A visitor could enjoy conversation about everything from languages to astronomy or mathematics within their walls, or simply relax in a comfortable environment in front of a good fire. Coffee remained a drink that was restricted to the cognoscenti, rather than enjoyed domestically; it was not drunk with milk or sweetened with sugar, practices that did not come in until the eighteenth century, but was instead served ground with boiled water.

In the early days of coffee drinking, it was a controversial substance. Some thought it had dangerous effects on the mind and temperament, others praised its medicinal and other virtues. A 1660 broadside in praise of coffee suggested that it should be drunk on an empty stomach and that no food should be eaten afterwards. The anonymous writer states that 'this drink will very much quicken the spirits, and make the heart lightsome. It is very good against sore eyes, and the better, if you hold your head over it, and take in the steam that way', before lauding it further for its properties in combating headaches, coughs and gout; the writer concludes (rather fancifully) by claiming, 'it is observed, that in Turkey, where this is generally drunk, they are not troubled with the stone, gout, dropsy, or scurvy; and that their skins are exceeding clear and white'.

The association of coffee with the Turkish infidel was worrying enough for an anonymous satirist to write another broadside three years later, *A cup of Coffee, or, Coffee in all its Colours*, which was scathing in the extreme about the new vogue:

> For men and Christians to turn Turks and think
> To excuse their crime because 'tis in their drink!
> Is more than magic, and does plainly tell
> Coffee's extraction has its heart from hell.

By 1666, the coffee craze was established in London, following the opening of Pasqua Rosée's shop the previous decade. Such establishments as the Temple Bar and the Turk's Head prided themselves on offering 'contentious but civil, learned but not didactic' debate. Even the king was a fan;* Alexander Man, of Man's coffee house on the Strand, was known as 'coffee-man to the King' and was well rewarded for his efforts. A particular favourite among the wits and writers of the time was Will's, where Dryden, Pepys and Wycherley consorted. Run by the cantankerous Will Urwin, it had originally been known as the Rose, but soon became one of the most exclusive places in town.

---

* In 1675, however, Charles would issue a proclamation ordering the closure of coffee houses as the 'great resort of idle and disaffected persons'. Such was the outcry, however, that he backtracked almost immediately and the edict never came into force.

Like the inns and alehouses, coffee houses were open to everyone, but they appear to have been male-dominated places, where men gathered to discuss such matters as business and politics.* A satirical document of 1674, 'The Women's Petition Against Coffee, representing to public consideration the grand inconveniences accruing to their sex from the excessive use of that drying, enfeebling liquor', railed against the deadening effects of coffee on male sexual energy:

> ...to our unspeakable grief, we find of late a very sensible *Decay* of that true *Old English Vigor*; our gallants being every way so *Frenchified*, that they are become mere Cocksparrows, fluttering things that come on *Sa sa*, with a world of Fury, but are not able to *stand* to it, and in the very first Charge fall down *flat* before us.

Tea, meanwhile, had first appeared in England just before the Restoration, at Thomas Garraway's establishment in Exchange Alley. Garraway made unblushingly grandiose claims for the drink, with a pamphlet describing it as 'by all physicians approved', but it was not commonly available until 1662 when Queen Catherine, who had been used to taking it in her native Portugal, continued to drink it. As a result, it became one of the most popular imports of the British East India Company, and had great cachet among aristocrats at court. Its supposed medicinal properties continued to be popular; Pepys

---

* The exceptions were if women were attending the coffee house on business, or in Bath, where the more open-minded attitudes in that town saw women drink and talk just as freely as men.

noted on 28 June 1667 that it was a drink that 'Mr Pelling the apothecary tells [Elizabeth] is good for her colds and defluxions'.* This tea was green, rather than black, and, like coffee, did not have anything added to it.

Drinking was popular, but dining was an essential part of life. In microcosm, the ways in which food was eaten represented every sector of society. The reasonably affluent visited eating-houses, where an unexceptional but acceptable dinner could be expected to cost around five shillings a head and be prepared by the local baker. The menu was fixed and there was no choice of dishes, so diners would know how much the meal would cost at the start, including their wine, which was normally plentiful, if seldom of high quality. The taverns served an 'ordinary' of a hot meal, cheese, bread and ale, and this might cost as little as ten pence.

In the towns and cities, itinerant street vendors wandered the streets, selling fruit, fish and asses' milk. The latter was believed to be beneficial to the health of young children. Market traders competed with one another to broadcast – as loudly and theatrically as possible – the taste and quality of their produce. Most everyday food items were purchased from markets where producers from the country came to the city in order to sell everything from vegetables and fruit to dairy produce and meat. In London, there was a clear class divide between City freemen (who were only allowed to sell their wares in shops) and market stallholders, who had neither the means nor the inclination to move beyond their basic pitches.

---

* Literally 'a runny nose'.

Animals were slaughtered all over London, whether in the market at Newgate Street or at Smithfield, and sold on from those premises. There were also smaller butchers, such as Eleanor Davies of the Maypole butchers on the Strand, who were licensed to kill and serve meat from their own shops. The contemporary appetite for beef, the staple meat, was enormous; the Italian diplomat and author Lorenzo Magalotti estimated that up to 3,000 oxen a day were butchered in London. The noise, and the smell, were apparently horrendous. The quality of the meat was generally poor, as the animals were often old and weak; the best beasts, of course, went to royal and aristocratic tables.

Those who desired higher-class fare could visit the Royal Exchange in Cornhill or the New Exchange in the Strand, where expensive and imported food and wine could be obtained, including peacock, larks' tongues and 'brisk', as champagne was then called. Even the destruction of the Royal Exchange in the Great Fire (leading to a sharp upturn in trade for its rival, which had previously been considered old-fashioned) could not stem a general interest in seeking out better-quality food and drink than had been available before. Perishable items were preserved in ice houses, which Charles had observed on his travels in France. Having originated from Turkey in the sixteenth century, they were now much in demand in London and in the country, from St James's Palace downwards.

Ironically, for all the xenophobia and nationalist contempt that most English people felt towards Europeans, their culinary influence was being felt in London more than ever before, whether in the form of the Portuguese wine that was drunk or the French or Italian styles of dining that were imported. Such hitherto unknown ingredients as anchovies and capers were used to flavour dishes, and ragoûts and fricassées were as common a feature of the better tables of London as any stew or pie. So prevalent was the French style of cookery that it even gave a new word, 'kickshaws', meaning 'fancy dish', to the language; a bastardization of 'quelquechose', or 'something', it summed up the casual acceptance of the new additions to the dining table.

It would be wrong to suggest that the Restoration saw the explosion of an unfettered Bacchanalian spirit hitherto absent in England. To misquote Philip Larkin, sexual intercourse did not begin in 1663. Before that date, people had still got drunk, behaved with personal immorality, visited the theatre and enjoyed public entertainments, albeit with some restrictions during the Protectorate. The difference was that the casting-off of the previous regime seemed to bring a giddy sense of release, which meant that anyone from the humblest apprentice or grandest lord could justify their behaviour to themselves and others as being dictated by a national excess of joy.

By the end of the year, Pepys was driven to describe Whitehall as consisting of 'a sad, vicious and negligent court, all sober men there fearful of the ruin of the whole kingdom'. Yet, while public life sometimes seemed a never-ending search for new sensations, what occurred at home was often, in a quieter way, the heart of the Restoration. A new style of living began to emerge, far away from the glittering chaos of the streets. Its repercussions persist to this day.

Dressing Up and Staying In

'I must go handsomely whatever it costs me'
– Samuel Pepys

Ironically, for a period in which appearance was all-important, Restoration portraiture was not always flattering to its subjects. Perhaps subconsciously following in the lead of Cromwell, who apocryphally demanded to be depicted 'warts and all', Charles commissioned the artist John Riley to paint him, late in his reign. The resulting portrait was less than kind. Charles looked preoccupied and haggard, the breastplate he was painted in less a testament to kingly success than a mocking reminder of the unsuccessful conflicts he had been involved in, from the failed attempt to regain his throne in 1651 to the disasters of the Second Anglo-Dutch War of 1665–7. It is no wonder that, when Charles saw the eventual result, he exclaimed: 'Is this like me? Then odds' fish I am an ugly fellow.'

Charles was at least at liberty to have his portrait painted as many times as he wished by the finest artists in the land. Such was the prerogative of a king. Those lower down the social scale, such as Samuel Pepys, needed to choose their painter more carefully. It was a considerable mark of prestige to afford to be immortalized in oils, and was often extremely expensive. The leading female portraitist of the day – and the first woman who could be described as a professional portrait painter – was named Mary Beale, and she charged £10 for a three-quarter-length painting, with £5 for a head and shoulders representation. This was the equivalent of a year's rental for a middling home in the City: an impressive sum.

The painter whom Pepys chose was John Hayls, who had established a considerable reputation in England by 1666; the writer Sir William Sanderson had described him as one of the leading portraitists in the country in 1658, and he specialized in either classical or classically influenced pictures such as his 1655–9 composition *A Portrait of a Lady and Boy with Pan*. Pepys initially encountered Hayls through his friend Thomas Hill, a fellow naval commissioner and assistant to the secretary of the Prize Office. Visiting the artist for the first time on 14 February to see Hill's portrait, Pepys pronounced himself impressed, writing, 'it will be mighty like him, and pleased me so, that I am resolved presently to have my wife's and mine done by him, he having a very masterly hand'. He did not tarry; his wife's portrait was started the next day. She was painted sitting in the fashionable pose of the Christian martyr St Catherine, an allusion to Charles's queen, Catherine of Braganza. Its creation went smoothly (even if, on 3 March, Hayls complained that 'her nose cost him as much work as another's face') and, on 17 March, Pepys recorded being 'infinitely pleased' with the portrait, and did not begrudge the cost of £14, with a further twenty-five shillings for the frame.

That same day, Pepys himself began sitting for a portrait by Hayls, wearing a borrowed Indian gown and holding a musical setting of William Davenant's poem 'Beauty, retire', which Pepys had written himself. The sittings were not always easy. The diarist complained: 'I sit to have it full of shadows and so almost break my neck looking over my shoulders to make the posture for him to work by.' Although Pepys enjoyed Hayls's 'very merry, pleasant discourse', he was less enamoured of having to sit 'til almost dark upon working my gown'. Despite a late disagreement ('he would have persuaded me to have had the landscape stand in my picture, but I like it not and will have it otherwise, which I perceive he do not like so well'), the picture was completed and collected on 16 May. Pepys again paid £14 for it, and twenty-five shillings for the frame, meaning that his total outlay for the two portraits was more than £30; however, the 'great pleasure' with which he hung them, along with his belief that they were 'very like', meant that the expenditure was a reasonable and highly satisfactory one.

For the contemporary observer viewing the picture in its present-day home, London's National Portrait Gallery, Hayls's portrait gives a fine insight into the thirty-three-year-old Pepys. The neck-breaking posture that he was asked to adopt by Hayls gives him an air of complicity with whoever sets eyes upon him. Pepys has a faintly roguish look– as if he was sizing up Elizabeth Knepp for a night on the town – but also a certain confidence. He has the countenance of a man who is utterly sure of himself, his status in the world that he inhabits and in the quality of the portrait that is being painted. It will be a good one, he seems to think, because I am a man of means, and men of means can afford such luxuries: in return, I will pay the artist handsomely. And, even if Hayls was frustrated by being unable to include a landscape, the painter seems to like and respect his subject. A bond of artist and patron developed between the two, with Pepys commissioning further portraits from Hayls of friends and family, although he was careful to note that nothing quite matched the quality of his own.

In borrowing a luxurious gown for his painting, Pepys was following the tradition whereby the well-to-do and the middle classes dressed in as lavish a fashion as they could afford. However, a misconception has existed that it was only with the death of Cromwell and the Restoration that colourful and rich attire became the norm. In fact, the privileged had dressed as lavishly in the Protectorate as they would do over the following years. Pepys wrote a letter to his patron Edward Montagu a decade earlier, in November 1656, in which he noted, 'I have sent swords and belts black and modish, with two caps for your honour... two pairs of spurs for yourself and two for [your sons], with two riding coats for them, as handsome as the Monsieur can make, and I hope they will please.' The involvement of a French tailor in making 'modish' clothes even during the Protectorate indicated that many in England had not taken up the proverbial sackcloth and ashes. Periwigs had arrived in the late 1650s, and, although not nearly as widespread as they would become, were still a notable fashion of the age. Two of the most sartorially conscious men associated with the interregnum were Cromwell's sons Richard ('Tumbledown Dick') and Henry. The disaffected Parliamentarian Matthew Alured said of them in 1659 that 'there was no apparel good enough to be gotten in London for the Lord Richard and Lord Henry to wear', and that 'they did keep courts higher than ever the prince... did'.

Nor was it only the late Protector's sons who exercised such self-indulgence. Anthony à Wood criticized Cromwell's chaplain John Owen for his expensive dress, singling out his 'powdered hair, lawn band,* a large set of ribbons pointed at his knees, and Spanish leather boots with large lawn tops, and his hat mostly cocked'. Even black, a shade traditionally associated with gloominess and a lack of sartorial vanity, was in fact produced by an expensive and carefully chosen dye that had been prevalent in the earlier Stuart court of the 1630s. While Cromwell can be accused of hypocrisy for employing a liveried footguard when he and his family 'removed to Whitehall' in the 1650s, he cannot be accused of ignoring the evolution of the fashions of the time. Perhaps appropriately, at his funeral in 1658 his coffin was covered with robes of purple velvet and ermine, and his body was attired in 'a rich suit of uncut velvet made up of a doublet and breeches of the Spanish fashion', as his biographer Samuel Carrington later described it.

At the start of the Restoration, linen and silk began to be imported in greater quantities, and thereby came within the reach of the aspirant middle classes. Fine clothing was thus democratized and – for those who could afford it – dressing stylishly and expensively became the expected norm for both

---

* A linen collar.

sexes. Clothes in 1666 were mainly made from wool, cotton, hemp and flax, or combinations of these materials. The well-to-do imported linen from the Continent, particularly Holland and France. After a failed attempt by James I to encourage the native growth of silk, it too was an imported luxury, albeit with a papist taint as it was predominantly an Italian product. Silk looked impressive, especially if it was brightly coloured with dye or ink printing, but it was quickly ruined in wet weather. Very few undamaged examples of silk garments have survived the Restoration.

Men favoured petticoat breeches or 'pantaloons', which were immensely popular at court thanks to their wide, billowing legs, which made them comfortable for wearing on horseback. Such breeches were also adorned with coloured lace and ribbons, and no self-respecting man of quality was without them in his wardrobe. Shirts, meanwhile, were thin affairs, made either of silk or linen (for the aristocracy) or wool (for others). In winter, most men, including Pepys, found it necessary to wear more than one shirt, a thinner linen undershirt next to the skin and then a thicker silk garment that bore more resemblance to a contemporary waistcoat than it did to a shirt.

Men also adorned themselves with lace or muslin cravats (generally tied in a bow under the chin), knitted silk stockings with sash garters below the knee, fine linen shirts and dress swords. The latter item was more a fashion accessory than a weapon, and was normally kept in a decorated sheath. Gowns, too, were considered desirable for wearing at home or around town. Pepys had at least three, of varying degrees of ornateness, size and cost, in addition to the borrowed one in which he was painted.

Having risen from modest beginnings as a tailor's son, Pepys knew the necessity of keeping up with the fashions of the day if he wanted to attain preferment; he wrote, 'I must go handsomely whatever it costs me; and the charge will be made up in the fruits it brings.' His diary records how he discarded his long black cloak in favour of a short one, 'long cloaks being now quite out', but then this was eventually superseded by his wearing a coat and sword 'as the manner now among gentlemen is'. Men wore a variety of outer garments including the 'Brandenburg', named after the German city, which was a long, loose-fitting overcoat that was considered both stylish and warm; and the 'jump', a long jacket that had a slit at the back and reached down to the thighs. Often in velvet, the 'jump' was an essential item for the dandy-about-town. It was commonly ornamented with embroidered flowers, allowing the wearer to strut around the streets in a passable imitation of a peacock.

Pepys also purchased a black silk suit for himself at the extremely high price of £24. Such garments eventually developed into more elaborate outfits that encompassed a silk doublet, adorned with a 'shoulder-knot' of ribbon or cord worn on the right shoulder, and a knee-length waistcoat, gorgeously decorated with gold and silver threads and tassels. Lurking under these garments was the recently introduced vest, which was designed to be collarless, loose-fitting and comfortable, and a loose tunic or 'surcoat' which hung over it. Pepys wore breeches on his legs, which were tight-fitting and decorated colourfully, trimmed with ribbon; in his diary on 15 October 1666, he wrote of how his legs were 'ruffled with black riband like a pigeon's leg'. Clearly, likening oneself to a strutting pigeon was intended to be a desirable, rather than embarrassing, comparison. It soon became as much a patriotic duty as a sartorial one to wear the kind of flamboyant clothing that celebrated the new order. This practice had already become so entrenched by 1662 that Charles – himself no mean dresser – noted in a speech to the House of Commons that 'the whole nation seemed... a little corrupted in their excess of living... all men spend much more in their clothes... than they used to do'.

This smacks somewhat of hypocrisy, given that the king was far from conservative when it came to spending serious money on his own clothes; when he first arrived back in England, he ordered five suits and cloaks from his Parisian tailor, Claude Sourceau, at the extraordinary cost of £2,000,* and he even paid £20 12s for a cravat. In late 1666, John Evelyn observed him dressed 'solemnly in the Eastern fashion' in clothing that was inspired by the Polish ambassador's national costume, a black three-piece silk outfit which immediately became the most popular style of dress at court, and also bore some resemblance to the suits that have subsequently become de rigueur throughout Western society. It even contained a narrow piece of coloured linen, or, in other words, an early tie. (Pepys sardonically commented that the purpose of this outfit and its inevitable emulation at court was 'to teach the nobility thrift'.) In this, as in many other things – including replacing

---

* See Chapter 2, 'King and Court', page 28.

the jerkin and doublet with the waistcoat – Charles was both an innovator and a sartorial omnivore, eagerly devouring every idea and fashion that he came across. It is little wonder that he needed a Gentleman of the Bedchamber, a Master of Robes and a barber to attend to his everyday attire.

The Restoration new look *pour homme* was seen by some as aesthetically controversial. Anthony à Wood, writing in 1663, described the time as 'a strange effeminate age when men strive to imitate women in their apparel'. Nor has posterity been any kinder. The judgement of the nineteenth-century historian F. W. Fairholt was typical, when he claimed that 'taste and elegance were abandoned for extravagance and folly; and the male costume, which in the time of Charles I had reached the highest point of picturesque splendour, degenerated and declined from this moment'.

A further show of ostentation came in the shape of an elaborate and expensive periwig. These were adopted in England for the first time just before the Restoration, but had been popular in France since Louis XIII, seeking to cover his baldness, had an elaborate periwig made in 1624. Like much that Charles saw on his European wanderings, it was initially an affectation, but soon became the norm. By April 1665, a life on the run followed by the demanding early years of the Restoration had so exhausted Charles that his hair turned 'mighty grey', prompting him to have it shaved off and to invest in increasingly elaborate and magnificent wigs. He had worn these before 1665 – Pepys refers to him being seen in one 'not altered at all' in April 1664 – but they now became a necessity rather than a luxury. Wigs were made from women's hair, and could cost anything up to £10 – that is, up to double the average worker's weekly wage.

Many men in society who were losing their hair greeted the arrival of wigs with pleasure and relief. As anyone who wore a wig had to have his scalp shaved, it had the happy effect of rendering many men's appearance the same. Wigs were visible and obvious status symbols; the size and quality of a man's periwig reflected his social standing just as much as other items in his wardrobe. For the cash-strapped individual who wanted to elevate himself in society, the purchase of a wig was yet another expense that could not be avoided if he wished to show his face at court. And all this because of an ageing king's vanity.* Those who retained their locks normally kept them short, as they were less prone to attract vermin.

Initially Pepys was unimpressed, noting in a diary entry of 9 May 1663, 'I have no stomach for [them]', but as 'the pains of keeping my hair clean is so great', he purchased two wigs in October that year, one for three pounds and the other for forty shillings. He was pleased with his acquisition, writing the next month, 'after I had caused all my maids to look upon it... they conclude that it do become me'. By now clearly a convert, Pepys proudly mentions his wig four times in his diary in 1666, and notes that he paid £4 10s for two periwigs the following year. The new hairpieces were not without their problems, however: in time once-grand wigs could become

* Charles had mixed feelings about wigs. Displeased by the sight of Nathaniel Vincent, fellow of Clare Hall and doctor of divinity at Cambridge, preaching a sermon while attired in a more than usually splendid wig, Charles wrote to the university instructing its members 'not to wear periwigs, or smoke tobacco, but to read their sermons'.

both dirty and ridden with vermin such as nits and fleas, and they also needed constant combing (a chore that was sometimes ostentatiously carried out in theatres or coffee houses). A more serious concern was that wigs might carry disease; Pepys wrote on 3 September 1665, at the height of the plague, that 'my new periwig, bought a good while since, [I] durst not wear, because the plague was in Westminster when I bought it'. He also wondered whether anyone would buy wigs any more after the plague was over ('for fear of the infection, that it had been cut off the heads of people dead of the plague'), but his fears proved groundless.

As with female clothing, male attire drew attention to masculine attributes. Breeches contained no fly, but instead were surmounted by a codpiece, which, although more modest than the penis-jutting ones of a century earlier, were an obvious statement of masculine endowment, as well as allowing ease of access for any purpose. Men's undergarments, or 'drawers', were made of linen and were lengthy, close-fitting affairs, much like long johns. Night attire was simple, consisting of long nightgowns that stretched down approximately to the knees, and embroidered nightcaps that kept shorn heads warm.

Even those who were not wealthy took great care over what they wore. The Lancashire tradesman Roger Lowe wrote in January 1666, 'I hired Thomas Leech's horse and rode to Standish on purpose to buy me a suit of brown shag, but there was none.' Lowe's unsuccessful journey of eight and a half miles was a considerable distance, but even relatively humble garments were hard to obtain outside London. As for the material of the suit he was after, 'shag' was a cloth usually made of worsted but occasionally silk, and which was made more fashionable by the addition of a velvet nap* on one side.

Shoes worn for everyday purposes – by both men and women – were straight and made no distinction between the left foot and the right, which sometimes made walking in them awkward. For social functions, men wore elaborate high-heeled leather shoes, which not only boosted height but also made movement difficult thanks to their pinched ends, which had the unfortunate side effect of crushing toes if worn for too long. Fastened by either ornamental or plain bows, they were fashionably tight-fitting. Given the filthy condition of the streets, it was necessary to wear galoshes to prevent such elegant footwear being ruined. Boots were associated as much with outdoor pursuits, such as riding, as they were with indoor activities, and so had to combine elegance with hard-wearing practicality.

Unless they were sporting wigs, convention dictated that men wore hats at virtually all times, whether inside or out. These could be anything from cheap and humble caps of the sort worn by workmen to the grandest headgear, which could be made with beaver fur from Canada† and ornamented with ostrich feathers. In 1666, there was a particular fashion for the so-called 'boater', a low, wide-brimmed hat, normally adorned with ribbon or lace. Men wore their formal hats indoors in public, and removed them in the presence of superiors, or

* The raised surface of a piece of material.

† The first permanent settlements had been established there earlier in the seventeenth century.

whenever their name was mentioned in conversation. Hats were also doffed when the wearer sneezed or laughed. Such hat-tipping was so prevalent that there was even a Turkish curse, 'I wish you as little rest as a Christian's hat'. The grander types of formal hat were expensive, with the beaver-trimmed and warmer types costing up to £5. Domestic headgear was straightforward, with many preferring to wear simple and comfortable caps that were covered with fur.

⸎

For women it was Whitehall that dominated contemporary fashion. For women of the highest quality, either those at court itself or the wives or mistresses of great men, formal outfits for state banquets and royal receptions were essential, and required considerable expenditure.* These women advertised their wealth and status by dressing in the most lavish attire that money could buy whenever they appeared in public. They often wore dazzlingly coloured and hugely ornate gowns of silk or velvet, with a lengthy train and a petticoat underneath. The effect was then set off by coloured braids and different linings, all of which made women look like exotic birds that might be found in nearby St James's Park.

Their hair was often an elaborate construction of frills, curls and extensions, and could take a couple of hours of preparation to give it the curled and bunched effect often seen in

---

* Some of the few remaining examples of clothing from 1666 tend to be of this type, rather than the more normal attire of the day.

portraits. Fashion accessories such as fans, purses and gloves were obligatory for ladies of quality, and often had symbolic connotations; a gaudily painted fan rapidly opened and closed, for instance, denoted sexual availability, just as dropping one's scented glove was often intended as a hint to one's gallant or other nearby admirers that picking it up might lead to later bedroom favours. Meanwhile, their most obvious means of showcasing their wealth remains familiar today. Jewellery was hugely desirable as both a status symbol and means of adorning oneself, and could cost the earth; Charles II was said to have spent nearly £10,000 on a 'great pair of diamond pendant' earrings, presumably for the rapacious Barbara Castlemaine. When the average gentleman was lucky to earn £500 per annum, this was a staggering sum.

Women wore very different outfits for 'best' and everyday occasions. At home, or in private, most would wear an unadorned skirt and a loose jacket, or a plain dress that could be opened and closed at the front without any difficulty. While performing domestic tasks, women would often wear a substantial plain pinafore or apron, the very opposite of an erotic item of clothing.

In public it was another story. A woman wore a stiff bodice and corset that would emphasize her breasts by pushing them upwards and together and minimizing the size of her stomach. (It must have been nightmarish for the pregnant, except when they were confined to their homes in the final months.) Reinforced with either wood or bone, corsets were tight, restrictive and painful, but that was the price women paid to look fashionable in public. Sometimes they covered themselves demurely with a scarf, but this was often felt to be an unnecessary waste of assets. Sleeves were worn to the elbow, with the mouths edged with lace, allowing the hands to emerge from a stylishly embroidered muff.

Skirts, underskirts and petticoats, meanwhile, were worn beneath, and by October 1666 there was a vogue for extending the skirt to one's feet; Pepys described it as 'graceful' but it is equally likely that most women, finding themselves traipsing through the mud and filth of London's streets, would have found this convention anything but. The skirts were usually open at the front, and were made of silk or fine cloth, lined with gold or coloured lace. Those who had little interest in their appearance, such as the Quakers or the impecunious, tended to favour wool, which was at least hard-wearing and cheap.

Underclothes, if the wearer could be bothered with them, were simple and made largely of white linen and ribbons, although the wealthier wore garments embroidered with several inches of lace, sometimes even with quilting. Lacking elastic, they were kept in place via attachment to the bodice; it is little wonder that many eschewed underwear in favour of ease of mobility. In the absence of brassieres, women's breasts were constricted by corsetry or bodices. If a woman wanted to carry her personal items about her, she had to place them in a concealed 'pocket' that was a detachable proto-wallet, sometimes richly decorated and embroidered and an easy target for opportunistic thieves, who took a bawdy delight in reaching under a lady's skirts in search of both money and more pleasurable rewards. The writer Henry Peacham tells an anecdote about a tradesman's wife in his book *The Art of Living in London* in which the tradesman, aghast that his wife has lost her purse at the playhouse, asks her whether she placed it under her petticoat. 'Aye', came the reply. 'Did you feel nobody's hand there, searching for your purse?' inquired the disbelieving husband. 'Yes', she replied, 'but I did not think that he had come for that.'

Women's outside clothing was a gamble, depending on the ever-mercurial English weather. Heavy, padded cloaks and coats were considered suitable against the worst of the rain or snow, as well as keeping the wearer warm. They were similar to men's, especially the so-called 'Justico',* which was primarily used as a walking garment. The colder winter weather saw the appearance of fur muffs, delicately fringed gloves (which were carried in more clement weather as a fashion accessory) and brightly coloured stockings made of silk or wool. In the summer, meanwhile, parasols were the fashionable accessory. As for headgear, a high-crowned hat helped to protect the wearer from both heavy rain and (atypically) hot sun, but a small hood or headscarf, known as a 'chaperone', was more attractive and fashionable. Masks tended to be worn by prostitutes or the wealthy, but were expected attire at balls, banquets and large-scale social gatherings. 'Vizard' masks covered the entire face, while 'loo' masks concealed only its top half.

The most popular place in London for women to buy clothes, at least before the Great Fire, was Paternoster Row; Pepys visited it to buy his wife's petticoats and frequented Creed's

* A close waistcoat or short coat.

the tailor, and the historian and biographer John Strype said of the street that it was 'taken up by eminent mercers, silkmen and lacemen; and their shops were so resorted to by the nobility and gentry in their coaches, that oft times the street was so stopped up that there was no passage for foot passengers'. Those who wished to adorn themselves with fine jewellery normally visited the Exchange, where Pepys bought a pearl necklace for Elizabeth in 1666 that cost £80 – a staggering sum for a man who was lucky to earn more than six or seven times that annually. Those less affluent individuals who wished to buy a small item to impress restricted their purchases to glass beads or 'river pearls', which cost no more than £5 for a string of beads, and, at a distance, looked much the same as the real thing.

Not all who visited Paternoster Row did so out of a desire to be fashionable. Some were there to buy the outfits that custom or observance required. Prostitutes were notorious for attiring themselves in 'black satin and rouge', normally acquired from the cloth market at Blackwell Hall in the City. Black was also worn in mourning, often for periods that might seem ridiculously long to present-day observers. Three months was the minimum, whether or not you truly cared about the person who had died, and Elizabeth Pepys reluctantly wore it for just such a length of time to mourn her detested mother-in-law. But mourning also offered opportunities for a striking sartorial display, and some of the greatest ladies in the land took a perverse pride in wearing as elaborate and grandiose an outfit as they could find – all while, of course, remaining in clothes as black as night. This was, it should be noted, equally true for men, who were required to wear 'dark' and 'dull' clothing for mourning, normally made out of unostentatious wool rather than glamorous silk. But it was a less expensive business for them; Anthony à Wood spent a grand total of two shillings on 'black buckles to my vest' and sixpence for 'blacking my russet shoes' for mourning his late mother; frugal in the extreme, he even borrowed a mourning gown.

When it came to everyday attire, there was a casually ostentatious eroticism about many women's clothes, whether or not they were available for hire, which spoke volumes about the lasciviousness of the court. Bosoms accentuated by deliberately tight bodices could be part-concealed by a piece of neckwear known as a 'pinner', a sort of scarf that nonetheless left a certain amount of décolletage on show. Even the skirt was designed specifically to allow tantalizing glimpses of the petticoat and underskirts beneath it.

Some women's dress made them instantly famous – or notorious, as in the case of the writer and natural philosopher Margaret Cavendish, the duchess of Newcastle. Her freethinking outlook was mirrored in her highly individual dress sense. Sometimes she donned breeches and a Cavalier hat, with such masculine attire reinforced by her refusal to shave an allegedly noticeable amount of facial hair. But at other times she could take sartorial conventions to an absurd level; when she visited the Royal Society in 1667, she was accompanied by an eight-foot train on her gown, borne by six attendants. She was content to scandalize – one evening she visited the theatre in a dress in antique style that bared her breasts – or simply to mystify. The diarist Philibert de Gramont in his (admittedly unreliable) memoirs recounted an occasion when 'as I was getting out of my chair, I was stopped by the devil of a phantom in masquerade... it is worthwhile to see her dress; for she must have at least sixty ells* of gauze and silver tissue about her, not to mention a sort of pyramid upon her head, adorned with a hundred thousand baubles.' Charles reportedly did not blink an eye, merely saying, 'I am ready to wager that it was the Duchess of Newcastle.'

Fine clothes might have created a veneer of style and beauty, but the physical realities of life in 1666, including such disfiguring conditions as smallpox or syphilis, meant that looking one's best was often difficult. Diseases often left unsightly blemishes and pockmarks upon faces. Both sexes applied cosmetics in generous quantities, made up of a variety of bizarre substances that could include everything from urine and extract of crushed snail to white lead and rosewater. Egg white was often used, but this had the disadvantage that it set hard, and subsequently cracked, or alternatively faded to an unpleasant grey colour. An especially popular concoction was 'water of talc and pearl', a mixture made up of an Arabian mineral, the 'talc', and ground pearls. This would be slathered all over faces, hands and any other exposed body part. Eyes were tinted and artificially brightened with belladonna drops,†

* A cubit, or approximately 18 inches (45 cm).

† A substance derived from deadly nightshade that was highly regarded as a beauty

female facial hair was treated with such would-be depilatories as cat dung mixed with vinegar and lips were painted red with a crude crayon. Excessive rouging, however, was regarded as vulgar; Pepys criticized his cousin's wife for it, declaring that she was 'still very pretty, but paints red on her face, which makes me hate her'.

Even as the plays of the time mocked courtesans and fops – the latter personified by the character Sir Fopling Flutter in Etherege's *The Man of Mode*, for example – who spent huge sums and effort on delicate beauty products, there seemed an ever-growing appetite for more elaborate ways of concealing one's true identity. The quacks and beauty doctors rubbed their hands and set up shop, claiming that eyebrows could be shaped, hands whitened, foreheads lifted and wrinkles removed, all with the aid of 'natural' products. Old wives' tales were revived and taken as gospel; oil of vitriol* was said to lighten hair, May dew was believed to be a beauty product and a powder made of snuff, tobacco, gum and myrrh was used as a crude toothpaste. Cheeks were filled out with small balls known as 'plumpers', which were made of cork or cloth, and were designed to guard against skin looking drawn and tight.

And there were those who died in the pursuit of beauty. At least one great lady of the time succumbed to mercury poisoning, having used so much of it as a cosmetic on her face that she was killed by it. If all else failed, there was one sure-fire, if rather ostentatious, means of covering pox scars, namely the application of small patches made of velvet or

---

treatment. The ancient Romans used it as a poison.

* Better known today as sulphuric acid.

leather. Shaped as stars, crescents and even small animals, these 'beauty spots', also known as 'mouches', were worn by men and women alike. The faces of some, among them Barbara Castlemaine, were almost overwhelmed by beauty marks.

Hairstyles, like dress, were strongly influenced by royal and courtly practice. Charles was dark-haired (and accordingly referred to as a 'black man' as far back as 1651, when he was on the run across England) and it was because of his influence that the most desirable hair colour was brunette or black. Blondes and redheads either had to resign themselves to their natural colouring, or attempt a primitive means of dyeing it, which could involve anything from a tincture of lime and 'a powder of gold' to a barberry or saffron wash. At best, this would be an effective short-term option; at worst it would kill the hair's roots and lead to baldness.

Women devoteded a great deal of care and attention to their locks. In the interests of enhancing their beauty, they put themselves through agonizing sessions with ivory or bone combs or heated curling tongs, which often resulted in singed hair. As ever at the Restoration court, fashion trumped practicality at every turn. Those who did not wish to endure such discomfort simply purchased extra locks of human hair, which they would tie to their heads with concealed threads, or attach to grand and elaborate wigs. Only a small number of women donned such wigs; most liked to accentuate their hair with a variety of ribbons and curls. The vogue of the day was for corkscrew curls, worn over and above the ears and with the hair pushed up into a bun at the back.

Beards, so popular in the reign of Charles I, were rare by

1666. Few men had the skill or equipment to shave themselves at home, so would head to the barbers, whose presence
was announced by the red and white striped poles that hung
outside their premises. However, they were less competent
than they should have been, and nicks and more serious cuts
were commonplace. Those who did not wish to expose themselves to the risk of a daily visit to the barber would have
to put up with a few days' worth of stubble. Pepys, upon
shaving for the first time after the Great Fire, wrote on 17
September, 'Lord! How ugly I was yesterday, and how fine
today!' Moustaches were worn occasionally – Charles culti-
vated one, as can be seen in contemporary portraits of him by
Lely and John Michael Wright – but the fashion was for them
to be thin and carefully maintained rather than bushy.

What lay under the clothes and make-up was generally less
appealing than their beautified exteriors. People smelled, especially when it was hot, although such was the general odour
of the city that individual aromas may have gone unnoticed.
There was a substantial difference between the attention paid
to 'external' parts of the body, such as the hands and face
(and sometimes feet), which were washed and rewashed with
near-obsessive attention to detail, using soap that had been
imported from Spain or Italy, and the 'hidden' areas, which
were only occasionally rubbed down with a cloth that had been
doused in herbs or water. Washing of the more private parts
of the body might take place in public baths such as Agnes-
le-Clair in Tabernacle Square or Queen Elizabeth's in Charing
Cross; the latter was so called because Elizabeth I was said
to have had one of her annual baths there. These places were

closer to saunas than to conventional tubs, enabling visitors to sweat away their various layers of filth and grime; Pepys described them as a 'hothouse' where one would take a 'sweat'. He was cynical about the benefits of cleanliness, writing of his wife attending the steam baths that 'she now pretends to a resolution of being hereafter very clean. How long it will hold I can guess.' She had her revenge, denying him the marital bed until he had washed himself with warm water.

There is evidence that people availed themselves of early forms of underarm deodorant; Hannah Woolley recommended that armpit sweat was combated with a mixture of white wine and rosewater boiled with the spice cassia lignum, which was to be applied to the newly plucked axilla. The ingredients involved, however, were rare and expensive and so this was not an everyday remedy.

Laundry was similarly sporadic. Some households followed a comparatively modern once-a-week washing cycle; but for some of the largest houses in town, it was a twice-yearly occurrence. The most basic, and ineffectual, means of washing clothing was simply to dunk it in a nearby river, but this was next to useless, given that river water was often filthy, especially if it was drawn from the Thames.

In middle-class and well-to-do homes, the household linens were placed in a large barrel-shaped tub, the so-called 'buck tub', into which a mixture of lye made of beech ash and animal urine was poured, followed by a vigorous rinsing with cold water. No soap was used. When this operation had been performed, the now sodden linens would be beaten and hung up in the garden in the summer, or in the kitchen in winter, and left to dry. Alternatively, there were a small number of professional laundry services, known as 'whitsters', who specialized in washing, bleaching and whitening.*

❦

Where you lived in 1666 depended on where you could find work and how much money you could afford to pay for a home. A middle-class house in London of the time probably had between three and six rooms in total, although in the country such houses tended to be larger, boasting up to ten rooms. These were not generally high: a man of average height, around 5 feet 6 inches (1.6 m) at the time, could easily touch the ceiling with his hand. Two or three of these rooms would be on the ground floor, with the main area of the house – the so-called parlour or hall – being where meals were eaten and where domestic activities such as washing and cooking took place. The central focus of many of the living rooms was the fireplace, which was the house's main source of both light and heat. Coal rather than wood was now used, which caused difficulties as many of the hearths had originally been designed to burn timber. Coal burnt at a lower temperature, and, as a result, fireplaces generated a good deal of smoke, necessitating regular cleaning to prevent the rooms being covered in ash and soot; it also left an unpleasant smell throughout the home. When it came to lighting, candles had the advantage of

* In *The Merry Wives of Windsor*, Shakespeare referred to some whitsters having been traditionally based at Datchet Mead, near Windsor.

being portable, but they lasted little time and also could set fire to hanging cloths or tapestries if left unattended, or if a sudden gust of wind knocked them over. Many preferred to use enclosed iron lanterns, which reduced the danger of fire considerably.

Keeping one's status among the neighbours was important; in addition to the cushions and soft furnishings that vendors such as Philip Harman could supply, collecting valuable items, such as china or ornaments, was considered a mark of attainment. These special objects were kept in a small closet or 'cabinet' in the parlour and shown to visitors on special occasions. Meanwhile, mirrors were expensive and normally consisted of a hotchpotch of small pieces of glass that were crudely placed together; this differed from the Continent, where mirror glass was used to decorate rooms in grandiose ways.

Upstairs were the 'chambers' or bedrooms, which had to house servants, children and adults. These were often cramped and squalid, normally comprising of a crudely subdivided 'great chamber', as Pepys referred to his upper floor. The bed was the main item of furniture in these rooms, consisting of four posts which supported a thick, straw-stuffed undermattress, then a wool or feather-stuffed top mattress, then sheets, with blankets and sometimes furs kept on top for warmth. To allow some privacy, curtains were normally suspended around the posts, allowing them to be drawn. (Nobody would want to be caught in carnal congress by a servant – or indeed by one's husband or wife, if entertaining another lover.) It was, however, considered normal for the servant to sleep in the same room as their employer, on what would be either a humble folding bed or, in the poorer households, a straw mattress on the ground, sometimes without even a blanket.

Houses had no bathrooms as such, meaning that the chamber pot saw a great deal of use. No particular effort was made to be discreet in such matters, regardless of the wealth and privilege of the house; men and women urinated in corners and in convenient pots. In September 1664 Pepys records walking in on Lady Sandwich 'blushing' while she was 'doing something upon the pot', which led to much mutual embarrassment as Pepys attempted to continue his conversation as if nothing had happened. John Evelyn, meanwhile, bemoaned the constant spitting inside and outside the house, which required both domestic and street spittoons.

When it came to interior decoration, houses were embellished in a variety of ways, whether with wall paintings (which often consisted of bright and garish depictions of biblical scenes and allegorical figures), wallpaper, which had been reintroduced in London in 1660 after being curtailed for being 'frivolous' during the Protectorate, and tapestries and silk screens for the wealthiest. These came in a variety of colours, shapes and sizes, and were cut up and redistributed as was believed appropriate round the house. The overall effect would have been overwhelming and perhaps even confusing; the home furnishings of the middle-class home of the 1660s were all too rarely marked by restraint or consistency. Walls were panelled either with oak, which was expensive and scarce, or pine, which was cheaper but less durable.

Such furnishings were a significant drain on household

resources. The average income of a middle-class family was somewhere between £50 and £200 a year, depending on the amount of patronage and custom that they managed to attain. Fifty pounds was generally thought to be a barely adequate amount to support a family, which typically consisted of between four to five living children and their parents. For those who enjoyed an income of more than £200 a year, such as Pepys, a good standard of living, rich in fine dress and domestic comfort, awaited. For those who earned less than £50, the Restoration brought no relief, just the continued realization of a drab, hand-to-mouth existence unameliorated by the trappings of wealth. It is their story that remains largely unwritten, owing to the illiteracy of the participants, but it is one that casts the grandeur and fancifulness of the time into particularly sharp contrast.

Dining at home was as simple or as grand an affair as individual taste and finances dictated. The largest houses cooked joints of meat or fish on large spits in front of the fire in the kitchen, which were either turned by hand, by crude mechanical devices such as a primitive clockwork jack (as in Pepys's home) or, in some wealthy homes, by the bizarre but practical expedient of putting a small but active dog, such as a spaniel, on a treadmill attached to the spit itself. Ovens, meanwhile, were simple structures built by or into fireplaces, heated by burning logs and designed to retain heat long enough to cook stews and small joints of meat. Preparation of more complex dishes, such as pies and pasties, tended to be the preserve of local butchers. Most people ate with forks, which were in common use by 1666, and the well-off ate from pewter plates;

the poor continued to use cruder wooden dishes or bowls.

In cases where the cook was indisposed – or incompetent – there were a few other options available, at least for households in the larger towns. So-called 'victualling houses' supplied takeaway food, which a dishonest or lazy host or hostess might pass off as their own, and bakers were regularly called upon to finish cooking pies. Pepys's diary entry for 10 July 1666 describes how, because of 'the yard being full of women... coming to get money for their husbands and friends that are prisoners in Holland... my wife and I were afeard to send a venison-pasty that we have for supper tonight to the cook's to be baked for fear of their offering violence to it; but it went, and no harm done'. Pepys set great store by the quality of the pies he consumed, noting with disappointment that he had had 'a bad venison pasty' at the naval contractor Sir William Rider's house on 9 September. Poor food was always a possibility, even at the greatest of houses; the following week, Pepys visited the home of Admiral Sir William Penn, where he recorded that he had had 'so sorry a dinner: venison baked in pans, that the dinner I have had for his lady alone hath been worth four of it'.

For a well-to-do household, the morning began with a feast that could have consisted of anything from oysters (then commonplace and dredged up from the Thames Estuary daily) and kippers to venison or turkey pie and sweetmeats, washed down with wine. For those with smaller appetites (and purses) bread and butter and weak or 'small' beer would start the day. Once breakfast was over, it was almost time for the main meal of the day, the midday lunch. This was an even larger affair that was intended to showcase the abilities of the cook and the wealth of the household to guests and visitors, or simply to feed everyone who happened to be at home at the time. In a grand house, lunch was eaten in the great parlour, the main downstairs space, which might have had a couple of partitioned rooms off it for visiting tradespeople and tutors to eat in. In a middle-class household, it was most likely to have taken place in a room that was becoming associated with eating, known as the 'dining room'.

Lunch did not proceed along the linear lines we know today of starter, main course and then pudding. Everything would have been placed on the table at the same time and then eaten, or abandoned, including food left over from breakfast. The menu might have included ox tongues, stewed carp, roasted pigeons, lampreys, chicken or mutton. On a feast day, such as Christmas, even more substantial meals were taken; Pepys records that on Christmas Day 1666 he ate roast rib of beef and mince pies, noting that his wife was 'desirous to sleep, having sat up til four this morning' supervising the making of the pies by her maids.

Feasts were not limited to religious or secular festivals. Pepys held a 'stone feast' every year in early spring, to celebrate the successful removal of a painful gallstone in 1658. Although there is no record in his diary of his dinner in 1666, a particularly sumptuous spread was held on 4 April 1663:

> Very merry at, before, and after dinner, and the more for
> that my dinner was great, and most neatly dressed by our
> own only maid. We had a fricasee of rabbits and chickens,

a leg of mutton boiled, three carps in a dish, a great dish of a side of lamb, a dish of roasted pigeons, a dish of four lobsters, three tarts, a lamprey pie (a most rare pie), a dish of anchovies, good wine of several sorts, and all things mighty noble and to my great content.

Meat was the staple of the diet, except at Lent, when a proclamation was issued that the eating of fish was obligatory. Anyone, whether they were an 'innholder, keeper of ordinary tables, cook, butcher, victualler, ale-house-keeper or taverner' was forbidden to serve meat at Lent under pain of the enormous fine of £60. (This was also true of Fridays both during and outside Lent.) The only exceptions to this were the young, infirm and elderly, who had to obtain a special licence to be allowed to eat anything other than fish. Fishmongers and fishermen were not permitted to profit unduly from this apparently captive audience; the only sales permitted were at 'moderate and usual rates and prices'. The heavy quantity of protein in many diets meant that gout was commonplace, and well-meaning but ultimately unsuccessful attempts to combat it (including placing one's feet in ice until they were nearly frozen) often caused more harm than good.

Vegetables and fruit such as carrots, oranges and possibly lettuce, purchased from kitchen gardens or stallholders, were also served, although these were regarded as cheap peasant food and not seen as an integral part of the lunch; many people eschewed them altogether, believing that they caused 'wind' and poor humour, a tradition dating back to the medieval belief that fruit affected the humours adversely. A typical judgement was that of John Goodyer, writing some four decades before, when he described Jerusalem artichokes as causing 'a filthy loathsome stinking wind' that 'pained and tormented' the belly.

For the well-to-do or the newly emergent middle class, the more modest entertainments of the home probably came as something of a relief after the roistering and hurly-burly of court, park or tavern. People entertained themselves with reading, if they were literate and could afford the books and pamphlets that were sold by the local booksellers, or dancing, which was considered a gentlemanly or ladylike way to comport oneself. Music occupied a key position in many households, and it was common for well-to-do folk to keep virginals and 'a chest of viols' for home music-making. In September 1666, Pepys noted that when the Great Fire was causing people to flee their homes, around one in three boats contained a pair of virginals. It was considered a normal and enjoyable pastime to invite friends to one's house to play music and sing an accompaniment. Public concerts, for small instrumental ensembles, only began in England in 1672, and took place at the house of the court composer John Bannister, who had composed the incidental music for Howard's and Dryden's *The Indian Queen*; Pepys referred to him approvingly in his diary on 18 June 1666, saying of another young musician, 'impartially I do not find any goodness in their airs (though very good) beyond ours when played by the same hand, I observed in several of Baptiste's* (the present great composer) and our Bannister's'.

* This is an allusion to Jean-Baptiste Lully (1632–87), the Italian-born opera composer who worked at the court of Louis XIV of France.

A popular daytime and evening activity – and an exclusively female preserve – was embroidery, on which Hannah Woolley offered advice and tips in her book *A Gentlewoman's Companion*. It was a delicate and difficult skill, requiring a good eye and thinly spun silk, along with coloured thread. Surviving tapestries and designs often drew on biblical scenes – implying that the aim behind their creation was instructive as much as it was aesthetic – or alternatively celebrated Charles and his Restoration.

Board games were popular, whether familiar ones still enjoyed today such as chess, draughts and backgammon, or archaic and now forgotten ones such as gleek (a game played by three people with counters, for a small financial bet). Tennis was played at the grand houses of the day, and was enjoyed by Charles, just as it had been by Henry VIII before him. Amid the changes and upheavals of the Restoration it was a reminder that some things, at least, showed few signs of evolving in the dramatic fashion that the rest of society appeared to demand.

Crime and Punishment

'Who does cut his purse will cut his throat'
– Andrew Marvell, 'Last Instructions to a Painter'

The Restoration may have been a triumphant, bloodless coup for the newly installed monarch and his supporters, but the early years of Charles's reign were marked by paranoia and suspicion towards those believed to be lacking in loyalty to the restored king. Six years after the Act of Indemnity and Oblivion of 1660, which had theoretically pardoned all Puritans and their supporters for their involvement in the civil war, there was still an uneasy atmosphere in the country at large, which was hardly mitigated by the continued appearance of severed heads and limbs at key places in London, such as the City gates.

In April 1666, the recently launched newspaper the *London Gazette* gave an account of the trial and conviction of a group of disaffected Commonwealth soldiers for the planned murder of Charles and the overthrow of the government:

At the Sessions in the Old Bailey, John Rathbone, an old army colonel, William Saunders, Henry Tucker, Thomas

Flint, Thomas Evans, John Myles, Will. Westcot, and John Cole, officers or soldiers in the late Rebellion, were indicted for conspiring the death of his Majesty and the overthrow of the Government. Having laid their plot and contrivance for the surprisal [sic] of the Tower, the killing his Grace the Lord General, Sir John Robinson, Lieutenant of the Tower, and Sir Richard Brown; and then to have declared for an equal division of lands, &c. The better to effect this hellish design, the City was to have been fired, and the portcullis let down to keep out all assistance; and the Horse Guards to have been surprised in the inns where they were quartered, several ostlers having been gained for that purpose. The Tower was accordingly viewed, and its surprise ordered by boats over the moat, and from thence to scale the wall. One Alexander, not yet taken, had likewise distributed money to these conspirators; and, for the carrying on the design more effectually, they were told of a Council of the great ones that sat frequently in London, from whom issued all orders; which Council received their directions from another in Holland, who sat with the States; and that the third of September was pitched on for the attempt, as being found by Lilly's Almanack, and a scheme erected for that purpose, to be a lucky day, a planet then ruling which prognosticated the downfall of Monarchy. The evidence against these persons was very full and clear, and they were accordingly found guilty of High Treason.

Samuel Pepys would refer to the *Gazette* story in a diary entry for 13 December 1666, and was intrigued by the closeness of the date of the intended conspiracy to that of the outbreak of the Fire of London in early September:

> Up, and to the office, where we sat. At noon to the 'Change and there met Captain Cocke and had a second time his direction to bespeak 100*l*. of plate which I did at Sir R. Viner's being twelve plates more, and something else I have to choose. Thence home to dinner, and there W. Hewer dined with me, and showed me a Gazette in April last, which I wonder should never be remembered by any body, which tells how several persons were then tried for their lives, and were found guilty of a design of killing the King and destroying the Government; and as a means to it, to burn the City and that the day intended for the plot was the 3rd of last September. And the fire did indeed break out on the 2nd of September which is very strange, methinks, and I shall remember it.

The fate that awaited Rathbone, Saunders, Tucker, Flint, Evans, Myles, Westcot, Cole and others convicted of treason against the king was a terrifying one – the so-called 'Holy Trinity' of hanging, drawing and quartering. If the guilty individual was an aristocrat or a gentleman, however, he was likely to be spared this prolonged horror of a traitor's death. The Parliamentarian Sir Henry Vane the Younger, found guilty of high treason by a jury packed with Royalists in 1662 – having been exempted from the Indemnity and Oblivion Act despite not being a regicide – was granted a cleaner and more dignified mode of execution in the form of decapitation by axe blow.

Pepys had recorded the courage and dignity Vane displayed at his execution at on 14 June 1662:

> We all went out to the Tower-hill; and there, over against the scaffold, made on purpose this day, saw Sir Henry Vane brought... He made a very long speech, interrupted by the Sheriff and others there; and they would have taken the paper out of his hand, but he would not let it go... the trumpets were brought under the scaffold that he might not be heard.
>
> Then he prayed and so fitted himself, and received the blow... He... died justifying himself and the cause he had stood for; and spoke very confidently of being presently at the right hand of Christ; and in all things appeared the most resolved man that ever died in that manner, and showed more heat than cowardice, but yet with all humility and gravity. One asked him why he did not pray for the King. He answered, 'Nay,' says he, 'you shall see I can pray for the King: I pray God bless him!'

Hanging was the most common punishment meted out for offences that ranged from high treason and murder to the apparently trivial, such as shoplifting or cutting down a young tree. On average, around 150 people were hanged in London a year. Some of the crimes that resulted in execution seem absurd – witness the case, cited by Anthony à Wood, of a woman sentenced to hang at Tyburn 'for that the dog laid with her several terms'. The animal, naturally, was found equally culpable and executed alongside its mistress.

For non-capital crimes, justice often took on a more complex form. Many of the long-term inhabitants of the country's jails were those who had been imprisoned for unorthodox religious practices and for refusing to kowtow to the 1662 Act of Uniformity. Many crimes that are now regarded as serious were unknown in 1666 (financial or corporate fraud, or child molestation were not on the statute books as offences punishable by imprisonment or the death penalty), but this did not mean that there was any less in the way of crime. It was the prerogative of the crown to decide what constituted wrongdoing and what did not, so, while many of the strictures of the Commonwealth soon passed into history, other, more appropriate laws were brought in. It was, for instance, considered treasonable to make the (factually sound) observation that the newly minted coins, of inferior quality because of the cheaper metal used within them, were likely to devalue the national currency, because the Sedition Act of 1661 had made it illegal to criticize the actions of the monarch, and money was inextricably linked to Charles, whose head was on every coin.

The Sedition Act was designed to shore up the role of the monarchy by creating four new kinds of high treason. It became illegal to 'within the realm, or without, compass, imagine, invent, devise or intend death or destruction or any bodily harm tending to death or destruction, maim or wounding, imprisonment or restraint of the person of the King'; to deprive the monarch of his crown; to levy war 'within this realm or without'; or to 'move or stir' any potential invasion of England. The eight Commonwealth soldiers had certainly transgressed against the Act, and knew the fate that awaited them when they were found guilty.

Law-keeping in Restoration England was chaotic. The widespread use of the military to maintain order and quash dissent under Cromwell had been met with fear and resentment, and Charles knew that the reintroduction of martial law was not an option if he wanted to retain his initial popularity with his people; a standing army was regarded as the tool of a despot, such as Louis XIV. The only circumstance under which the army might be called in was to deal with an uprising, but even then they had to be deployed carefully, with the minimum of violence and disruption to the innocent. Having dispensed with Cromwell's New Model Army when he ascended the throne, Charles had to find both a new means of protecting the country and of keeping order within it. He created a small standing army by royal warrant in January 1661, but this on its own was not enough.

In their efforts to maintain law and order, Charles and his ministers were not helped by the status quo. There was no police force in England in 1666, either local or national. Each parish had between three and four constables or bailiffs, who were regarded as rather lowly figures. They were recruited more or less at random (and often reluctantly) and paid a pittance in consequence. Their assistance, such as it was, came from the local watchmen and the citizenry at large, whose zeal in catching criminals was often enhanced by the offer of a reward. However, especially in villages and small towns, catching petty criminals seldom required a great deal of detective work. Few possessed any objects of great value, so pickpocketing and theft of household items (as opposed to theft of, say, livestock, a more common occurrence) were all but unknown outside the large cities, and most of the crimes of violence that took place were between people known to one another.

More serious rural (and suburban) offenders were the marauding highwaymen, whose reputation – then as now – as gentlemen of fortune was something of a romantic myth, with the occasional high-profile exception. The most famous brigand of the age, Claude Duval (or Du Vall), came to England from France as a footman and stable boy of the Duke of Richmond, and soon realized that he could make more money on his own horse, so to speak. He haunted the roads leading to London, most notably those around Hounslow Heath and the northern lanes around Islington and Highgate. He acquired a reputation for both rapaciousness and charm, especially to women; a famous (and probably apocryphal) story told by Duval's subsequent biographer William Pope involved him allowing a victim of his to retain part of his money in exchange for Duval's dancing a coranto with his wife on Hounslow Heath. Duval was reputed never to use force or violence, although this did not prevent him from being executed in 1670 when he was eventually captured at the Hole in the Wall tavern in Covent Garden, much to the sorrow of many ladies. His popularity was such that many appeals for a royal pardon were made, but these were unsuccessful. He was buried in St Paul's Church, Covent Garden, and his memorial referred to his modus operandi with some affection:

> Here lies Du Vall, Reader, if male thou art,
> Look to thy purse. If female, to thy heart.

Much havoc has he made of both; for all
Men he made to stand, and women he made to fall.
The second Conqueror of the Norman race,
Knights to his arm did yield, and ladies to his face.
Old Tyburn's glory; England's illustrious Thief,
Du Vall, the ladies' joy; Du Vall, the ladies' grief.

In his eschewal of bloodshed, Duval differed from the majority of his fellow criminals, whose idea of courtesy was often to rape their female victims and then to murder their husbands and companions. Some of these men worked in organized packs, while others preferred to strike out on their own. The most successful highwaymen concentrated on a particular locale, knowing when a lucrative coach was likely to cross their patch and when to strike accordingly. Some were the disinherited or bastard sons of great men and called themselves gentlemen in consequence; others were former soldiers who had acquired, along with a taste for high living, a talent for fast and skilful horsemanship. One of the most famous of these soldiers-turned-felons was John Nevison, dubbed 'Swift Nick', allegedly by King Charles himself, following a reputed 200-mile dash from Gad's Hill in Kent to York in order to provide an alibi. (In York, 'Swift Nick' encountered the Lord Mayor of that city, and was thereby able to prove his whereabouts.) The only thing that these highwaymen had in common, other than robbery, was contempt for their criminal inferior, the footpad, whose modus operandi of skulking in the bushes ready to pounce on unsuspecting passers-by was regarded as both a lowly and a time-consuming way of committing theft.

It was unlikely that any of the great ladies of the day wept at their executions, as they did at Duval's and Nevison's.

Crime in London was of an altogether different order, and there was a great deal more of it. Crime existed at all levels of society – whether it involved pickpocketing or theft by the urban poor, brawling among the rough thespians of Covent Garden, or drunken tomfoolery on the part of wealthy young men. Murder or assault might be committed by virtually anyone. There were lawless parts of the City into which few dared to venture, most notoriously an area between Blackfriars and the Temple that was known as Alsatia, taking its name from a Dominican convent that had existed there before the Reformation. Since the fifteenth century, it had been a sanctuary for debtors and all kinds of non-violent criminals, who would not be pursued by the forces of the law there; the corollary was that it was ruled ruthlessly by the extremely dangerous, who would happily rob and kill anyone who fled there. Likewise, the area around the Marshalsea prison in Southwark saw all manner of wrongdoing taking place on its doorstep; perhaps not coincidentally, most of the city's low-grade brothels were situated near here, on Bankside, attracting a varied and undiscerning clientele who were prone to make their displeasure (or pleasure) known with acts of violence.

Nor were those higher up the social scale immune from crimes of violence. Alice Thornton, a once-wealthy and literate woman from Yorkshire, wrote about how her nephew, Thomas Danby, was killed in a street brawl in London around Christmas 1666. Her description of the proceedings provides an affecting account of Danby's death, in touching contrast to the coldly factual terms in which violent crime in the city was often described.

About this Christmas, 1666, [Thomas Danby] was inhumanly murdered at London, near Gray's Inn. It was the permission of God, for the affliction of us all, in the loss of so brave a gentleman, to let a dismal stroke fall heavy upon the person of my nephew Thomas Danby, being the hope of his family; and just at that time when he had engaged to clear of all debts, portions, etc., in the due performance of his father's will, when all things would have been done to all persons' satisfactions. But alas! This poor gentleman was suddenly surprised and murdered, without any provocation or malice begun on his side, committed with the most barbarous circumstances imaginable, by one Berridge, a stranger to him, but a comrade to Ogle and Jenny, which was then with Tom Danby, but did not assist. The pretence was about Ogle's sword, that Tom had redeemed from pawn, and unluckily had on that day, and which Berrige upbraiding him for, picked a quarrel. But it is too probable that they had a spleen against his life, because none assisted, but witnesses of this bloody tragedy. The murderer fled; they were catched [sic]; but by the too remissness of the jury, escaped punishment, notwithstanding the displeasure of the judge.*

If the criminal was caught, depending on the offence justice

* One crumb of consolation for Thornton was her note that Jenny was 'convicted in conscience' and he died shortly after the trial, in August 1667.

was either dispensed summarily or in court. A common punishment for minor wrongdoings, such as petty theft or libel, was to be placed in the local pillory and humiliated publicly by being pelted with rotten food and other missiles.* Whippings were administered for sexual misdemeanours such as prostitution, or for vagrancy. Debtors, and those who had committed the few financial crimes that were recognized at the time, were fined (unless they directly affected the king, in which case they were treasonable) and imprisoned – often indefinitely – if they could not pay up; they would only be released from the grim conditions of jail once they – or their families – had produced the money required.

For more serious crimes, such as murder or robbery, a trial was called for. If you lived in the country, you were dragged to the nearest county jail and thrown into it to await the next assizes, when the local magistrate or a visiting high court judge would pass sentence on the unfortunate miscreants arrayed before him. If you lived in a city, the administration of the law was faster, if no more merciful.

Justice, like many things in England in 1666, was both a matter of good fortune and of class. If the man on trial was an aristocrat, he could ask for the judgement of his peers in the House of Lords, who, knowing that they might one day find themselves in a similar position, were inclined towards leniency. As a result, many more 'great' men were acquitted than ordinary offenders. In the event of a peer being impeached – as happened when John, Viscount Mordaunt was accused of

---

* These could be stones or heavy rocks, which resulted in injury or even death for the seriously unpopular.

the false imprisonment of the surveyor of Windsor Castle and the rape of his daughter in 1666 – there was a good chance that Charles would offer a pardon. Mordaunt was not merely an aristocrat, but had been an active conspirator on Charles's behalf during the Protectorate, and at the Restoration was rewarded with the titles of Constable of Windsor Castle and keeper of Windsor Great Park; he could not, therefore, be expected to face the same justice as other men. However, the presumption of guilt was enough to make the transgressor a pariah thereafter.

Ordinary men who pleaded not guilty faced a jury of a dozen of their peers, whose task was to hear the evidence against the prisoner and come to a decision as to their guilt or innocence. To encourage them to make a speedy judgement, the jurors, who were ordinary men chosen at random, were kept without food, water or sleep until they had reached their verdict, based on the judge's summing-up. If the judge considered they had come to the wrong conclusion, they were sent back until they came back with the right one. Mid-seventeenth-century jury service was a harsh and unlovely business, especially in rural areas; jurors on the assizes might find themselves travelling from town to town on rough carts to finish the judgement of a case. And, as the acquittal of Danby's murderers showed, the eventual verdict returned might bear little relation to the rights and wrongs of the case.

Once they found themselves in court, the accused knew that their life was likely to be forfeit. Few were acquitted, as the defendant was allowed neither counsel nor sympathetic witnesses, and their only means of defending themselves was to question the evidence against them, which was normally hard to refute. When convicted of a capital crime, a prisoner automatically forfeited all their possessions and any property they owned. The only way that anyone might save their goods from confiscation was by publicly invoking 'the judgement of God', a guilty plea of sorts, which finished the trial automatically, but allowed the prisoner's family to retain their effects, as well as letting him die with some measure of dignity. The other alternative, and one that only the educated and literate had any chance of succeeding with, was to object to the indictment, which could theoretically be nullified if it could be shown to contain mistakes. However, the defendant was often thrown back into jail while the indictment was rewritten, as in the case of the Quaker George Fox in 1664.

There was, however, a strange legal quirk by which it was impossible to convict a prisoner of an offence unless they had pleaded guilty or not guilty; it was tempting for anyone who knew conviction was likely simply to refuse to plead, as this meant that their family would not be disinherited. This resulted in further imprisonment, but the legal system was able to threaten the most stubborn individuals with a particularly refined form of torture that, while seldom used in practice, inevitably led to a plea.

The process of *peine forte et dure*, literally meaning 'strong and hard punishment', or simply 'the press', was a barbaric process by which the prisoner was taken back to his cell, laid on his back and had stones or iron placed on his chest 'as great as you can bear', and denied food or water other than 'three morsels of the coarsest bread' on the first day, and 'three draughts of stagnant water from the pool nearest to the prison door' on the third. This punishment, with weights added as the jailer saw fit, continued either until death or until the unfortunate victim was prepared to plead. Sometimes, a particularly sadistic judge decided that this process might as well continue to the subject's end regardless. Only the hardiest managed to endure the agony for more than a couple of days. It was regarded as excessive and undignified to apply *peine forte et dure* to a female prisoner who refused to plead; instead, their thumbs were tightly bound together with whipcord, to agonizing effect.

There were a few instances in which, once found guilty of a capital crime, the defendant was not automatically condemned to death. A husband who murdered an adulterous wife would be found guilty of manslaughter rather than homicide, given a short spell in prison and branded on the hand, but with the judicial instruction, as with Justice Jones in a case of a husband murdering both his wife and her lover, that this mutilation should be done 'gently, because there could not be greater provocation than this'. If the homicide was considered justified in some way – having been committed, for instance, for reasons of self-defence – the killer might not even be charged. If they were brought to trial, they might well be acquitted (although their property would still be confiscated).

However, the majority of the malefactors who were convicted in court were condemned to death, and then the final process of the law began. Little time elapsed between conviction and execution – after all, what was the point of keeping a condemned man alive unnecessarily? As there was no appeal court, the only chance of a commutation or quashing of sentence came through application to the king for a royal pardon.

Sometimes this worked; on 25 April 1666, Sir John Towers, a former keeper of the Royal Seal, was convicted of high treason for counterfeiting the Seal and the king's signature, for which the punishment was hanging, drawing and quartering. Before the sentence could be carried out, however, Towers successfully petitioned Charles for his punishment to be commuted to transportation to Barbados, where he was eventually sent on 15 October, but not before he had suffered several months 'in a loathsome prison'. The reason for the delay in departure was that Towers had not been able to obtain any security for his safe transport; presumably a disgraced courtier who was shipped overseas was still entitled to some rights and privileges that ordinary criminals were not. Transportation was becoming an increasingly popular punishment for non-capital crimes, removing wrongdoers from society and offering a useful source of unpaid labour for British settlements in America's east coast and in the Caribbean.

Another way of having one's sentence reduced without royal intervention was to claim 'benefit of clergy'. This legal provision, which had existed in various forms since medieval times, allowed clergymen to seek to be tried by an ecclesiastical court (which could only offer civil rather than criminal penalties) as opposed to a secular one. Those who wished to claim benefit of clergy would take what was essentially a 'literacy test' in which they proved their clerical status by reading from the Bible. They would recite (having memorized the words, if they were illiterate) the so-called 'neck verse'* from Psalm 51, 'Have mercy upon me, O God, after thy great goodness: according to the multitude of thy mercies do away mine offences'. It had long since been accepted that the purpose of the provision was to allow the literate a chance of leniency for their first offences, but by 1666 the number of crimes for which benefit of clergy could be claimed were very limited. These included theft of an item with a value of less than five shillings from a shop, or goods worth less than forty shillings from a house. For those who successfully claimed benefit of clergy, the likely punishment for a minor misdemeanour was to be branded on the thumb or hand in court, followed by a public whipping or a sojourn in the stocks. Whatever sanction the malefactor received, it was preferable to incarceration.

The purpose of prison in 1666 was not rehabilitation, but punishment, and to act as a deterrent to other potential wrongdoers. Conditions inside prisons varied enormously. At best, it was possible to have a tolerable time of it inside, if the felon was wealthy and prepared to bribe his jailers to allow him extra food and drink and home comforts; some jailers even turned a blind eye to conjugal visits by wives and mistresses. Men of quality were incarcerated in the Tower;

* So called for its power to save one's neck.

Rochester was held there after his failed attempt to abduct his wife-to-be in 1665, and Buckingham found himself imprisoned there in 1667, accused of treason. They could at least expect to be treated with dignity. Conditions inside humbler English jails in 1666 were appalling, with prisoners often chained and manacled, crammed into tiny, stinking cells, deprived of food and water and prone to disease and other forms of suffering. Especially shocking for modern sensibilities, this was the fate of all those awaiting trial – the theoretically innocent – as well as the convicted. Not until the Habeas Corpus Act* of 1679 was any serious attempt made to prevent unlawful imprisonment, meaning that before then a prisoner could expect little in the way of decent treatment.

One of the most notorious jails, Newgate in London, burnt down in the Great Fire, but while it existed it was a byword for degrading and inhuman conditions. One inmate, Colonel John Turner, said of it in 1662 while awaiting execution that its condemned cell, known as 'the Hole' or simply 'Hell' was 'a most fearful, sad, deplorable place', where there was 'neither bench, stool nor stick for any person there. They lie like swine upon the ground, one upon another, howling and roaring – it was more terrible to me than death.' Turner, who knew what he was talking about, concluded, '[the law] had better take them and hang them as soon as they have their sentence'.

The reasons for the dreadful indignities of incarceration were relatively simple. In the first place, there was no money provided by Parliament for those imprisoned, hence the

---

* Which had its origins in Magna Carta.

privations that they endured unless they were willing to pay to improve their confinement. Ironically, it was their fellow inmates who offered what assistance they could. The Quaker Henry Jackson, in a petition to Charles of 3 September 1666, begging for clemency, stated that he had been imprisoned for over two years, after he had attempted to visit a friend in prison, but was instead accused of holding an unlawful meeting (for which the official penalty was 'only' three months' imprisonment) and thrown into jail without trial for failing to take the Oath of Allegiance. According to Jackson's description of the conditions he faced: '20 of us are thronged in a stinking room, where [we] cannot all lie down together, neither straw nor food allowed except at enormous rates, even 3*d*. for a quart of water, and what [our] friends bring [us] taken from [us] four or five days together, so that moderate people, though not of their opinions, in tenderness throw bread over a house top into the dungeon court for them; all bedclothes are taken away, and [we] are sometimes struck with a staff and chained one to another'.

Quakers tended to fare particularly badly in prison.* One especially notable resident of the grim Bridewell prison throughout the 1660s was the Quaker Thomas Ellwood, whose friendship with John Milton and refusal to stop holding meetings led to his being imprisoned sporadically between 1660 and 1670. In his account of his incarceration, Ellwood, who was kept separately from the ordinary criminals – perhaps because it was feared that he might try to proselytize them

* See also Chapter 3, 'Anglicans and Dissenters'.

– describes the kindnesses that he was offered by two 'honest, grave, discreet and motherly' widows, who managed to feed the Quakers from their own pockets, but also the difficulties he had in obtaining other food from other sources, as he only had ten pence on him.

It is interesting to read Ellwood's description of the variety of victuals available at the chandler's shop in the prison, including 'beer, bread, butter, cheese, eggs and bacon'. Ellwood himself, however, was able to afford only a penny loaf. His account reveals starkly both the manner in which money ruled the roost in prison, and also the way in which he was discriminated against because of his beliefs. Bridewell, a place for petty offenders and the socially undesirable, housed a range of wrongdoers of different types. It was Ellwood's fate to 'sit down with lower commons', and to be reduced to a state of near-starvation.

Some of the more unscrupulous lawmakers found an easy way of making money out of prisoners. City constables or watchmen would house criminals in their own homes for a few days, and charge them for the privilege of spending time out of jail. Most were only too happy to pay for the luxury of enjoying better living conditions for a short while. This was viewed with dismay by the city jailers, who themselves wished for a cut of the proceeds. One Oxford jailer, Bartholomew Arnold, complained to the city council about this state of affairs in early 1666. Their judgement, delivered in a decree on 2 March, was as follows:

It is now agreed that no serjeant, or deputy serjeant, of this

City shall on any pretence whatever keep any freeman, who has been arrested by any process out of the City Court, any longer than a week in his house or in any place other than the common jail of Bocardo, nor a foreigner more than three days, but shall, after a week for freemen and three days for foreigners, carry their prisoners to the common jail upon penalty of being dismissed from his office.

The common jail of Bocardo was not, admittedly, a place that many would have wanted to find themselves inside, being a damp, dismal and rat-infested hell-hole that was eventually demolished in 1771.*

Once inside these infernal institutions, the prisoner did well to make it beyond his or her trial, but the fate that awaited those condemned to death was grim. In London, they were initially taken from Newgate to Tyburn, the traditional place of execution situated on the northeast corner of Hyde Park. There were other settings for hangings, including Tower Hill and Leadenhall Street in the City, but Tyburn attracted the greatest crowds. The procession, which set out in the early morning, normally took three or four hours to cover the two-mile journey between Newgate and Tyburn. The condemned travelled either on foot or in a cart, with their coffins following behind. Armed guards ensured that no rescue attempts were made. Usually, the men would be allowed to stop at a tavern on the way, such as the Halfway House in Holborn or the Bowl Inn in St Giles, the intention being that they would arrive at the

---

* Perhaps ironically, it has now lent its name to an upmarket hotel in the city.

gallows either partially or fully intoxicated.* Sometimes the hangman might even join them for a drink, although it's hard to imagine what the conversation would have been like. It was a tradition for the departing prisoners to shout to the other customers, 'I'll buy you a drink on the way back!' Depending on the infamy of those convicted, they might either expect abuse and missiles to be thrown at them, or cheers and backslapping; in either case, their route was a congested and busy one.

At Tyburn convicts achieved, in the moments before and during their execution, a grim form of celebrity as leading players in this most brutal of public spectacles. Thousands turned out to watch public executions, from all sectors of society, and the best views were much prized; Pepys recorded in his diary in 1664 that he 'got for a shilling to stand upon the wheel of a cart, in great pain, above an hour before the execution was done'. The crowd, who were often given a day's holiday to watch the execution, screamed, shouted and bayed for blood. They were not to be disappointed.

Those who had been convicted of treason, such as the eight soldiers we encountered at the beginning of this chapter, were first hanged by the neck until they were nearly dead. Then, choking and weakened, they were dragged to the scaffold where they were castrated and disembowelled. Their intestines were then burnt before their eyes, and their hearts were cut out. Finally, they were decapitated before having their limbs severed, to be placed on display throughout the City at the various gates. If more than one man was to be executed

---

* Hence the number of pubs that have the grimly punning name the Last Drop.

in this fashion, the others were made to wait their turn and witness the death agonies of their fellows; it was probably a relief to be the first to die. An especially agonizing and cruel process of execution, hanging, drawing and quartering nevertheless appears almost merciful in comparison with some of the means of dispatch that were commonly practised in Europe, such as the French method of tying a man by his arms and legs to four horses, which then dismembered him as they pulled away.

Executions by hanging, drawing and quartering were relatively uncommon, although other forms of dispatch were painful enough. How quickly the hanged man died often depended on the skill of the hangman. At Tyburn at least, the hangman was a public servant (and often himself a reprieved criminal) whose task it was to perform the executions, and who was paid – quite literally – on a per capita basis. It was up to him to finesse the details of the hanging, dealing with everything from the length of the rope to whether or not the victim's relatives should be allowed to hasten their passing by tugging at their legs. A competent hanging could lead to almost instantaneous death, but a deliberately botched one could result in a slow and agonizing demise. In the most gruesome and long-drawn-out of cases, it was recorded that birds would peck out of the eyes of dying men. It comes as little surprise that hangmen were not only eminently bribable, but often demanded a bribe; when Miles Corbet, one of the regicides of Charles I, was awaiting execution in 1662, the executioner asked for payment that he 'might be favourable to him at his death', and upon being denied this, vowed that he would 'torture him exceedingly'.

Women found guilty of capital crimes met their end in a different but equally unpleasant way: they were burnt at the stake for reasons of 'the decency due to their sex', which 'forbids the exposing and public mangling of their bodies'.* In some cases the condemned woman was strangled or bludgeoned by the executioner before she was burnt, but sometimes – particularly if appropriate payment had not been forthcoming – this was not carried out with the necessary force, and the woman was still alive when the pyre was lit. The agonies suffered by the victim can only be imagined.

The question inevitably remains why the English were so prepared to accept a judicial system that not only seems barbaric, but frequently sadistic as well. If England was no worse than the European norm in this regard, this is less a testament to Charles's enlightened rule and more a reflection of how a people beaten down by years of war, Commonwealth repression and, latterly, plague simply accepted the state of things, however harsh it might have been. It is probably best to remember the words of Samuel de Sorbière, when he talked of there being 'no people in the world so easily frightened into subjection as the English' (see page 22). The draconian rule of law and order could only work in a country where most people accepted and obeyed their ruler; in this regard, the Restoration was less of a shift from the harshness of the Commonwealth than might have been imagined, or hoped for. Under Cromwell, the all-powerful 'major generals' who

* The quotation comes from an eighteenth-century jurist, William Blackstone, writing in his *Commentaries on the Laws of England*.

maintained order were much-feared figures, and imprisonment without trial for perceived dissent was common. Yet no greater number of people were executed before the Restoration; if anything, slightly fewer faced capital punishment owing to the comparative absence of politically motivated executions under the Protectorate. For all Charles's fine words of tolerance and reconciliation, punishment and penal conditions remained nasty and brutish, and the chances of decent treatment for those accused of transgressions remained scant indeed.

Foreign Affairs

'For what can war, but endless war, still breed?'
– John Milton, 'On the Lord General Fairfax
at the Siege of Colchester'

On 6 June 1666, London exulted at the news of a great naval victory against the Dutch, during what would become known as the Second Anglo-Dutch War. The initial news received at court was of an enemy retreat and of many of their ships being destroyed or captured. This entirely erroneous report led to fireworks being set off, bonfires being lit and general rejoicing. Pepys captured the mood vividly:

> Mightily pleased with this happy day's news, and the more, because confirmed by Sir Daniel Harvy, who was in the whole fight with the Generall, and tells me that there appear but thirty-six in all of the Dutch fleet left at the end of the voyage when they run home. The joy of the City was this night exceeding great.

This glee was to be short-lived. When Pepys arrived at his office on 7 June 'with the same expectation of congratulating ourselves with the victory that I had yesterday', he was given 'quite contrary news, which astonishes me' of a severe defeat, with several ships lost, not a single Dutch vessel taken prisoner and many men of all ranks killed. Exuberance and rejoicing quickly turned to disappointment and misery, as realization of the disastrous extent of the débâcle dawned on the country at large.

When Charles came to the throne in 1660, belligerence was the last thing on his mind. His long exile had given him a deep respect for many of the European monarchs he had dealt with, most notably his cousin Louis XIV. He had a far better relationship with the Dutch than either his father or Cromwell had had, having enjoyed their hospitality while he was in the United Provinces. Not only was the 1660 Declaration of Breda, which effectively sealed his return as king in exchange for a general pardon, written in the Netherlands, but upon his departure for England he was given many gifts of art, jewellery and gold by his Dutch hosts (see page 139). The intention, on both sides, seemed to be to bring about a lasting peace between the two countries after the belligerence of the First Anglo-Dutch War, and to ensure a harmonious and tranquil reign for Charles. He also knew that the Dutch ruling élite, the House of Orange, had been a key supporter of his father, lending him huge sums of money in the civil war.

Nonetheless, renewed conflict between England and the Dutch Republic was inevitable and the main reason for that conflict was trading rivalry. During the previous half-century, such matters as trade disputes, the rights to fish for herring in the North Sea and the race to dominate the lucrative international cloth markets had raised tensions between the two countries. The Dutch had developed the largest mercantile fleet in Europe and acquired a dominant position in European trade; their powerful navy had expanded at the expense of an England distracted during the years of the civil war. However, the First Anglo-Dutch War of 1652–4, waged by Cromwell, had ended in a decisive victory for a newly strengthened English navy under the command of Admiral Robert Blake. England gained outright control of the waters around her shores, and the United Provinces were obliged to accept an English trading monopoly. This rankled with the Dutch, who were intent on rebuilding both their naval and commercial strength after their ignominious defeat.

On 22 February 1664, Pepys reported the Duke of Monmouth's uncle's intelligence that everyone at Whitehall save Charles and the influential men of the City was 'mad for a Dutch war'. George Monck, by now Lord Albemarle and head of the Admiralty, claimed 'what we want is more of the trade the Dutch now have'. Charles was not ruling a wealthy country, but one that was deep in debt and desperately seeking a quick solution to its problems. A quick, easy and apparently winnable war, fought at sea, where England was traditionally strongest, seemed like the best idea both to secure funds and Charles's standing as a great king. Therefore, financial necessity won out over a desire for peace. Charles gave his blessing to attacks on Dutch ships by privateers, knowing the inevitability of counter-attacks. First, the privateers undertook some opportunistic forays against trading ports such as Cape Coast Castle, which had become a Dutch possession in 1663, in the Dutch Gold Coast (today known as Ghana), and New

Amsterdam in America (the latter captured bloodlessly and promptly renamed New York). Then, after many more attacks and skirmishes, a formal declaration of war was made by England against the Netherlands in March 1665.

Initially, the omens for a decisive and speedy victory were good. The English outnumbered and outgunned the Dutch, with 160 warships, 5,000 guns and 25,000 sailors against the United Provinces' 135 warships, and they considered themselves the foremost naval power in Europe. In an early battle fought off Lowestoft, on 3 June 1665, the English fleet triumphed, destroying 17 Dutch ships and taking 2,000 prisoners. The nation rejoiced; Pepys wrote, 'a greater victory was never known in the world'. Had England pressed home its advantage, a final reckoning would have led to annihilation of the Dutch within a matter of weeks, but instead complacency and a lack of organization resulted in the Dutch being able to regroup (under the inspirational leadership of first Johan de Witt and then the great admiral Michiel de Ruyter), rebuild the ships that they had lost, and generally prepare themselves for further battle.

After their strong start to the campaign in 1665, by the start of 1666 the English navy was in disarray. The previous year's plague had put paid to any serious attempts to conduct an expedition in the last few months of 1665, as had the lack of any finances to fight a war. John Evelyn, acting as a commissioner for the sick and wounded, wrote to the naval administrator Sir William Coventry on 10 October 1665 to complain that 'there are upon my hands at present 2700 prisoners and more than 2000 of our own sick men, who have neither bread, nor harbour, nor medicaments, nor attendance'. The reason, as Evelyn saw it, for this deplorable state of affairs was a simple one; 'for our money being exhausted', he wrote, 'our credit is lost.' The gamble of embarking upon a war in order to restore the country's finances had failed.

Another difficulty was that the range of enemies faced had widened considerably. Thanks to Dutch diplomacy, an arrangement was reached with Louis XIV to honour his 1662 treaty with the Netherlands. This treaty guaranteed armed support in the event of one or other country being attacked, and Louis XIV duly fulfilled his part of the bargain on 16 January 1666, when he declared war against England. Given Louis' good relations with his cousin Charles II and reluctance to imperil the French navy, this was a symbolic rather than practical action, but it was nonetheless a blow to English attempts to isolate the Netherlands from the rest of Europe. With Frederick III of Denmark being bribed to join the increasingly grand alliance, England seemed strapped for allies. The only European ruler to offer his support to Charles was the ineffectual Bernhard von Galen, prince-bishop of Münster, subsequently known as 'Bombing Bernhard',* whose personal eccentricities included fire-eating. He withdrew from the conflict in April after Louis gently suggested that he might be better off governing his bishopric, rather than facing annihilation from a European coalition.

Unsurprisingly, morale on board the English ships at the start of 1666 was low, despite the confident claims of future

---

* He acquired the nickname from the Dutch after an unsuccessful attempt to lay siege to the city of Groningen in 1672 involving bombs.

success in various almanacs, such as William Lilly's, which predicted 'prosperity, satisfaction and happiness of the English with their glorious victories'. Not only was there no money (Pepys, calculating the navy accounts at the year's beginning, worked out that there was a deficit of £800,000 owing, with a parliamentary grant of £2,500,000 being exhausted in five months when it was supposed to last a year), but the plague had left many naval personnel worried about their families and friends. One twenty-four-year-old sailor, Edward Barlow from Prestwich near Manchester, wrote in his journal of how, after hearing of the death of his brother, three cousins, mistress and 'divers neighbours and acquaintances more', he felt 'a great grief to heart'. Nonetheless, he was determined to 'go through many troubles and dangers more, for I had bound myself to a hard and miserable calling, and there was no way for me but I must endure it'. The 'hard and miserable' times that Barlow wrote of would worsen significantly throughout the course of the year, leading him eventually to claim that 'there are no men under the sun that fare harder and get their living more hard and that are so abused on all sides as we poor seamen'.

The ships' companies were made up of a variety of men. Some officers were experienced seamen who had proved themselves over years of fighting, but others were simply scions of aristocratic families for whom naval service was thought to be an easy and profitable means of currying royal favour. Rochester was a typical example of the latter. Having fallen from grace with Charles after attempting to abduct Elizabeth Malet, his future wife, he redeemed himself with sterling service and conspicuous bravery at the Battle of Vågen (in the port of Bergen) in August 1665. He later rejoined the fleet in June 1666, by now a veteran, when all able hands were needed and distinguished himself in the St James's Day Battle on 25 July by heroically carrying a letter from one ship to another under heavy fire.

Serving on board ships was widely thought to be a socially acceptable and (apparently) financially rewarding task. Pay for ordinary seamen was between nineteen and twenty-four shillings a month, with board included, although the financial difficulties of the Exchequer meant that many could expect to wait months to be paid, leading to desperation and poverty among the sailors. A 'humble petition' of 1667 claimed that wives and children had been reduced to starving in the streets because of their lack of pay. The unfortunate Barlow had to wait as long as nine months before being paid. When he eventually received his salary of £10 in one instalment, he was informed by the paymaster that his next payment would not be forthcoming for *another* nine months, since it was believed that a comparatively wealthy seaman was one more likely to desert.

Even when the seamen were paid, their lives in times of war were far from easy. Rations, which were supposed to consist of generous helpings of beef, bread, beer, fish and much else besides,* were in practice limited and often inedible after a long sea journey. Discipline was harsh and frequently enforced – necessarily so, as otherwise mutiny and desertion were

---

* Rations included no fruit or vegetables, leading to inevitable outbreaks of scurvy.

inevitable. The Navy Discipline Act of 1661 ordered seamen to obey instructions by their superiors, diligently defend their fleet in combat and never quarrel with officers or utter 'any words of sedition or mutiny', or face the invariably severe consequences. Coventry claimed that 'Nothing but hanging will man the fleet', and capital punishment was far from uncommon. Severe floggings with the cat-o'-nine-tails, meanwhile, were an everyday occurrence, their bloodthirsty nature regarded as an invaluable tool *pour encourager les autres*. Serious misdemeanours could lead to those responsible being publicly cashiered. The *London Gazette* of 4 May 1666 reported the case of the court martial of William Tyler, gunner of the *Matthias*, who was demoted to the rank of foremast man of the *Helverston* for drunkenness and endangering the ship by setting fire to his cabin by experimenting with fireworks.

One of the few incentives for serving on board ship was the possibility of acquiring plunder. The act of 1661 dictated that seamen should not 'take out of any prize or ship or goods seized for prize any money, plate, goods lading or tackle' before these had been appraised by the Admiralty Court, save when these were found 'upon or above the gun deck of the said ship, and not otherwise'. In other words, regular seamen could divide between them any merchandise that stood on the decks of prize ships. This was a tricky matter to adjudicate, especially in the heat of a victory, and reputations could be ruined if it was felt that merchandise had not been fairly divided. Pepys's patron Edward Montagu, earl of Sandwich, had attracted much criticism for what was felt to be ungenerous behaviour in late 1665 when some lucrative trading ships of the Dutch East India

Company were captured. It was hoped that the booty taken would go some way towards paying for the navy to continue to wage war on the Dutch, but Sandwich's determination to reserve the best for himself and his commanders caused significant damage to both morale and to his own standing.

It did not help England's cause that, by 1666, many were openly questioning the point of serving in the navy. Barlow wrote: 'I could wish no young man to betake himself to this calling unless he had good friends to put him in place or supply his wants, for he shall find a great deal more to his sorrow than I have writ.' There were also rumours of corruption and incompetence at the highest levels. These rumours were broadly accurate. The Navy Board, for which Pepys was an administrator, was an organization that, if not actively discreditable, certainly prized connections and greased palms above everything else. It was common for officials to be bribed with everything from gold and silver to wine and oysters by those anxious to obtain favours and preferment. Sandwich had explained to Pepys back in 1660 that he should not take the job for the meagre salary, but for 'the opportunities of getting money while he is in the place'.* This was not an organization fit for the purpose of running a naval campaign against the Dutch.

It did not help that, of the two men in charge, Lord Albemarle and Prince Rupert, neither was an experienced naval commander. Albemarle had acquired his considerable reputation by a long period of infantry service that had culminated

---

* Pepys soon learned his trade; he estimated that his worth by the end of 1666 was 'above £6200', whereas it had been a mere £40 at the Restoration.

in his carefully brokering Charles's return to the throne in 1660. Although he had served in the First Anglo-Dutch War as general at sea in 1652, he was now fifty-eight years old, and exhausted from a lifetime of constant battling and intrigue. Prince Rupert, meanwhile, was something of a national hero in 1666, having served with bravery on the Royalist side in the civil war and thereafter as a Royalist privateer.

Placing these two men in joint command of the navy seemed to be a wise move on Charles's part, with the old greybeard Albemarle able to balance Rupert's more impetuous tendencies, and the younger man instilling a sense of vigour and energy in the elder. However, it soon proved that Charles would have been far better off installing a more experienced naval commander in their stead, such as Sandwich, who was then Vice Admiral of England. He had been responsible for the transfer of the fleet from Protectorate to royal control in 1660, and was highly able.*

Some had questioned whether the two commanders – proud and opinioned men both – would get along; in fact, their working relationship proved to be one of the few successful aspects of the 1666 campaign. Clarendon, who acknowledged Rupert's desire to command on his own, also described their relationship as one of 'great unanimity and consent'. Such disagreements as there were between the two men must have taken place in private. This was not always the case with their supporters; a row developed in July between their protégés Sir Robert Holmes and Sir Jeremy Smith, who loathed each other

---

* He was also Pepys's patron, which accounts for the glowing references to him throughout his protégé's diaries.

so much that they were unable to exchange even basic courtesies, and had to be persuaded not to engage in a duel. By the early summer of 1666, however, the animosity between the two men was the least of England's worries.

Disaster did not visit the English fleet until the end of May, when Albemarle and Rupert, who had been formally placed in charge of the fleet by the Navy's de facto commander James, duke of York, on 22 February, decided to take a more aggressive stance and attack the Dutch. Albemarle's fifty-six ships were outnumbered by the enemy's superior force, who boasted a total of ninety-three vessels. However, he believed that the favourable wind would aid his victory, even though Rupert was not immediately available to lend him much-needed support, having been sent on a fruitless mission towards the English Channel to see if there were any French belligerents planning an attack. Albemarle wrote to Lord Arlington, the secretary of state, on 28 May to say:

> I could heartily wish his majesty would hasten away those ships that are to come out to us for at present we shall not be here above 56 ships. If we could make up 70 sail, I should be very confident to meet the Dutch anywhere; and on the other side, I should be loath to retreat from them, being as it goes against my stomach to do it.

Albemarle would have been better off exercising a measure of caution, given that he was a dozen vessels short of his desired number; perhaps he had been buoyed by Arlington's letter of 24 May, which claimed that the Dutch were 'very poorly manned and poorly spirited'. Much the same could be said of the English.

The root of what would become an English naval catastrophe lay in a simple misunderstanding of Albemarle's earlier letter to Arlington. The Duke of York's interpretation was that Albemarle was asking whether he was permitted to engage in battle with fewer than the seventy ships that he deemed the ideal number with which to take on the Dutch. The duke replied, 'I spoke also with His Majesty about it, who conceived it best to leave it to your prudence, to do what you shall think best for His Majesty's Service.' Albemarle read this as a royal indication that he was trusted to make up his own mind. He proceeded therefore to do just that – and made up his mind to engage in battle. English intelligence suggested that Admiral de Ruyter planned to engage with the English fleet within the next couple of weeks. On 30 May Rupert's detachment of ships was summoned in the expectation that battle would not commence before the second week of June. This would prove incorrect.

Instead, action was imminent. On 31 May the Dutch were seen at anchor off the Flanders coast and were believed to be heading towards the mouth of the Thames. In the early morning of 1 June, they stationed themselves around thirty-five miles from England, and twenty-five miles from Dunkirk, planning an advance towards the Strait of Dover. Albemarle and his ships, lying fifteen miles to the northeast, off the Kentish coast, sighted the enemy, who were around seventeen miles southwest of their position. After a hasty council of war, they decided to attack.

This decision was much criticized at the time, and has remained controversial subsequently. Although Albemarle claimed that his aim was to attack the Dutch fleet before they could be reinforced by the French, no obvious sign of a French attack presented itself, and his actions seemed dictated more by panic than good judgement. A later account presented by Albemarle in 1667 described how 'I thought fit to advise, if we might not get into the river without fighting, and in order thereunto I called together all the flag officers and captains on board, who after some consideration unanimously agreed, that in regard most of our fleet were heavy ships, we could not avoid fighting, and thereupon the resolution was to fall upon them as they lay at anchor.'

This used the benefit of hindsight to omit two obvious factors, firstly that battle was far from inevitable, and secondly that there was no consideration unanimously agreed; instead, a contemporary account of Albemarle's describes how 'about 7 of the clock, our scout gave the signal... after two hours chase we descried [the enemy] to be the Dutch. The Duke immediately called a council of war of his flag officers, which being done the signal was given to fall into a line of battle and so bore away to the enemy'. The decision lay with Albemarle alone, who contrived to ask his officers for their consent when they were faced with a fait accompli. The signal was given at half past twelve that day for the red flag of battle to be hoisted, and, in that immortal phrase beloved and feared by every seaman, 'the fleets met'.

In fact, the Dutch were taken entirely by surprise, as de Ruyter had formed the opinion that the English would not attack that day owing to the poor weather conditions and resulting inability to fire their lower-deck guns. Initially, this jolt favoured the English, who pressed home their advantage against Lieutenant Admiral Cornelis Tromp's ships, causing him to flee, before turning their attention to the centre of the Dutch fleet. De Ruyter had by then recovered his composure and engaged Albemarle's ships in battle; there was a substantial quantity of ammunition wasted, but very little achieved in strategic or military terms.

The fighting grew heavier throughout the afternoon of 1 June, with further Dutch reinforcements coming to de Ruyter's aid, and there were significant losses on both sides. The Dutch lost one of their key vessels, the *Hof van Zeeland*, and the English ship the *Swiftsure* was captured, with 80 men killed and its remaining 300 crew taken prisoner. Its captain, Vice Admiral William Berkeley, had fought valiantly, taunting the Dutch aggressors by shouting, 'You dogs, you rogues, have ye the heart, so press on board!' but to little avail; he was fatally wounded with a musket ball through the throat, after which the morale of his men plummeted. When Albemarle discovered what had happened, he was furious, writing in his eventual report that 'the *Swiftsure* by not keeping his station fell into their fleet'. Two other ships, the *Seven Oaks* (a Dutch ship captured the previous year and renamed) and the *Loyal George*, were also captured; such was the hubbub of the time that Albemarle was unaware of their loss until the end of the battle four days later. Jeremy Roch, a naval captain fighting on the warship *Antelope*, kept a journal in which he described the chaos of that day; he characterized the fighting as 'the most terrible, obstinate and bloodiest battle that ever was fought on the seas' and described the sudden death of a comrade who had offered him a better sword, and who was killed at the very moment that Roch shook his hand in thanks.

The fighting continued for several hours on 1 June, with neither side able to claim victory. Disasters abounded: Albemarle was slightly wounded by flying debris, which had the embarrassing effect of tearing off part of his breeches. (He was later mocked for this in a satirical poem by Andrew Marvell, which claimed 'But most with story of his hand or thumb/Conceal, as honour would, his Grace's bum.') When an English ship, the *Henry*, was attacked by the Dutch flagship the *Walcheren*, the boatswain sardonically replied to the chaplain's panicked inquiry 'What should we do?' that he jump overboard. The chaplain and dozens of other seamen promptly threw themselves into the water. The ship's captain, Rear Admiral John Harman, restored order by threatening to execute on the spot anyone who headed towards the rail, and went on to oversee his ship's successful escape. It was in keeping with the strange, topsy-turvy fortunes of the day that, as the *Henry* fled, its parting shot killed Lieutenant Admiral Cornelis Evertsen, who earlier in the fighting had asked Harman whether he wanted to surrender, only to be told, 'It is not come to that yet!' Harman was later praised for his bravery under fire, and was rewarded with a knighthood; Pepys wrote that the event was 'the greatest hazard that ever any ship escaped, and as bravely managed by him'. Such instances of success in the face of adversity proved to be rare.

Battle resumed on 2 June, with Albemarle in command of a

total of fifty ships and the Dutch facing them with seventy-seven vessels. The weather, as Roch noted in his journal, was now 'fair for the sport', and indeed the day was hot and sunny. These conditions, however, made the fighting – which began at first light – all the harder. From six o'clock in the morning the English sought to recover their advantage of the previous day by, as de Ruyter later put it, coming 'powering upon us'. The day's battle was bloody, confused and protracted, with little gained on either side in the morning, but with horrendous losses on both sides; by lunchtime, the Dutch were reduced to fifty-seven vessels, and the English to forty-three, the other ships either being lost or so badly damaged that they had to flee. The 'terrible and bloody' fighting, as a later report described it, nonetheless began to favour the Dutch, especially when a reinforcement squadron of twelve ships appeared in the evening – a crushing blow to English morale, and, as the official papers of the day later reported, 'some discouragement to our men, being also so overpowered with numbers'. Albemarle now gave the order to begin a withdrawal, knowing that victory with his damaged and diminished fleet was impossible. By the end of the day, he only had twenty-eight ships still in reasonable fighting condition; his impetuosity of a couple of days before had cost him and his men dearly. The English fleet thus began its westward retreat. Prince Rupert – still pursuing a non-existent French fleet – remained absent.

Edward Barlow, who was serving under Albemarle, was injured in the leg, 'striking me lame for the present', although it was little more than a flesh wound. However, when he headed down to the ship's sickbay where the wounded men were lying in often agonizing pain, it caused him to question his patriotic duty:

> I was forced to go down amongst the wounded men, where one lay without a leg and another without an arm, one wounded to death and another groaning with pain and dying, and one wounded in one manner and another in another, which was a sad sight to see – poor men thus slaughtered by the treachery of our nation and them who lived at home at ease and wanted nothing, but grudged to see their own nation flourish, striving what they could to bring in a papist power and sending the true-hearted subjects to fight against a trouble for to be devoured, we spending our dearest blood for our King and country's honour, not thinking it too much to spend our lives for the advance and liberty of our native country, whilst our traitorous countrymen lay at home eating and drinking the fat of the land, and rejoicing at our overthrow.

The bloodshed and horror of the past forty-eight hours weighed heavily on the combatants, but there was no prospect for them of a quick escape and return home.

The third day of the battle was to bring humiliation for the English Vice Admiral Sir George Ayscue. He had fought with conspicuous gallantry in the civil war, albeit on the side of the Parliamentarians rather than the Royalists. He was responsible for the capture of the Scilly Isles and Barbados from the Royalists in 1651, and he weathered a defeat in the First Anglo-Dutch War to come back after the Restoration as a commander of the fleet and a vice admiral, this time avowedly loyal to Charles. On 3 June 1666, Ayscue's flagship, the *Prince Royal*, presented a conspicuous target for the Dutch as it attempted to flee. Unfortunately for Ayscue and his men, the ship ran aground in the nearby Galloper Sand, and no other English vessels were in a position to assist them. Within a matter of hours, Lieutenant Admiral Tromp was able to board the ship and take the entire crew, including Ayscue, as prisoners, with barely any resistance at all. De Ruyter ordered the ship to be burnt, rather than taken as a prize, as the *Prince Royal* was badly damaged. Ayscue therefore suffered the ignominious disgrace of being the last admiral of the English fleet to be captured by the enemy. Barlow commented in his journal that 'we lost the second best ship in England, having ninety brass pieces of ordnance and eight hundred men, which was a great grief to all the rest of the fleet, for she did more good in a fight than five or six of some others'.

Ayscue was taken to the Dutch prison of Loevestein – a medieval castle that at least had a half-decent reputation for comfort – where he was allowed to retain his servants. However, Ayscue's status as a high-profile prisoner led him to a humiliating fate. His strong Lincolnshire accent made him incomprehensible to the Dutch, and before he was incarcerated he was paraded through The Hague as an object of mirth. Stories circulated that he had been painted and had a tail pinned on him. Once he arrived at Loevestein, he was imprisoned there until September 1667, and Pepys's eventual judgement that he did not have 'much of a seaman in him' seems all too apt, although it was generally considered that he had behaved with as much propriety and courage as could be expected, under the circumstances.

Conditions in Dutch jails at the time were dismal, as the naval surgeon James Yonge had discovered earlier that year when his ship, the *Bonaventure*, was taken in January and he was imprisoned in Amsterdam. While Ayscue was unlikely to have been shackled on to a long iron bar, as Yonge was, and might have been fed slightly better than the 'water, gruel, rusty pork and sad beef, filthy peas' that the prisoners (and Dutch seamen) had as their rations, he suffered the same 'damnably insulting' treatment at Loevestein as Yonge. The enemy gloated over the English defeat, and Ayscue was afflicted by 'the intolerable stink of the house-of-office' (otherwise known as the toilet). Yonge was fortunate enough eventually to be released on bail in September, although his relief at this was short-lived, as the first news he had on his emergence was of the destruction of London by fire.

However, given what had occurred in the Four Days' Battle, perhaps a dull and embarrassing imprisonment was better than death or lasting disgrace. The rest of the fighting of 3 June consisted of the English attempting to escape back to England, and the Dutch pursuing them. The noise of the guns was audible in London, a hundred miles away; at first it was dismissed as thunder, but it soon became clear that the sound of cannon fire was distinct, and getting closer. Wild rumours flooded the city of both imminent victory and, increasingly, ghastly defeat, as the damaged ships began to limp home, with huge numbers of dead and wounded. Pepys wrote that he spent the evening walking in the park, 'discoursing of the unhappiness of our fleet' and criticizing Albemarle for his part in their losses. The only source of comfort was that it was now clear that Prince Rupert and his fleet were heading to rendezvous with Albemarle and his ships. When he did so, this gave the English a combined force of sixty-five vessels; although this was considerably weaker than the Dutch, who still had around seventy-six ships, it still encouraged the commanders to rally and fight a final battle, which took place on 4 June.

By then, the hot and sunny weather of the first day of the battle had been replaced by cloudier conditions. Mist hovered between the two fleets. As the English fleet prepared to attack the Dutch, their adversaries were ready for them, in superior numbers. De Ruyter's tactic was to weaken the English fleet by cutting off vessels from their formations. Rupert's flagship the *Royal James* was hit by cannon fire, and had its mainmast destroyed, necessitating a swift exit from the battle, along with the supporting ship, the *Breda*, which had to tow it. It was an inglorious end to Rupert's involvement in the battle, albeit preferable to being captured, as was the fate of four other English ships that day. Eventually, exhausted, low on ammunition and demoralized, the remaining ships headed for English ports. De Ruyter pursued them for a time, but a combination of thick fog, his own exhaustion after fighting an extended battle and the risk of pursuing the English ships into their own enclave led him to abandon the chase and return to his own port with his fleet. As Barlow put it, '[the] fleet made no great haste to follow us, being willing to leave off, having their bellies full as well as we'.

The Four Days' Battle was over. The fate of many of the

missing ships became all too clear. Ten ships had been lost, and nearly as many damaged; more than 1,000 were dead, including many captains and flag officers; around 1,500 were wounded and nearly 2,000 had been captured and now languished in Dutch jails.* One-fifth of the crews of the English ships that took part in the battle were therefore incapacitated. The English injured were dispatched to hospitals around the country; Barlow recorded that he was sent to Rochester with his injured leg, where he received seven shillings a week as payment for the three weeks that he spent recuperating there. Many were less fortunate, dying either on the voyage home or shortly after their arrival back in England.

The aftermath was grim and fractious, dominated by arguments as to who should be held responsible for the English defeat, although it was never openly acknowledged as such in Whitehall. Albemarle, who refused to accept any blame for the loss and persisted in claiming that only seven ships were destroyed, was an obvious target for scorn. Although an official report, disingenuously entitled the 'True Narrative' of the conflict, claimed that ten ships small and great were lost in total, and that the Dutch had 'concluded themselves beaten', few were fooled. The only comfort was that the French had not honoured their agreement to support the Dutch, either during the battle or subsequently; an exhausted, ill-equipped and damaged English navy could hardly have withstood a French attack.

England's display of incompetence in an area where they

---

* The Dutch, by contrast, lost 1,550 men, as a result of four of their ships being burnt, with around 1,300 wounded. However, no other ships of theirs were destroyed.

had traditionally excelled was a target for mockery. Andrew Marvell produced a satirical poem, 'Last Instructions to a Painter', that parodied Edmund Waller's 1666 patriotic poem 'Instructions to a Painter', in which Waller (somewhat pompously) wrote of how he hoped a painter would commemorate England's 1665 victory against the Dutch at the Battle of Lowestoft. Waller was unfortunate in that the rapid change in military fortunes made his poem seem absurd, but nonetheless the sycophantic manner in which he praised the court of the day seemed ripe for mockery, which Marvell duly supplied, as he ridiculed the perceived venality that had seen a 'race of Drunkards, Pimps, and Fools' prosper, and the righteous suffer in consequence. Marvell had been an arch-Parliamentarian and supporter of Cromwell, and so some of his vitriol was deeply partisan. Tellingly, Albemarle escaped Marvell's general criticism of a regime in which the former Commonwealth general occupied so central a position, but the poet's depiction of 'Gross Bodies, grosser Minds, and grossest Cheats' feels uncomfortably accurate. It is little wonder that Marvell wrote these poems anonymously; the consequences for him had their authorship been discovered would have been unpleasant.

Despite England's humiliation of 4 June, the issue was not yet decided. The Four Days' Battle had ended not with a glorious and definitive Dutch victory that guaranteed their dominance at sea, but in a stalemate that left the two rival navies exhausted and depleted. Both sides knew that further fighting was inevitable. This duly came the following month, on 22 July, with the English forces, again led by Albemarle and Prince Rupert, seeking to re-establish themselves by heading off from the King's Channel in the northern part of the Thames Estuary to encounter the Dutch off Harwich. The two fleets prepared themselves to fight on 25 July – St James's Day.

The English ships were superior in size and firepower to the Dutch vessels, having 87 ships of the fourth rate or bigger* along with two fifth-rate ships, one sixth-rate and sixteen fire ships, armed with 5,100 guns and holding around 24,000 men, compared to their opponents' 72 ships, 17 frigates and yachts, which bore around 1,500 fewer men and 500 fewer guns. When the fighting began, their dominance led to a welcome English victory, which was eventually achieved after two full days' fighting. They were helped by a factor of which they were unaware, namely a dispute between de Ruyter and Tromp over the latter's perceived dereliction of duty, which led to Tromp's immediate dismissal. The eventual losses were between 1,000 and 1,200 English seamen and two ships, with the Dutch losing twice as many sailors, as well as a pair of vessels of their own. It is likely that greater damage would have been done had the wind favoured the English; as Barlow noted, 'it proved little wind, and afterward quite calm, or else we would have destroyed the most part of their fleet, but we burnt only two ships, the Vice-Admiral and another. And chasing them all night, but it being so little wind we could not come near to do them much harm.'

Hostilities continued throughout the remaining months of 1666 and well into the following year. In June 1667, in the 'raid on the Medway', de Ruyter attacked the laid-up English fleet,

---

* 'Rate' being a reference to the number of guns on board each ship; thus, a third-rate ship held around eighty, a fourth-rate between fifty and sixty, and so on.

burning a number of vessels and capturing the English flag-ship HMS *Royal Charles*. The shock of the raid, combined with the ruin of the Great Fire and the country's general poverty, led England to sue for peace on 31 July. The Dutch victory – and England's humiliation – was complete. Far from being a source of national pride and general exultation, the Second Anglo-Dutch War had proved a waste of lives and money, and a damaging distraction from the more pressing problems that dominated life in England. One anonymous and sedi-tious document claimed 'the people curse the King, wish for Cromwell, and say "come Dutch, come Devil, they cannot be worse"'. Charles's apparent lack of interest in the war, and greater interest in his sexual dalliances, was mocked in the same pamphlet, which stated, 'People say "Give the King the Countess of Castlemaine and he cares not what the nation suffers."' Whatever the justice of that claim, the conflict had been a disastrous one, leaving nobody in any doubt that English sea power was not the mighty force it had once been. And the morale of the exhausted, penurious and disgruntled seamen was at its lowest ebb. Barlow eloquently described the plight of England's seamen:

> There are no men under the sun that fare harder and get their living more hard and that are so abused on all sides as we poor seamen, without whom the land would soon be brought under subjection, for when once the naval forces are broken, England's best walls are down. And so I could wish no young [man] to betake himself to this calling unless he had good friends to put him in place or supply his wants,

for he shall find a great deal more to his sorrow than I have writ.

England's 'best walls' did not fall down in 1666 because of foreign invasion. An even greater disaster was about to be visited upon the country in an entirely different, and unexpected, fashion.

– 10 –

The Great Fire of London

'He wept the flames of what he loved so well'
– John Dryden, *Annus Mirabilis*

By midday on Sunday, 2 September 1666, Sir Thomas
Bloodworth, Lord Mayor of London, knew that he had
made the gravest of errors. As he watched the city that he
was supposedly responsible for burn around him, in the most
serious conflagration that England had ever known, he began
to regret his rash words of the previous day. Summoned to the
part of London where the fire had begun in the early hours
of the morning, still half asleep and vexed that he had been
roused from his bed, he had dismissed its seriousness. Pepys
reported his (possibly apocryphal) comment that, looking at
the smouldering conflagration, he sneered, 'A woman could
piss it out!' He then headed home, unaware that, in a few
hours, dozens of important buildings and hundreds of houses
would be destroyed, and, as the wind helped spread the fire,
the inferno would seem to be uncontrollable. London, it
appeared, was to be reduced to ashes.

The summer of 1666 had been unusually hot and dry.
Anthony à Wood wrote in his diary that it was typified by

'rivers almost dry, rivulets quite dry, notwithstanding divers violent flashes of rain and hail. The like hath not been known in the memory of man, or at least for 60 years. Plentiful year of corn. To the great impoverishment of the boatmen.' Apart from the unfortunates who made their living on the Thames, most had welcomed the long spell of good weather, but, by Saturday, 2 September, London was wilting under a heatwave that had reduced everyone, from aristocrats to apprentices, to a state of dizzy fatigue.

Conditions were not ameliorated by buildings that, in the City at least, were closely packed, badly maintained and filthy. They were covered in an omnipresent cloud of smoke, a by-product of the innumerable small fires that were lit by tradesmen, hawkers, brewers and builders in the course of their everyday work. John Evelyn reflected public opinion when he complained of 'this horrid smoke which obscures our churches and makes our palaces look old, which fouls our clothes and corrupts the waters'. The smoke was accused of rendering women infertile and killing off the fruit of orchards. Despite the deaths of so many during the plague, houses in the City remained overcrowded warrens, and an unparalleled source of human misery.

The outbreak of the fire was not entirely unexpected. Charles himself had written to the aldermen and Bloodworth in April 1665 to warn them of the likelihood of a disastrous occurrence if something was not done about the abundance of cheaply and poorly constructed buildings in the City. These were theoretically in breach of the Building Acts that had been put in place at the Restoration, and could be pulled down and their builders imprisoned. In practice, little was done about them; there were too many other concerns of greater importance.

There were other, more portentous, warnings as well. Ever since the Restoration, there had been murmurings that divine judgement was imminent. While some had relished the free-spirited permissiveness of the early 1660s, others were less enamoured of what they saw as a combination of the restrictive and the hypocritical. Rumours of unrestrained libidinousness at Whitehall sat uneasily with the news of military defeat in the Anglo-Dutch War, the forced implementation of the Book of Common Prayer and the continued persecution of Dissenters. Pamphleteers and booksellers made a good profit out of sensationalist works that prophesied fire and brimstone raining down on London in punishment for the city's sins. Almanacs talked of a year of fire and blood; one particularly mischievous poet and pamphleteer, George Wither, noted that the expression 'Lord Have Mercy Upon Us', as represented as 'LorD haVe MerCIe Vpon Vs', when rearranged came to MDCLXVI, or the year 1666 itself. The late Quaker seer Humphrey Smith had had a vision, warning that:

> in the foundation of all her buildings and there was none could quench it... The burning thereof was exceeding great... All the tall buildings fell and it consumed all the lofty things therein... And the fire continued, for though all the lofty part was brought down yet there was much old stuff and parts of broken down, desolate walls, which the fire continued burning against.

While few were foolish enough to state their convictions publicly, for fear of being accused of conspiracy against the king, there was a growing feeling in the sweltering heat that a reckoning was coming.

The appropriately named Pudding Lane was home to several bakeries and eating-houses, including one owned by Thomas Farriner. The street was a jam-packed row of uneven, tottering buildings, all of timber, with the wood covered in pitch in an attempt to render it waterproof; that this made it far more susceptible to fire seemed not to have occurred to anyone. It was said to be one of the narrowest roads in the City, and the contemporary writer Rege Sincera* described its current state as reflecting 'the covetousness of the citizens and connivancy of magistrates'. It was typical of the area: cramped, squalid and deeply dangerous.

Farriner, who was then in his early fifties, was a widower and a moderately prosperous baker, who lived above his shop with his three children, maid and serving man. On the night of Saturday, 1 September, he went to bed as usual just after midnight, his work done for the day. He had neglected to douse a pile of faggots that he had left smouldering by his oven. Perhaps he was drunk, or maybe he had simply forgotten. In either event, he was awoken by his servant about an hour later to find the house full of smoke and the oven on fire. He woke his family and they escaped to a nearby house, but their unfortunate maid was left behind and so perished, probably suffocated by the thick smoke.

* The name is presumably a pseudonym; the identity of the writer is unknown.

For the first hour or so after the fire had begun it was Farriner's tragedy, but there was no reason why it should have become anyone else's. The building burnt solidly, but his neighbours were able to leave their homes with their families and possessions intact before their own houses, bone-dry after the summer drought, were set alight by the scattered sparks that were billowing from the baker's. The conflagration soon gained in intensity, spreading as far as St Margaret's church, on New Fish Street. As it blazed from home to home, sleeping Londoners were roused from their beds by the smoke and fled their houses, gathering what few possessions they could lay their hands on.

Despite the shock and inconvenience, the blaze was not yet regarded as anything wildly unusual. There were frequently small fires caused by bakeries or street hawkers, and the majority burnt themselves out after an hour or two. The Lord Mayor's airy dismissal of what he saw before him was the moment that transformed a serious but containable local conflagration into a city-wide inferno that would transform London forever.

The reasons for the rapid spread of the fire were many, but one of the most critical was that Pudding Lane was very close to Thames Street, adjacent to London Bridge, where many of the City's most flammable materials were stored, ready to be placed on ships and transported abroad. Coal, barrels of oil, timber and tallow were piled high in warehouses and sheds, awaiting distribution. It was little surprise that, by eight in the morning, London Bridge itself was fully ablaze. Those watching closely might have seen the grisly spectacle of some of the severed heads of traitors illuminated by the flames, as if in ghastly approval of the horror unfolding below.

Shortly before nine that morning, waking Londoners began to recognize the potential danger at hand. Pepys, who lived in Seething Lane, in the heart of the City, wrote, 'I did see the houses at that end of the bridge all on fire, and an infinite great fire on this and the other side the end of the bridge', and said that the 'lamentable spectacle' made his 'heart full of trouble'. Swiftly, the fire had spread into the public buildings, which were destroyed like brittle pieces of firewood. The great Fishmongers Hall soon perished, as did the Thames water-house, which had been responsible for supplying piped water to the nearby houses. Churches such as St Botolph-without-Billingsgate and St Margaret's were ruined within a matter of hours. The contrast between the encroaching destruction and the clear, bright and cloudless day could not have been greater.

At this point, Bloodworth could still have prevented the fire from spreading. Many of the houses that had been destroyed were rotten, cheap and easily replaceable. Most of those that were yet to be destroyed by the fire were similar. If they had been pulled down at this point to create firebreaks, it would have stopped the blaze in its tracks, and the damage, while serious and costly to make good, would have been merely in the thousands of pounds. However, the panicking Bloodworth (described by Pepys as looking like 'a fainting woman') failed to take the necessary bold decision. When it was suggested to him that houses should be demolished to prevent the fire from spreading, his weak response was to ask: 'Who shall pay the cost of rebuilding the houses?' He refused to take such an action without the agreement of the owners, which was impossible to obtain in such frenetic and dangerous circumstances. When Bloodworth finally ordered the demolition of the houses, after hours of vacillation, it was nearly noon on Sunday, 2 September, and he had sealed London's fate.

Initially, those who were not immediately threatened by the fire regarded it with a relaxed curiosity. Blazes were not uncommon in the City, and it did not seem particularly impressive by daylight. However, as rumours spread that the French or the Dutch were attacking, or that a Catholic plot to unseat Charles was under way, insouciance gave way to fear as a strong wind helped speed the progress of the fire. One Westminster School pupil, William Taswell, who had sneaked away from a service in Westminster Abbey, recorded that 'the ignorant and deluded mob, who upon occasion were hurried [sic] away with a kind of frenzy, vented forth their rage against the Roman Catholics and Frenchmen'. As fists flew and shops were looted, the mob claimed that their acts of violence were motivated by patriotic fervour. Scapegoats were needed, and the French and Dutch found themselves accused of starting fires virtually at random and thrown into prison on the slightest pretext; unless, that is, they had already been beaten senseless by the frightened and enraged mob. One unfortunate man was torn to pieces in Moorfields because he was said to be carrying 'flaming spheres'; his great balls of fire were, in fact, nothing more than tennis balls.

The mob's energies would have been better channelled into fighting the fires, rather than visiting retribution on their perceived enemy. London was ill-equipped to deal with a blaze of this size: primitive fire-hooks were the principal means available for tearing down burning buildings; and the brass hand pumps or 'engines' that provided the jets of water needed to combat fires held rather less than a gallon each. A more productive fire engine had been invented in Nuremberg in 1651, but nothing like it was yet available in England.

By mid-afternoon on Sunday, the fire was gathering in strength. The power of the blaze created an unstoppable momentum, which in turn transformed a fire into a firestorm. Pepys was sufficiently frightened to flee his home west of the Tower, having first taken steps to secure his most treasured possessions – rather than his wife. These included his gold, money and his best wines, which he either hid in his cellar or had transported to a friend's house in Bethnal Green early the next morning, on a carriage that he drove himself, dressed in his nightgown. He wrote of how the 'most horrid malicious bloody flame' lit up the sky, and, as he saw the wreckage of the houses, and displaced and panicking people swarming the streets with what little they could salvage, noted 'it made me weep to see it'. Even the wings of the pigeons were singed, causing them to fall helplessly to the ground.

Until then, Charles, who was at Whitehall, had been unaware of the blaze taking place a few miles to the east. In 1666, Westminster and the City might as well have been in separate counties, so different were their worlds. However, when he was informed of the catastrophe engulfing his city, Charles was swift to act, unlike the hapless Bloodworth. His first response was to send in the few soldiers that he could spare, although the Duke of York's offer of the Royal Life

Guards as firefighters was initially refused, and to attempt to instil some sense of civic responsibility into the Lord Mayor, who, encountering Pepys after visiting Whitehall, cried 'Lord! What can I do? I am spent.' Charles and his brother James headed down the Thames on the royal barge to view the full extent of the damage. One Italian observer claimed that the king was so moved by the destruction of Watermen's Hall that he jumped out of the boat and attempted to assist in the pulling down of nearby buildings with such zeal that his attendants had to physically restrain him, for fear that he himself would be consumed by the flames. As Pepys wrote, 'Their order was only to pull down houses apace, and so below bridge the water-side; little was or could be done, the fire coming upon them so fast. Good hopes there was of stopping it at the Three Cranes above and at Botolph's Wharf below bridge, if care be used; but the wind carries it into the City, so as we know not by the waterside what it do there.'

As night fell, the fire seemed unquenchable. It exerted a hideous fascination on all who saw it, who seemed transfixed by what looked like a divine judgement on mankind. Those who had been made homeless by the blaze gathered what few possessions they had been able to salvage and headed for open ground, either to nearby Finsbury and Moorfields or to the hills of Highgate and Hampstead to the north. The houses of a fortunate few, such as Pepys, were unharmed by the fire because of the direction of the wind, and they took in refugees. Pepys headed home 'with a sad heart' when it became dark, and, shortly after his return, took in 'poor Tom Hater', the naval clerk Thomas Hayter, whose house in nearby Fishstreets

Hall had been burnt. Unfortunately for Hayter, Pepys wrote, 'he got very little rest, so much noise being in my house'. Fear and paranoia were exacerbated by the absence of any information as to the cause of the disaster, or any reassurance from anyone in authority.

The fire burnt through the night, destroying many of the landmarks of the old City, from the great Skinners' Hall, one of the original fifteenth-century City companies responsible for skin and fur, to the legendary Boar's Head tavern in Eastcheap, which had been immortalized in Shakespeare's *Henry IV Part II*, and had been a regular drinking haunt for the virtuous and wicked alike of London for hundreds of years. Now, it was no more. Even the Post Office of Cloak Lane, Dowgate, then the only one in London, was burnt to ashes, giving the intelligence services of the day a substantial headache; the building had been used as a centre for gathering information and forging letters. The postmaster James Hickes saved what little he could, but wrote a despairing letter to his superior Lord Arlington's secretary saying, 'how we shall dispose of our business only the wise God knows'.

As the fire raged out of control, wild rumours continued to flourish. A later letter by a Dutchman living in London at the time claimed that Charles was woken by the sounds of terrified people shouting, 'Fire! Fire! God and the King save us!' The latest issue of the city's newspaper, the *London Gazette*, did little to deny these stories when it was published on 3 September, merely saying that 'it continues still with great violence'. With residents unable to contact their families and friends, fear and paranoia took even greater hold. In a letter written on the morning of Monday, 3 September to her Buckinghamshire friend Sir Ralph Verney, the aristocrat Lady Anne Hobart, who lived on Chancery Lane, vividly described both the extent of the devastation and the predicament of her and her husband Sir Nathaniel: 'I am sorry to be the messenger of so dismal news, for poor London is almost burnt down.' By then, it was common knowledge that the fire had begun at a baker's in Pudding Lane, although she ascribed its cause to 'a Dutch rogue' who '[has] attempted to fire many places'. She was fully aware of the seriousness of the fire, writing ' 'tis thought Fleet Street will be burnt by tomorrow... there was never so sad a sight, nor so doleful a cry heard, my heart is not able to express the tenth, nay the thousandth part of it'. Profiteering was rife; Lady Hobart complained that the price of a cart that would take their property to safety was now £10, and expressed the fear that 'I shall lose all I have and must run away'.

In the end, the Hobarts were spared; a friend helped provide them with a cart, and their home escaped destruction. However, they were among the few fortunate ones. The fire had expanded north and west, briefly endangering Southwark on the south bank, but fortunately a firebreak on London Bridge ensured that the blaze did not cross the river. In the morning of Monday, 3 September, the fire headed north, destroying Gracechurch Street as it went, until it arrived at the heart of the mercantile district in Lombard Street and Cornhill. This was one of London's most commercially important and affluent areas, where wealthy bankers and merchants both lived and worked, and home to many of the City's most upmarket and fashionable shops. It was to be entirely destroyed by the Great Fire, ruining the livelihoods of many successful men. The businessman and philanthropist Thomas Firmin had to take lodgings in nearby Leadenhall Street when his house on Lombard Street burnt down; he was obliged to rebuild his business from scratch, which he eventually did with some success. The churches continued to burn, leading gloomy onlookers to conclude that the conflagration was a sure sign of divine disaffection; the Puritan minister Thomas Vincent took a perverse joy in watching the main shopping area, the Royal Exchange, fall,* writing, 'the glory of the merchants is now invaded with much violence... by-and-down [sic] fall all the Kings upon their faces... with such a noise as was dreadful and astonishing'.

Even by day, the remorseless progress of the inferno was a ghastly spectacle, thanks to what Vincent called 'the smoke of a great furnace' billowing out from it, which so obscured the sun that, if it could be seen, it was as red as blood. Contemporary estimates were that the smoke from the burning city could be seen as far as fifty miles away. The philosopher John Locke, then studying meteorology at Oxford, noted a 'dim reddish sunshine' and a 'strange dim red light' – perhaps a distant glimpse of the destruction of the capital.

The fire raged on, consuming such famous landmarks as St Mary Abchurch and the Painter-Stainers' Hall with it. Famous thoroughfares such as Threadneedle Street and Thames Street

---

* The Royal Exchange was rebuilt after the fire in 1667, only to be destroyed again in 1838. On both occasions the statue of its founder, Sir Thomas Gresham, was undamaged.

were reduced to ash and rubble within the space of a few hours. No respecter of class, background or wealth, fire reduced many of the City's leading citizens to pauperdom within a matter of moments. Those who had not fled to other parts of London remained and helped as best they could with the efforts to combat the blaze, either by pulling down burning buildings, throwing water on the flames or simply by transferring possessions to the crypts of churches or cellars.

As they struggled, a growing sense of panic was instilled in the hearts of those who saw their livelihoods being taken away from them and their homes destroyed. The authorities were virtually powerless in the face of the onslaught. Bloodworth had disappeared when he saw that the fire had become uncontrollable; this led to Charles, still uncertain as to the cause of the fire, appointing a Privy Council to attempt to keep some sort of order, which mainly consisted of placing what troops they could on the streets in an attempt to calm a difficult situation. This was a matter of some controversy, with the city magistrates maintaining an antipathy to soldiers being deployed on the streets of London, but it was a necessary matter of last resort in the absence of the hopeless Lord Mayor.

One of the few useful edicts issued on Monday afternoon was a ban on carts in the vicinity of the fire, which simultaneously ended the profiteering and halted the build-up of heaped wooden carts cluttering the streets, which, far from saving people's possessions, only added ballast to the all-consuming flames. Nonetheless, the brave or foolhardy continued to carry off as much as they could bear, with the wealthy desperately paying anyone strong enough to transport what remained of their gold and coins.

By the time Billingsgate was burning down on Monday evening, it was clear that the fire could not be checked by human effort. A combination of luck and brute strength saved Leadenhall, one of the City's greatest markets, from destruction, the buildings around it being torn down briskly and efficiently before the fire could spread beyond its western side. The prestigious East India House, which housed one of London's major trade companies, was spared in similar fashion. But such examples of buildings escaping the fire's progress were rare. The fifteenth-century Baynard's Castle, situated close to Blackfriars, took all night to burn, and was still blazing on Tuesday morning. Thomas Vincent claimed that the spread of the fire resembled 'a dreadful bow... it was a bow which had fire in it, which signified God's anger, and his intention to destroy London with fire'. The noise was indescribable; Vincent compared it to the sound of a thousand iron chariots beating against the cobbled stones. Evelyn took the more compassionate view that it was a 'miserable and calamitous spectacle', and wished 'God grant mine eyes may never behold the like, who now saw about 10,000 houses in one flame.' Evelyn estimated that the area of the City that was ablaze was two miles in length and one mile in breadth. If anything this seems a conservative estimate, given the extent of the damage that had been caused. By now, half the City had been consumed completely, destroying streets and roads and churches that had existed for hundreds of years. It seemed impossible that things could get worse. Yet, on 4 September, they did.

As the sun rose on Tuesday, the jewellery quarter of Cheapside was consumed by the blaze; the famous church of St Mary-le-Bow was burnt to the ground, leaving only its crypt intact. The loss of Cheapside was as much symbolic as it was practical, this being the part of the City through which kings and queens had passed on their way to Westminster; only six years before, Charles himself had travelled through it to Whitehall, greeted by cheering crowds and hosannas. Now, the only sound to be heard was the ghastly crash of timber and stone, interspersed with weeping and shouting from the unfortunates trapped by the fire. The goldsmiths and silversmiths had managed to save what they could of their possessions in the night and moved them to the Tower, but the damage was incalculable. Famous inns such as the Mermaid and the Mitre were gutted. The fire was now at its height, and even the Fleet river failed to provide the expected check to its progress; the strong wind instead blew it inexorably forward. People stood around as if paralysed by horror; the lawyer and politician John Rushworth wrote: 'When Cheapside was on fire, not ten men stood by helping or calling for help, I have been an eyewitness and can verify this and 100 times more.'

Over at Whitehall, Charles was beginning to realize that the blaze could eventually engulf the palace itself. Calm in the face of enormous adversity, he arranged for the Exchequer to be removed to Henry VIII's great construction, Nonsuch Palace in Surrey, and then he and his brother James rode into the City to begin the hard and difficult task of fighting the conflagration themselves. The Duke of York had been placed in charge of firefighting operations on Monday evening in the absence of anyone responsible in charge of the City; what might have been greeted with controversy in other circumstances now seemed like the only sensible course of action.

Ignoring the ever-present danger that he faced, both from the fire and from his frightened and angry people, Charles rode around with a small retinue, alternately encouraging those who were engaged in firefighting or getting involved himself, whether manning the water buckets or helping make falling buildings safe. One observer wrote to the aristocrat Edward Conway to credit the 'incredible magnanimity' with which both Charles and James had acted in London's bleakest hour, and the 'reverence and admiration' with which their work was regarded by their subjects.

The heroic efforts of the two royal brothers were largely unavailing as the fire continued its greedy assault on the City's historic buildings and institutions; the Merchant Taylors' Hall, St Anthony's Hospital and Founders' Hall all fell to the blaze, with those attempting to fight the conflagration driven back in terror by the merciless encroachment of the inferno. The Drapers' Hall, built by Thomas Cromwell in the last century and widely believed to be the high point of Tudor architecture in London, was also destroyed. Only its gardens survived largely intact.

At last, inevitably, the fire arrived at Guildhall, the centre of administration and pageantry in London. Its sturdy walls had been constructed in the early fifteenth century, and they lasted even the fire's most frenzied destruction, which laid waste to the gallery, windows and the oak roof. Thankfully, the records and documents were preserved in the vaults, otherwise they would have been destroyed irreparably, and our knowledge of London before 1666 would have been the poorer as a consequence.

As the afternoon continued, the fire spread out to its furthest extent, burning the entire City between the Tower of London in the east and Newgate in the west, and pressing up to Fleet Street and Temple. The frantic efforts to tear down buildings, spearheaded by the royal pair, were beginning to bear fruit, preventing the blaze from advancing beyond Aldgate. Gunpowder was used to destroy burning houses, which Pepys reported 'did frighten the people more than anything else'. The air, thick with smoke and heat, was hard to breathe, and even the offer of significant financial reward for helping clear the debris and wreckage was not enough for many, who fled as far as they could from the horrific scene before them. By this point, nearly 15,000 houses had been destroyed, and as many as 100,000 citizens (or a quarter of the population of London) had been rendered homeless. Disaster made everyone equal; as Evelyn noted, those who had lived in 'delicateness, riches and easy accommodation in stately and well-furnished houses were now reduced to the extremest misery and poverty'.

By about five o'clock, the inferno sailed down Fleet Street, and prepared to claim its most ostentatious prize. St Paul's Cathedral was, then as now, one of London's most iconic landmarks, but it had evaded destruction over the previous days, despite the razing of the nearby Stationers' Hall. It was believed that the cathedral would provide safe refuge; many of the stationers who conducted their business in the shadow of St Paul's fled into the eastern part of the crypt, praying that the thick walls would withstand the full force of the conflagration outside. They were joined by scores of other tradesmen, including mercers and booksellers, all of whom hoped that divine providence would protect them and that their sanctuary would go undamaged.

The cathedral might even have survived the fire had it not been for a stroke of ill fortune. Shortly before the fire began, the Deputy Surveyor of the King's Works, the thirty-three-year-old architect Christopher Wren, had drawn up preliminary plans for its renovation, and highly flammable pieces of wood had been placed against the walls in preparation for the building work. The scaffolding predictably caught fire, and by nine o'clock the flames had surrounded the building. After a couple of hours, the timbered roof beams also went up and melted the lead roof; the enormous heat caused the walls and ceiling to explode. Evelyn described the stones flying like 'grenadoes'. The spectacle of vast chunks of masonry and scaffolding crashing to earth, destroying tombs and statues and shattering the cathedral's stained glass, must have been a terrifying one. The horrified booksellers and stationers watched as the floor of the crypt was destroyed by the intense heat above and the burning timbers, and their prized stock was set alight, causing an estimated £150,000 worth of damage. The stock was still burning a week later. The blaze was so vivid that the scholarly William Taswell, passing by, was able to read an edition of the Roman playwright Terence that he was carrying in his pocket by the light of the flames.

Charles and James, still firefighting, watched the great building burn. What went through the king's mind can only be imagined. On a practical level, the cathedral's destruction was a ruinously expensive disaster, which would take a huge amount of money to repair; the proposed renovation, itself a huge commitment for a depleted Exchequer, would have been trifling in comparison. Yet more importantly, on a symbolic level, the burning of St Paul's could hardly have been a more devastating blow for the city and country. It seemed entirely possible that the inferno would remain unchecked, and could eventually spread to devour Whitehall itself, leaving London reduced to little more than a few disconnected streets and countless piles of rubble. Were that to happen, Charles's — and England's — future would be bleak indeed. In the interests of self-preservation, therefore, he returned to Whitehall, and gave instructions that he would head to Hampton Court early the next day.

At around midnight on Tuesday, relief finally came. The strong wind, which had speeded up the progress of the fire, finally dropped in its intensity, thereby preventing the much-feared scenario of the blaze reaching Charing Cross and Somerset House. The progress of the fire was arrested by blowing up buildings on the Strand with gunpowder, in order to isolate the most important structures and prevent their destruction. It was too late for most of the significant buildings on the edge of the City — the Custom House was razed to the ground and the Temple was badly damaged — but fortune, which had been so absent in the burning of St Paul's, seemed at last to be on the side of the firefighters. In the east, the blaze had spread almost to the Tower of London, but was stopped by the demolition of nearby houses and businesses. Had it reached the Tower, and detonated the gunpowder stored in the White Tower, it would, in the words of John Evelyn: 'not only have beaten down and destroyed all the bridge, but sunk and torn all the vessels in the river, and rendered the demolition beyond all expression for several miles about the country.'

The fires continued to burn through the night, but daybreak on Wednesday the 5th revealed the first signs that the blaze was beginning to extinguish itself. Somewhere around Pye Corner, by Cock Lane in Smithfield, the westward advance of the fire was halted. Pepys, looking out at the ruined city, described it as 'the saddest sight of desolation that I ever saw; everywhere great fires, oil cellars and brimstone and other things burning'. Like many others, he had not eaten for days, hunger being outweighed by anxiety about the potential loss of property and life; the previous day he wrote that he and a friend 'did dig another [pit] and put our wine in it, and I my Parmesan cheese'.* He had to forego his usual lavish meals, not least because many of his local haunts had been destroyed.

As the immediate threat to life appeared to have passed, Londoners started to ponder the enormous loss that they, and their fellow citizens, had suffered. Sir William Denton, the court physician, wrote to Sir Ralph Verney† to tell him that 'the short account of the fire is that more than the whole city is in ashes', and that 'we had sent away all but my books so

---

* Pepys was acting not from indulgence but out of pragmatic good sense; imported Parmesan cheese was hugely expensive and regarded as an investment, so was well worth attempting to save.

† Although Verney lived in Buckinghamshire, he, like many others, was tangentially affected by the fire; he wrote in his diary that he was having difficulty buying a cradle for a newborn baby, 'such things being very dear now, as all their stores are burnt'.

that we were fain to lie only on blankets'. Denton's account also hinted at a growing sense that the fire was the result of a Catholic conspiracy ('it is generally believed, but not at court, that the Papists have designed this, and more, many and strong presumptions there are for it'). He also briefly described the crippling social effect of the devastation ('here nothing almost is to be got that we have not in possession, bread, beer, meat, all in scarcity & many want it'). Finally, he bemoaned the fact that most able-bodied men were being forcibly recruited in the dangerous act of firefighting, saying, 'I dare not send a man out of doors for fear of being pressed to work at the fire, James & Jack were both pressed this morning.'

The fires in the City were still burning in many buildings, which gave onlookers the impression that the wider conflagration was continuing to expand, but the apparently unstoppable momentum that had claimed so many houses and churches had been checked. Pepys was able to walk into the centre of town, finding 'Fenchurch Street, Gracious Street and Lombard Street all in dust [and] the Exchange a sad sight, nothing standing there of all the statues and pillars but Sir Thomas Gresham's picture in the corner'. The streets that he was walking through were unpleasantly hot, and full of chaos, due to the mixture of impromptu firefighters, citizens attempting alternately to bury or retrieve their possessions and occasional (and false) rumours of new fires starting in other parts of London. William Taswell echoed this when he wrote, 'the ground [being] so hot as almost to scorch my shoes; and the air so intensely warm that unless I had stopped some time upon Fleet Bridge to rest myself, I must have fainted under the extreme languor of my spirits'. Over the course of the day, those fires that were still burning began to die down. By the time the sun rose on Thursday, the Great Fire of London had extinguished itself, leaving chaos and exhaustion in its wake.

—— ⚬⚬⚬ ——

Even after the flames had finally abated, the city remained in turmoil. William Denton wrote that 'we are in such a confused condition that we know not what favour of friends to make use of, though we have need of them all'. Charles and his councillors were faced with the necessity of both restoring a semblance of order and of helping the vast numbers of destitute and homeless citizens, many of whom had barely eaten since Sunday morning. The king issued two Royal Proclamations on Thursday, setting up temporary food markets at a variety of locations in Bishopsgate, Tower Hill, Islington and other sites, and decreeing that all surviving churches, chapels and schools should be open to receive people's property.

The damage caused by the fire was hard to assess at first. The City surveyors Jonas Moore and Ralph Gatrix described it as having claimed 13,200 houses, 87 parish churches, 400 streets and courts and over 400 acres within and without the city walls. Its after-effects lingered for many weeks; Pepys reported in his diary of 16 March 1667 seeing 'smoke remaining, coming out of some cellars, from the late great fire, now above six months since'. Whether or not its appearance was coincidental, it remained prominent in folk memory.

As for the death toll, a fiction has subsequently grown up

that no more than seven or eight people died in the blaze, which can be credited to the propaganda of the time deliberately playing down the seriousness of the destruction; the *London Gazette* claimed that nobody died at all, and the eventual Bills of Mortality put the number of deceased at six. Both of these estimates seem ludicrously low, and due at least in part to a lack of records of the deaths of 'ordinary people', the poor and less affluent. The extreme heat of the fire was such that many bodies would have been incinerated entirely, and the associated deaths from exposure, starvation and, in one case, 'being frighted' seem likely to have been in the hundreds, if not the thousands. A couple of deaths were directly reported, beginning with Farriner's maid; Taswell, for instance, recorded seeing:

> A human body presented itself to me, parched up as it were with the flames; whole as to skin, meagre as to flesh, yellow as to colour. This was an old decrepit woman who fled here for safety, imagining the flames would not have reached her there. Her clothes were burnt and every limb reduced to a coal.

Once people realized that their lives were no longer in immediate danger, and that the worst of the destruction had passed, then thoughts turned to blame and retribution. Despite Charles addressing the largest of the refugee camps at Moorfields on Thursday and explicitly telling them that the destruction had not been caused by any papist, French or Dutch plot, suspicion lingered amid the panic. This was then affirmed judicially with the spurious arrest of a French watchmaker, Robert Hubert, who was said to have confessed to beginning the fire deliberately as an agent of the pope, and a trial that found him guilty despite clear inconsistencies in the evidence against him. Hubert was swiftly executed at Tyburn, but it soon became embarrassingly clear that he had not even been in London at the time of the outbreak. However, anti-Roman feeling was running rife, and it was widely believed that Catholics were responsible for the fire. The irony in the case of Hubert is that he was most likely to have been a Huguenot (French Protestant), and that his so-called 'confession' was extracted under duress. Clarendon wrote of him that he was 'a poor distracted wretch, weary of his life, and chose to part with it in this way'.

The case of Anthony d'Elora was also typical. D'Elora was a man of St Andrew's in Holborn who was tried at the Middlesex Sessions on 8 September as being suspected 'to be in the plot of the late great fire'. While d'Elora was innocent of the accusation, he was believed to have papist sympathies, and was summarily executed. Suspicion spread as far as Whitehall, thereby making it even more difficult for Charles's broadly Catholic sympathies to be openly expressed; despite his gallant behaviour in helping quench the fire, rumours spread that his brother James was in fact a papist stooge, and his 'gay countenance' during the blaze was held up as evidence that he was fanning the flames, rather than fighting them.

As often with false rumours, there was a nugget of truth at the heart of them: the Duke of York was indeed a Catholic sympathizer, and would convert to the faith in 1668. Meanwhile, gossip continued to spread until there was a widely believed consensus that the fire had been caused by a conspiracy, rather than by an accident. When Parliament resumed on 28 September, a motion was carried for the immediate deportation of Catholic priests and Jesuits, and all members of the Commons were forced to take Anglican communion and restate their belief in the English church on pain of immediate arrest.

The other, less publicly expressed, belief that many held was that the fire was a divine judgement on England and the decadence of Charles's court.* Sir Nathaniel Hobart, writing to Sir Ralph Verney shortly after the blaze, talked of how 'the image of this terrible judgment has made such an impression in the souls of every one of us, that it will not be effaced while we live' and that 'God was not pleased, & we must submit to his will'. The Quakers, who had been persecuted since the Restoration, were especially sure in their belief that the blaze was a sign from God. Their founder, George Fox, was released from prison on 1 September, and described the fire in his journal, claiming, 'I saw the Lord God was true and just in his word that he had showed me before in Lancaster jail, when I saw the angel of the Lord with a glittering drawn sword southward, as before expressed. The people of London were forewarned of this fire: yet few laid it to heart, or believed it; but rather grew more wicked, and higher in pride.' Satisfied that the destruction was a punishment for this wickedness, he

---

* Although there was an alternative, somewhat perverse, view that it was divine retribution for the execution of Charles I; Thomas Oxinden, a trooper in the Lifeguards and the son of the Kent vicar Henry, wrote to his father on 14 September, saying, 'I suppose have you already too often heard of the destruction of the wicked City of London which all but the ignorant conclude to be just for the murder of our late King.'

wrote that 'the Lord has exercised his prophets and servants by his power, and showed them signs of his judgments. And some they beat and evilly entreated and imprisoned, both in the other power's days and since. But the Lord is just, and happy are they that obey his word.'

Fox was brave to have written down such sentiments; had they been made public, he would certainly have been arrested and probably executed for treason. Others rejoiced in the destruction; an anonymous Spanish writer, probably an ambassador, wrote a pro-Catholic account of the fire, *Relacion Nueva y Verdadera del formidable incendio que ha sucedido en la grande ciudad de Londres,** in which he stated 'at the sight of a Catholic temple the fire acknowledged itself to be conquered' and wished 'may God open their eyes to the truth, and enable them to take a lesson from the destruction of their own hundred and forty churches and the safety of the one Roman Catholic temple'.

In the aftermath of the fire, Clarendon continued to behave as if he was the most powerful man in the kingdom. He was soon to be disabused of this belief. Earlier in the year, he had commissioned the architect Roger Pratt to build Clarendon House on Piccadilly; it was completed in 1667. Described by Evelyn as 'the most magnificent house in England', and set within eight acres of prime land, its grandiosity and expense – an estimated £40,000, a staggering sum of money that equates to roughly £3.2 million in today's terms – soon led to Clarendon's downfall. It was an act of thoughtlessness or hubris on his part to have continued to build a home of this

---

* Roughly translated as 'The new and true account of the great fire that has engulfed the great city of London'.

nature when thousands of his countrymen were homeless after the Great Fire, and his many enemies accused him of having used the stones of the destroyed St Paul's to construct his palatial new home, as well as being a papist, polygamist and sodomite. Despite the accusations lacking veracity, Clarendon lacked friends and supporters, and he was dismissed from office shortly after the house was completed. His fate was soon sealed once he had irreparably lost royal support and he fled to France, fearing the worst. When Parliament convened on 10 October 1667, Clarendon was sentenced to exile and stripped of his office *in absentia*. Eventually, he was informed that if he returned to England again he would be impeached for high treason and executed. It was an ignoble end to one of the great political careers of the time, with Clarendon as the exemplum of how anyone could be brought down by innuendo and a wave of public hostility.

As blame and accusation flew around, it was clear that London could not continue to lie in ruins, but had to rise, phoenix-like, from the ashes. Charles issued a Royal Proclamation on 13 September 1666, referring to 'this our native city', and talked of how the 'lamentable' events would instead give way 'to a wonderful beauty and comeliness'. He went on to state that 'if any considerable number of men... shall address themselves to the Court of Aldermen, and manifest to them in what places their ground lies upon which they design to build, they shall in a short time receive such order and direction for their proceeding therein, that they shall have no cause to complain'. Fine words, but, as so often, they dodged practical realities, instead landing the city authorities with the responsibility of reconstructing London with no funds.

The Lord Mayor and aldermen met to discuss the ways in which the damaged city could be rebuilt, and their first proposal was put to Parliament on 24 September. This impressively swift reaction had much to do with the fact that the City of London was an international centre for banking, trade and commerce, and as such was of critical importance to England's economy. Not to have acted quickly would have been disastrous for national morale; as around 80 per cent of the City of London had been destroyed by the fire, reconstruction was a priority. Since there was no money in place for repairs to be carried out on a vast scale, piecemeal and makeshift mending dominated. The Post Office found new lodgings at Bishopsgate Street, and Leadenhall Market expanded its remit to include the sale of meat, fish and leather, replacing the destroyed places in which they were normally sold.

London remained impoverished; the Second Anglo-Dutch War had taken its toll, and so the desired pot of money to bring the new city into being was sorely lacking. Funds were so stretched that a general plea for assistance was issued by representatives of the City parishes, and distributed both through London and throughout the country. Many gave as generously as they could. Lyme Regis in Dorset subscribed £100, Marlborough in Wiltshire £50 and the tradesman Roger Lowe of Ashton-in-Makerfield was called upon by the local vicar to organize a collection in the village with his friends Naylor and Chadocke. Lowe noted in his diary of 16 October that he was asked 'to see what people would give towards the relief of such needy persons as had sustained loss by the great fire in London, and to set their names down, which we did over the one half of Ashton'. Clearly the perception of London as a metropolitan bubble did not dissuade those who dwelt outside the capital from coming to the aid of its citizens *in extremis*. A total of nearly £13,000 was raised through church collections, with a further £1,000 from private donations. Although this was a fraction of what needed to be raised – estimates of the cost of the damage caused have varied between £7 million and £11 million, in 1666 prices – it was better than nothing. This spirit of neighbourly amity was encouraged by Charles's Proclamation of 13 September, which stated 'all cities and towns whatsoever shall without any contradiction receive the said distressed persons and permit them the free exercise of their manual trades'.

Perhaps surprisingly, many of those who had been more directly affected by the fire chose not to offer assistance, although this stemmed more from their straitened financial circumstances than from callousness. When the Pewterers' Company was asked by the aldermen to make a donation to offset the suffering caused by the poor, they replied: 'In consideration of the late calamities by fire in which the Company hath been very great sufferers, and the generality of the poorer sort of people hath been in some measure gainers, it was concluded nothing should be given.'

The Great Fire caused a huge deficit in the English economy that would not be fixed for the rest of the century. Taxation was increased for such everyday items as coal and wool, and many of those who had enjoyed a rise in their financial fortunes since the beginning of the Restoration found that rise suddenly checked. It served as a severe blow to the traditional guild system, doing away with centuries of custom and allowing 'all carpenters, bricklayers, masons, plasterers, joiners and other artificers, workmen and labourers… [to] have and enjoy such and the same liberty of working… [as] the freemen of the City of the same trades and professions have and ought to enjoy'.

The chance to rebuild, or at least remodel, an entire city was one that few architects might ever expect to receive, but out of disaster came opportunity. Wren produced his first plan for the rebuilding of London on 10 September, and others also offered their ideas for the city's reconstruction, including Evelyn, who wrote to his friend Sir Samuel Tuke, 'Dr Wren got a start of me, but both of us did coincide so frequently that his Majesty was not displeased.' Evelyn's ideas had a more European slant than Wren's, making the Guildhall a central feature of a grand square and creating piazzas and well-ordered streets; his stated intention was to 'create variety in the streets… there should be breaks and enlargements, by spacious openings at proper distances, surrounded with piazzas and uniformly built with beautiful fronts'. Another idea, from Robert Hooke, envisaged the city being remodelled on a utilitarian grid system; while it was not adopted, it was sufficiently in favour to see Hooke raised to the post of City Surveyor.

In September 1666, Wren, in concert with Hooke, had a far greater canvas before him than simple refurbishment. Within a matter of days, he had made a preliminary sketch for his idea of what a rebuilt London should be, which replaced the cramped medieval streets and pathways with wide, tree-lined boulevards, a triumphal arch celebrating Charles II where

Ludgate once stood, a grand Romanesque building for the Royal Exchange and, most spectacularly of all, a vast and ornate new building for St Paul's, crowned with an enormous dome, which would become the iconic landmark of the new city, just as the old one had dominated all it surveyed.

Had unlimited funds been forthcoming, it is likely that Wren's vision for London would have come about. Charles was a great admirer of his work, having come to know Wren through his association with the Royal Society, and had been enthusiastic about his designs for St Paul's, which had been submitted on 27 August, just days before the fire rendered his plans moot. However, his vision for a new city was never executed, owing to lack of money, and also an absence of enthusiasm for a project as large and ambitious as his. A compromise was reached; Wren was placed in charge of redesigning fifty-one of the City churches, and the master craftsman Edward Jerman was responsible for many of the other public buildings, including the Royal Exchange and the company halls. The greatest of all the religious buildings, St Paul's, did not formally become Wren's project until 1669, whereupon it took thirty-six years between commencement of building in 1675 and its completion in 1711, at a total cost of over £1 million.

Another of Wren's contributions to the rebuilding of London is the famous Monument to the Great Fire of London, which stands on the spot where St Margaret's, the first church to be destroyed, once stood. Its inscription boldly claims: 'London rises again, whether with greater speed or greater magnificence is doubtful, three short years complete that

which was considered the work of an age'.* This was technically untrue, but it served the purpose of a narrative that was
being constructed by then. Much of the old street plan was
recreated, and, as well as the new buildings being constructed
of brick and stone as Charles directed, the streets were
widened and access to the river made easier.

However, full rebuilding of the city was not accomplished
in three years, because there was no means of doing so. Those
who could afford to rebuild their houses and places of business
did, but there was no homogeneity of design; Wren's grand
scheme of a transformed London never came to pass. The clergyman Samuel Rolle wrote in 1668 that around 800 houses
had been built in the affected parts of the City, calling it 'an ill
prospect and a ghastly sight'. It took decades for the churches
and markets to be brought back, and the only new streets
of any note were King Street and Queen Street between the
Thames and Guildhall. The dream of a new London seemed
to be at an end.

<hr>

Faced with the legacy of this disaster, what the court needed
was a propagandist, who could make the official version
the one most believed, and even beloved. The fire had to be
portrayed as less an apocalyptic disaster and more the symbol
of the Restoration rising once more.

It was an opportunity that an ambitious man would find

* It also had a 1668 addition, ascribing the fire to 'the malicious hearts of barbarous
papists', including the unfortunate Hubert; these were removed in 1830.

hard to refuse, and John Dryden was certainly ambitious. Thirty-five years old in 1666, he had already written a poem in 1660, *Astraea Redux*, in which he both recanted his previous support of Cromwell and hailed Charles as a 'happy prince, whom Heaven hath taught the way'. Dryden was unembarrassed by a reputation for playing both sides, having published his respectful *Heroic Stanzas* on Cromwell's death in 1658.* But by the beginning of 1666, his fortunes appeared becalmed, not least because his fellowship of the prestigious Royal Society had been annulled for non-payment of his subscription, indicating that his finances were far from flourishing. A change in his situation was much longed for. Observing how other writers at court had attracted royal patronage by producing work to Charles's taste, he began what would be his most significant work to date.

Dryden's poem about the events of 1666 – specifically (apparent) English victory in the Second Anglo-Dutch War and the Great Fire – *Annus Mirabilis* first appeared the following year. He had begun it as a response to the victory of the St James's Day Battle on 25 July, and intended it to have Virgilian overtones, and had probably written most of it before the fire. It was a self-conscious attempt to construct a poetic national language, both in terms of the epic style that he was attempting to achieve, and also the elevated register of language he chose – 'poesy' rather than 'poetry' was its description. His 'account of the ensuing poem' addressed to Sir Robert Howard claimed:

---

* A friend of both Milton and Marvell, he had even walked in Cromwell's funeral cortège with them.

I have chosen the most heroic subject, which any poet could desire: I have taken upon me to describe the motives, the beginning, progress and successes, of a most just and necessary war; in it, the care, management and prudence of our King; the conduct and valour of a Royal Admiral, and of two uncomparable generals; the invincible courage of our captains and seamen, and three glorious victories, the result of all.

At 1,216 lines, it was an epic work, filled with classical allusion and continued praise of the 'mighty monarch'* Charles, who is described in terms befitting Zeus/Jupiter, and as being the possessor of a 'sacred face', along with his family and supporters such as, James, Rupert and Albemarle. The poem was also a celebration of the indomitable spirit of the English as displayed in battle against their enemies, and its final verses talk in grandiose fashion about the reborn and newly built London emerging from the ashes of the fire, the 'scourge' that the city needed to undergo before it could rise once more. Unavoidably, Dryden's major source was the *London Gazette*; Pepys's vivid and colourful diaries were not available to him.

From the beginning, *Annus Mirabilis* was explicit about its aims and intentions. Dryden set out to celebrate English endeavour and the city in which he lived, writing in the opening dedication 'to you, therefore, this Year of Wonders is justly dedicated, because you have made it so; you, who are to stand a wonder to all years and ages; and who have built

---

* Although this possibly contains a double entendre about Charles's sexual prowess.

yourselves an immortal monument on your own ruins'. What became of the people who had inhabited these 'ruins' was described with compassion and skill:

> Those who have none, sit round where once it was,
> And with full eyes each wonted room require;
> Haunting the yet warm ashes of the place,
> As murder'd men walk where they did expire.
> Some stir up coals, and watch the vestal fire,
> Others in vain from sight of ruin run;
> And, while through burning labyrinths they retire,
> With loathing eyes repeat what they would shun.
> The most in fields like herded beasts lie down,
> To dews obnoxious on the grassy floor;
> And while their babes in sleep their sorrows drown,
> Sad parents watch the remnants of their store.
>
> While by the motion of the flames they guess
> What streets are burning now, and what are near;
> An infant waking to the paps would press,
> And meets, instead of milk, a falling tear.

Despite its patriotic tone, *Annus Mirabilis* was less an application for the then barely existent post of Poet Laureate[*] than it was Dryden attempting to elevate himself above his contemporaries as the commentator best placed to articulate the country's concerns. It is a conservative, monarchist work

[*] Court poets to have held the position before it became an official royal office included Edmund Spenser, Ben Jonson and Dryden's predecessor, William Davenant.

that rejected those radical political elements (the 'bold fanatic spectres') that he saw as attempting to bring about the country's destruction, and instead celebrated the events of 1666 as the basis for a new covenant between Charles and his people. Such a development never took place.

Nonetheless, the poem worked well as propaganda, and Dryden was duly rewarded by being appointed England's first official national poet and Historiographer Royal in 1668, with an annual salary of £300 for his pains. Like many others at court, Dryden would find obtaining recompense from the perpetually impecunious Charles a difficult task. Perhaps it was because of this that his later work, such as his 1681 political satire *Absalom and Achitophel*, would adopt a vitriolic and scornful, rather than celebratory, tone.

Annus Mirabilis ends with a look forward to the rebirth of London after the events of 1666:

> Methinks already from this chymic flame,
> I see a city of more precious mould,
> Rich as the town which gives the Indies name,
> With silver paved, and all divine with gold.
> Already, labouring with a mighty fate,
> She shakes the rubbish from her mounting brow,
> And seems to have renew'd her charter's date,
> Which Heaven will to the death of time allow.
> More great than human now, and more august,
> Now deified she from her fires does rise:
> Her widening streets on new foundations trust,
> And opening into larger parts she flies.

London, battered and downhearted though she was by the end of 1666, would rise again. Wren, Hawksmoor and others would make virtue out of necessity, creating some of the city's most beloved buildings, many of which still stand today. Shops would reopen. Streets gutted by fire would be rebuilt. Communities would reform. For all Dryden's hyperbole, he hit upon an inescapable truth; that London, and England in general, could not be cast down. This indomitability remains a deservedly praised aspect of the national character and it was seldom better illustrated than by the strange, destructive and unexpected events of 1666. The year might have ended up being Charles's tragedy. But for ordinary people, tested by fire, plague, war and all other kinds of adversity, it would become their own restoration.

Acknowledgements

A story like this is never told in isolation. There are many to thank who have been involved in its genesis and production, whether directly or indirectly. Georgina Capel is the agent that every writer hopes that they will be lucky enough to have. Utterly committed to the project from start to finish, it is the very best of fortune to be represented by someone as superb as her. Meanwhile, I have had similar luck in my editor, Richard Milbank, whose patient guidance and constructive criticism about the book continue a more than harmonious working relationship. Thanks also to the rest of Head of Zeus, especially Anthony Cheetham, whose enthusiasm and vision was a constant inspiration. My research assistant Thomas Lalevee was a similar delight to work with, expertly unearthing rare and fascinating material with the nonchalance of one who is to in-depth detective work of this nature born.

Anyone writing a book about the Restoration is following in the footsteps of the great Liza Picard, whose seminal Restoration London was the single greatest assistance and inspiration to me. I was saddened to hear of Lisa Jardine's death while in the final stages of editing; she offered much useful advice about the period, especially the lives and work of Wren and Hooke.

The book was composed with the aid of many libraries and research institutes, but the most constant of these was the London Library, a place I have come to regard as a second home of sorts: my thanks to the endlessly patient and helpful staff. There were many historians and academics who I have turned to in the research for this and *Blazing Star*, but Dan Jones, in particular, offered some invaluable discussion on the book's themes and structure at its conception, as well as acting as a good-humoured source of practical advice for those (thankfully rare) moments when the entire project seemed on the verge of becoming overwhelming.

Sophie Gregory offered similar help and guidance, which had its intended effect of making me laugh as well as think. As ever, Joseph Wilkins, James Douglass and Simon Renshaw – the 'three wise men' – offered their own stimulating thoughts and opinions on the chapters as they progressed. My thanks also to my grandparents, Barbara and Raymond Stephenson and Therese Larman; they will, deservedly, be the first recipients of this book.

I started thinking about *Restoration* in 2012, albeit in the context of another book altogether. Now, as I write this four years later, a great deal in my own life has changed. It is to my wife Nancy who I owe the deepest debt of thanks, for being a constantly ameliorative presence in my life, for being the kindest and best of people, and, last but not least, for being the mother of my daughter, Rose. 'It is a far, far better thing that I do, than I have ever done', and it is to them that the book is dedicated. I can think of no worthier pair of recipients.

Sussex, January 2016

Bibliography

A text is listed upon its first reference in the book. Many of these were used throughout.

CHAPTER I: THE STATE OF ENGLAND

Baron, Xavier, ed., *London 1066–1914*, Helm Information, 1997

Keeble, N. H., *The Restoration*, Blackwell, 2002

Latham, Robert, ed., *The Illustrated Pepys*, BCA, 1978

Morrah, Patrick, *Restoration England*, Constable, 1979

Pepys, Samuel, *Diaries 1660–1670*, edited by Robert Latham and William Matthews, Bell & Hyman, 1971

Picard, Liza, *Restoration London*, Weidenfeld & Nicolson, 1997

Roberts, Stephen, *Recovery and Restoration in an English County*, University of Exeter Press, 1985

Sachse, William L., *Restoration England*, Cambridge University Press, 1971

Sarasohn, L. T., 'Who Was Then the Gentleman?: Samuel Sorbière, Thomas Hobbes, and the Royal Society', *History of Science*, vol. xlii, 2004

Thorold, Peter, *The London Rich*, Viking, 1999

Tomalin, Claire, *Samuel Pepys*, Viking, 2002

Two East Anglian diaries, 1641–1729: Isaac Archer and William Coe, Boydell Press, Suffolk Records Society, vol. 36, 1994.

CHAPTER 2: KING AND COURT

Barker, Brian, *The Symbols of Sovereignty*, Westbridge Books, 1979

Coote, Stephen, *Royal Survivor*, Hodder & Stoughton, 1997

Fraser, Antonia, *King Charles II*, Weidenfeld & Nicolson, 1979

Harris, Tim, *Restoration*, Penguin, 2005

Larman, Alexander, *Blazing Star*, Head of Zeus, 2014

Ogg, David, *England in the Reign of Charles II*, Clarendon Press, 1955

Schramm, Percy, *A History of the English Coronation*, Oxford University Press, 1937

Stedman, Gesa, *Cultural Exchange in Seventeenth-Century France and England*, Ashgate, 2013

CHAPTER 3: SCIENCE AND SUPERSTITION

Hill Curth, Louisa, *From Physick to Pharmacology*, Ashgate, 2006

Hunter, Michael, *Science and Society in Restoration England*, Cambridge University Press, 1981

Jardine, Lisa, *The Curious Life of Robert Hooke*, HarperCollins, 2003

Wright, Thomas, *Circulation*, Chatto & Windus, 2012

CHAPTER 4: ANGLICANS AND DISSENTERS

Apetrei, S. L. T., *Women, Feminism and Religion in Early Enlightenment England*, Cambridge University Press, 2010

Birchwood, Matthew, *Staging Islam in Britain: Drama and Culture, 1640–1685*, Boydell & Brewer, 2007

Hill, Christopher, *Turbulent, People and Factious Seditions*, Clarendon Press, 1988

Matar, Nabil, *Islam in Britain, 1558–1685*, Cambridge University Press, 2008

Walsham, Alexandra, *Charitable Hatred*, Manchester University Press, 2006

CHAPTER 5: THE GREAT PLAGUE

Bell, Walter George, *The Great Plague*, Folio Society, 2001

Moote A. Lloyd, and Dorothy Moote, *The Great Plague*, Johns Hopkins University Press, 2004

Porter, Stephen, *The Great Plague*, Amberley Publishing, 2009

CHAPTER 6: GOING OUT

Barr, Andrew, *Drink*, Bantam Press, 1995

Boswell, Eleanore, *The Restoration Court Stage*, Harvard University Press, 1932

Cameron, David Kerr, *London's Pleasures*, Sutton, 2001

Evelyn, John, *London Revived*, Clarendon Press, 1938

Fisk, Deborah, ed., *The Cambridge Companion to English Restoration Theatre*, Cambridge University Press, 2000

Hopkins, Graham, *Constant Delights*, Sutton, 2002

Horner West, Francis, *Rude Forefathers*, Bannisdale Press, 1949

Howe, Elizabeth, *The First English Actresses: Women and Drama, 1660–1700*, Cambridge University Press, 1992

Roberts, David, *Thomas Betterton*, Cambridge University Press, 2010

Stevens Curl, James, *Spas, Wells & Pleasure Gardens of London*, Historical Publications, 2010

Summers, Montague, *Restoration Theatre*, Kegan Paul, 1934

CHAPTER 7: DRESSING UP AND STAYING IN

Cunnington, C. Willett, and Phillis Cunnington, *Handbook of English Costume in the 17th Century*, Faber & Faber, 1972

Drummond, J. C., and Anne Wilbraham, *The Englishman's Food*, Jonathan Cape, 1957

Hartnell, Norman, *Royal Courts of Fashion*, Cassell, 1971

Laver, James, *A Concise History of Costume*, Thames & Hudson, 1969.

Little, Patrick, 'Cromwell's "Gay Attire"', *History Today*, vol. 58, issue 9, 2008

Sambrook, Pamela, and Peter Brears, eds, *The Country House Kitchen 1650–1900*, Sutton, 1997

Weatherill, Lorna, *Consumer Behaviour and Material Culture in Britain 1660–1760*, Routledge, 1988

CHAPTER 8: CRIME AND PUNISHMENT

Babington, Antony, *The English Bastille*, Macdonald, 1971

Halliday, Stephen, *Newgate*, Sutton, 2006

Marshall, Alan, *The Strange Death of Edmund Godfrey*, Sutton, 2009

CHAPTER 9: FOREIGN AFFAIRS

Boxer, C. R., *The Anglo-Dutch Wars of the Seventeenth Century*, HMSO, 1974

Fox, Frank L., *The Four Days' Battle of 1666*, Pen & Sword, 2009

Hainsworth, Roger, and Christine Churches, *The Anglo-Dutch Naval Wars, 1652–1674*, Sutton, 1998

Jones, J. R., *The Anglo-Dutch Wars of the Seventeenth Century*, Longman, 1996

CHAPTER 10: THE GREAT FIRE

Bardle, Stephen, *The Literary Underground in the 1660s*, Oxford University Press, 2012

Bell, Walter George, *The Great Fire of London in 1666*, Folio Society, 2003

Hammond, Paul, *The Making of Restoration Poetry*, D. S. Brewer, 2006

Hanson, Neil, *The Dreadful Judgement*, Doubleday, 2001

Jardine, Lisa, *On a Grander Scale*, HarperCollins, 2002

Maclean, Gerald, ed., *Culture and Society in the Stuart Restoration*, Cambridge University Press, 1995

Miller, William, *London Before the Fire of 1666*, J. H. Woodley, 1867

Reddaway T. F., *Rebuilding of London After the Great Fire*, Jonathan Cape, 1940

Tinniswood, Adrian, *By Permission of Heaven*, Jonathan Cape, 2003

Ward, Charles E., *The Life of John Dryden*, University of North Carolina Press, 1961

Winn, James Anderson, *John Dryden and His World*, Yale University Press, 1987

Zwicker, Steven N., ed., *The Cambridge Companion to English Literature 1650–1740*, Cambridge University Press, 1998

Index